THE ARCHAEOLOGY OF THE JERUSALEM AREA

THE ARCHAEOLOGY OF THE JERUSALEM AREA

W. HAROLD MARE

BAKER BOOK HOUSE
Grand Rapids, Michigan 49506

Copyright 1987 by
Baker Book House Company

ISBN: 0-8010-6126-1

Library of Congress
Card Catalog Number: 85-073719

Printed in the United States of America

Unless otherwise indicated, all Scripture quotations are from
the New International Version copyrighted 1978 by the New
York International Bible Society and published by the Zondervan
Corporation.

Photographs not otherwise credited are property of the author.

The author expresses sincere appreciation to the following individuals for
permission to use their copyrighted materials:

Biblical Archaeologist, American Schools of Oriental Research
Biblical Archaeology Review
Raymond E. Collins, commercial artist
Doubleday and Company
École Biblique et Archéologique Française, Jerusalem
Franciscan Printing Press, Jerusalem
Michael J. Fuller, architect
Israel Exploration Society
McGraw-Hill Book Company
Oxford University Press
Palestine Exploration Fund, London, and Naseeb Shaheen
Palestine Exploration Quarterly
Princeton University Press and Jack Finegán
J. K. T. Richie, Legate for Kathleen Kenyon, Clwyd, England
Yigal Shiloh, Head of the Institute of Archaeology, The Hebrew University of
    Jerusalem
Harold G. Stigers, architect
Weidenfeld Publishers, Limited

To

Donald W. Burdick

and

Edwin M. Yamauchi

and all the Colleagues in the

Near East Archaeological Society

Contents

6

Panoramic view of Jerusalem.

Preface

Of all the places revered by the Christian and the Jew, none can compare with the sacred and hallowed city of Jerusalem. The city is also revered by Muslims as one of their most sacred areas. Jerusalem figures prominently throughout the historical events recorded in the Bible. As a matter of fact, the first reference to the city occurs in Genesis 14—the account of the meeting between Abraham and Melchizedek, the king of Salem (Jerusalem). This city, the holy city of God here on earth, was a center of worship, religious interest, and power in both the Old and New Testament periods. Struggles to control it continued in the era of the early church and beyond—through the Islamic, Crusader, and Turkish periods, and even into the present. In addition to the kings and governors who have ruled here, in addition to the nations and armies that have battled over this religious center, thousands of pilgrims over the centuries have made their way to this city of God.

Jerusalem! A city commanding such allegiance and international interest warrants our attention. Intriguing questions come to mind. Just how far back does the history of this holy city go? What was the nature of the struggles waged over it by pagan, Jew, Christian, and Muslim? What archaeological evidence is there of religious practices? What was the lifestyle of the people who inhabited Jerusalem over the centuries? What was the economic status of the city in the various segments of its history? How strong were its defenses and, accordingly, how readily was it conquered?

The approach of this study is basically chronological, covering the archaeological history of the Jerusalem area from earliest times to our modern day. While the archaeological evidence is stressed, care is taken to fill in the picture with historical details gathered from the Bible and from other literary sources. Maps, photographs, and sketches are included in order to illustrate fully the archaeological data discussed in the text. A select bibliography is added for the benefit of the reader who wishes to delve further into various aspects of the history and archaeology of Jerusalem.

I express my gratitude to Covenant Theological Seminary for the sabbatical granted me in the spring of 1980. I spent some of that time writing the last part of this manuscript in the delightful setting of the Albright Institute of Archaeological Research near the Old City of Jerusalem. I also express indebtedness to my wife, Betty, for her sacrificial labor in typing the manuscript.

I hope this study will not only add to the reader's knowledge of Jerusalem but also that it will be of spiritual and inspirational help.

Chart of Archaeological Periods in Palestine[1]

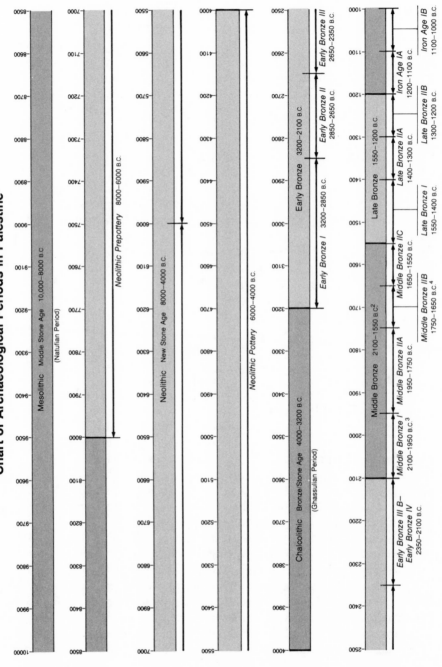

Mesolithic Middle Stone Age 10,000–8000 B.C.
(Natufian Period)

Neolithic Prepottery 8000–6000 B.C.

Neolithic New Stone Age 8000–4000 B.C.

Neolithic Pottery 6000–4000 B.C.

Chalcolithic Bronze/Stone Age 4000–3200 B.C.
(Ghassulian Period)

Early Bronze 3200–2100 B.C.
Early Bronze I 3200–2850 B.C.
Early Bronze II 2850–2650 B.C.
Early Bronze III 2650–2350 B.C.

Early Bronze III B–
Early Bronze IV 2350–2100 B.C.

Middle Bronze 2100–1550 B.C.[2]
Middle Bronze I 2100–1950 B.C.[3]
Middle Bronze IIA 1950–1750 B.C.
Middle Bronze IIB 1750–1650 B.C.[4]
Middle Bronze IIC 1650–1550 B.C.

Late Bronze 1550–1200 B.C.
Late Bronze I 1550–1400 B.C.
Late Bronze IIA 1400–1300 B.C.
Late Bronze IIB 1300–1200 B.C.

Iron Age IA 1200–1100 B.C.
Iron Age IB 1100–1000 B.C.

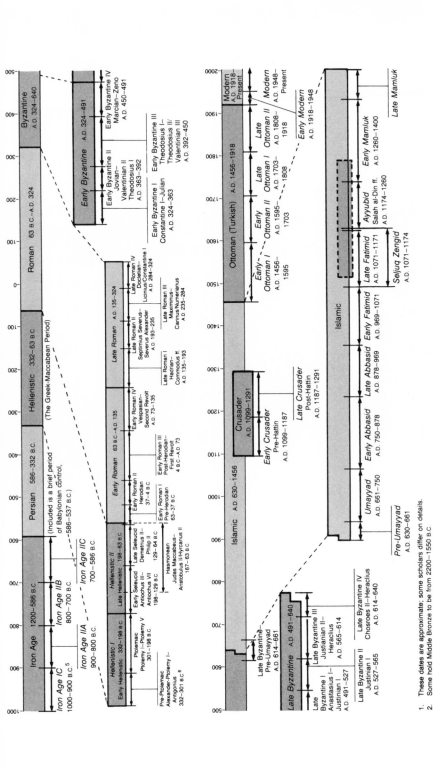

1. These dates are approximate; some scholars differ on details.
2. Some hold Middle Bronze to be from 2200–1550 B.C.
3. Or, 2200–2000 B.C.
4. Some do not divide Middle Bronze IIB into MB IIB and MB IIC.
5. Some hold that Iron II extends from 1000–586 B.C.
6. These dates agree with those from J. A. Sauer, *Heshbon Pottery* (Berrien Springs, Michigan: Andrews University Press, 1971), pp. 3, 4.

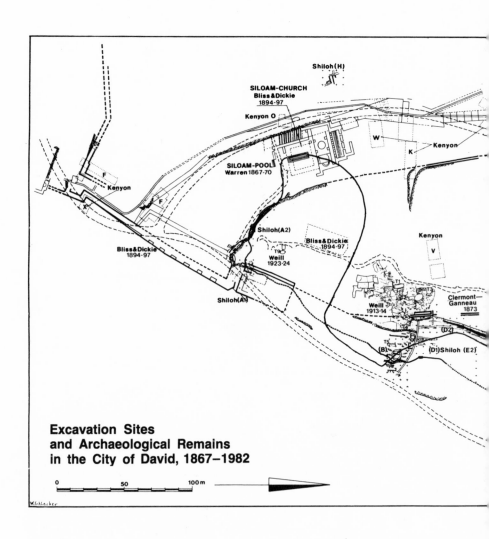

**Excavation Sites
and Archaeological Remains
in the City of David, 1867–1982**

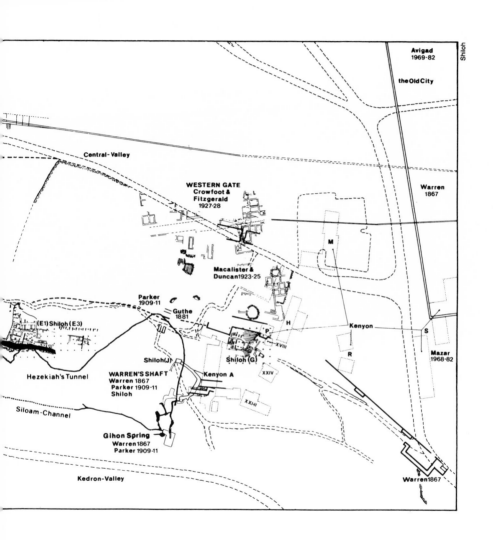

Avigad
1969-82

the Old City

Central-Valley

WESTERN GATE
Crowfoot &
Fitzgerald
1927-28

Warren
1867

M

Macalister &
Duncan 1923-25

Parker
1909-11

Guthe
1881

H

(E1) Shiloh (E3)

Kenyon

S

Shiloh (J)

Shiloh (G)

P

XVIII

R

Mazar
1968-82

Hezekiah's Tunnel

WARREN'S SHAFT
Warren 1867
Parker 1909-11
Shiloh

Kenyon A

XXIV

Siloam-Channel

XXI-II

Gihon Spring
Warren 1867
Parker 1909-11

Kedron-Valley

Warren 1867

Introduction

Jerusalem! The very word has a mystique. It is strongly religious in character. This city is not famous as a center of military or political power. No great military leader has come forth from it to conquer the world. Yet men have fought and died to possess and to preserve it.

Jerusalem, situated as it is between the Eastern and the Western worlds (though it exudes the aura of the East), is really famous for something else. It has always gained strength and renown from the moral and religious precepts taught within its walls. This has been true from the times of the Old Testament prophets into the time of Jesus, the apostles, and the church fathers, and on through the period of Islam. Today the religious atmosphere still permeates the city through a variety of faiths, each practicing its own tenets.

Jesus' statement in Luke 13:34 epitomizes the age-old concern with the religious life of Jerusalem: "O Jerusalem, Jerusalem, you who kill the prophets and stone those sent to you, how often I have longed to gather your children together, as a hen gathers her chicks under her wings, but you were not willing!"

Up to and including the present day, religious interest in Jerusa-

15

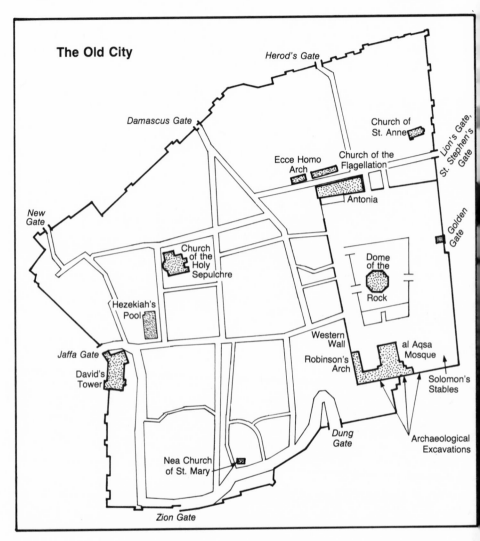

The Old City

Herod's Gate

Damascus Gate

Church of
St. Anne

Ecce Homo
Arch

Church of the
Flagellation

Lion's Gate,
St. Stephen's
Gate

Antonia

New
Gate

Golden
Gate

Church
of the
Holy
Sepulchre

Dome
of the
Rock

Hezekiah's
Pool

Western
Wall

al Aqsa
Mosque

Jaffa Gate

Robinson's
Arch

David's
Tower

Solomon's
Stables

Dung
Gate

Archaeological
Excavations

Nea Church
of St. Mary

Zion Gate

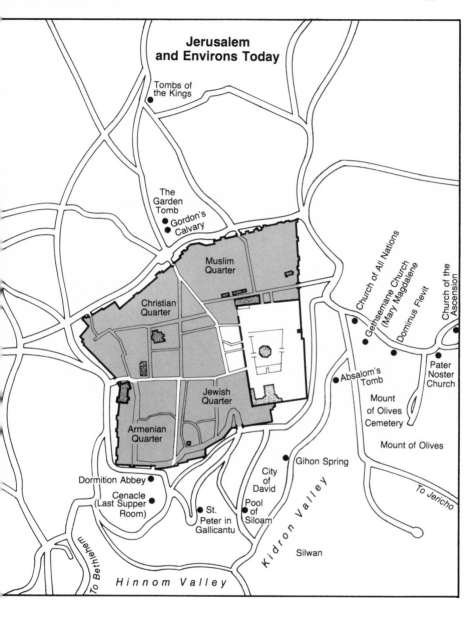

Jerusalem and Environs Today

Tombs of the Kings

The Garden Tomb

Gordon's Calvary

Muslim Quarter

Christian Quarter

Church of All Nations

Gethsemane Church (Mary Magdalene)

Dominus Flevit

Church of the Ascension

Pater Noster Church

Absalom's Tomb

Jewish Quarter

Mount of Olives Cemetery

Armenian Quarter

Mount of Olives

Dormition Abbey

Gihon Spring

City of David

Cenacle (Last Supper Room)

St. Peter in Gallicantu

Pool of Siloam

Kidron Valley

To Jericho

Silwan

To Bethlehem

Hinnom Valley

lem has flourished. The walled city itself is presently divided into four quarters: the Armenian (southwest), the Christian (northwest), the Muslim (northeast), and the Jewish (southeast). The division indicates the intense religious interest present in that section. This same interest is apparent on the Mount of Olives and in other nearby areas, as well as throughout the entire land which has an abundance of Muslim, Christian, and Jewish holy places and shrines.

The intense religious interest focusing on the city of Jerusalem is further seen in the number of pilgrims that have come to visit and worship throughout the centuries. For instance, it is estimated that in the time of Herod the Great and Jesus (first centuries B.C. and A.D.) Jerusalem swelled from a normal population of 55,000 inhabitants to 180,000 when the Passover was celebrated.[1] There was also an additional influx of pilgrims and soldiers during the period of the Crusades.

In addition to the religious fervor, there is a romance attached to the name *Jerusalem*, an aura of the Oriental. This is true in part because of the area's connection with traders from the East who brought here a part of their Oriental culture together with their exotic spices and other goods. One is reminded of the Ishmaelite-Midianite merchants who came through Palestine near Dothan with their camel loads of spices, balm, and myrrh to be sold down in Egypt (Gen. 37:23–28). And the area of Jerusalem had many other contacts with the surrounding world—with Egyptians to the south and west (Gen. 12:10), with the Phoenicians and Tyrians to the north (2 Sam. 5:11), with the Greeks to the northwest. The Hellenistic culture spread by Alexander the Great and his generals did much to affect this area. The Babylonians, Assyrians, and Persians from the east, the Syrians from the north and east, and the conquering Romans from the west all had their influence on Jerusalem and left their stamp on its culture. Greatest of all, perhaps, was the cultural impact of Christianity and of Islam on the city.

1. Joachim Jeremias, *Jerusalem in the Time of Jesus* (Philadelphia: Fortress Press, 1969), p. 83.

Jerusalem Through the Centuries
An Overview

The city of Jerusalem has had a long and inspiring history. Settlement in the area goes back several millennia; in fact, the earliest pottery fragments at the site date from the Neolithic period.

One may think that the name and the physical limits of the ancient walled city remained the same throughout the centuries, but such is not the case. Almost everyone has seen a picture of modern Jerusalem with its crenelated walls. The outline of the Old City formed by these walls is basically the same today as it was in A.D. 135, when the Emperor Hadrian rebuilt Jerusalem as a pagan Roman city, naming it Aelia Capitolina.

Kathleen Kenyon has said regarding this:

> Jerusalem to-day therefore received its form in A.D. 135. Almost the only link with the form of Jerusalem of New Testament times is the great platform of the Temple built by Herod the Great. . . . Archaeological examination. . . . starting a hundred years ago, down to the campaign begun in 1961, has at least succeeded in tracing the outlines of the successive towns, and we can therefore now claim that we have

available some material for a picture of the town in which the events
of the Old and New Testaments took place.[1]

This is not to say, however, that the boundaries were always the
same in those periods before A.D. 135, nor that the boundaries have
remained unchanged since that date.

The Name *Jerusalem*

The name *Jerusalem* seems to have been attached to the city at
least as far back as the nineteenth–eighteenth centuries B.C., when it
appeared in the Egyptian Execration Texts in the form *Rushalimum*.
There is a possibility the name also occurs in the Ebla tablets found
at Tell Mardikh in Syria, which date about six to eight hundred
years earlier. In the Amarna Letters from Egypt (fourteenth century)
the name is written *Urusalim*, and in the inscriptions of Sennacherib
the Assyrian (seventh century) it is written *Ursalimmu*. The short-
ened form *Salem* is used in Genesis 14:18 and Psalm 76:2.

The elements composing the name *Jerusalem*, *yeru* and *shalem*,
which are of Semitic derivation, have been interpreted as meaning
"foundation of peace." The element *yeru* ("foundation") is seen in
the form *Yeruel*, meaning "founded by God" (2 Chron. 20:16; cf. Job
38:6); and *shalem*, meaning "peace," is found in Genesis 14:18. The
word *shalom* ("peace") of course, is found in many Old Testament
references. According to an alternate interpretation, the word *Jeru-
Shalem* means "foundation of (the god) Shalem." Benjamin Mazar
states that "Shalem is known from a Ugaritic mythological text as
one of the two 'beautiful and gracious gods,' Shohar and Shalim
('Dawn' and 'Twilight,' respectively)."[2] If this latter interpretation is
correct, the Hebrews took over the word from a heathen context. In
view of their ordinary use of the word *shalom*, the Hebrews may
have come to think that the city was founded on peace, that is, on
Jehovah, the God of peace.[3] In this connection note that Jerusalem
is often referred to in terms suggesting that it belongs to God; for
example, "the city of God," "the city of our God," "O city of God,"
"the city of the Lord" (Ps. 46:4; 48:1, 8; 87:3; Isa. 60:14). In Greek

1. Kathleen Kenyon, *Jerusalem* (New York: McGraw-Hill, 1967), p. 197.
2. Benjamin Mazar, "Jerusalem in the Biblical Period," in *Jerusalem Revealed*
(Jerusalem: Israel Exploration Society, 1975), p. 1. Ugaritic is a Semitic language of
about 1400 B.C. which is related to Hebrew.
3. "Jerushalim," in *Hebrew and English Lexicon of the Old Testament*, ed. Francis
Brown, S. R. Driver, and Charles A. Briggs (Boston: Houghton Mifflin, 1907), p. 436.

and Latin the name occurs as *Ierousalem*, as well as *Hierousalem*, *Hierosolyma*, and *Solyma*.

Another biblical name for the city is Jebus (Judg. 19:10; 1 Chron. 11:4). At least a portion of the city in the time of Solomon was called Mount Moriah. The threshing floor which David purchased from Araunah the Jebusite and which became the site of Solomon's temple was in this area (2 Chron. 3:1). The name *Moriah* no doubt has some connection with the account in Genesis 22, which speaks of Abraham going to Mount Moriah to offer up Isaac. In other Old Testament passages Jerusalem is spoken of as "Ariel" (i.e., the lion of God—Isa. 29:1), "Zion" (Isa. 31:9), "the Daughter of Zion" (Isa. 52:2; Lam. 2:1), "the Virgin Daughter of Zion" (Isa. 37:22; Lam. 2:13), "the Daughter of Jerusalem" (Isa. 37:22; Lam. 2:13, 15) and "the daughter of my people" (Lam. 4:6, KJV). Isaiah also calls it the "City of Righteousness, the Faithful City" (Isa. 1:26); and in the Psalms, besides "the city of God," it is called "the city of the Great King" (Ps. 48:2) and "the city of the Lord Almighty" (Ps. 48:8). In Psalm 74:7 it is called "the dwelling place of your name." This concept may have led to the use of the term *the holy city* in both the Old Testament (Neh. 11:1; Isa. 48:2; 52:1; Dan. 9:24) and in the New (Matt. 4:5; 27:53). In similar fashion Joel (2:1) speaks of it as "my [God's] holy mountain" (KJV), "my holy hill" (NIV). Since Jerusalem is particularly connected with David, it is called "the City of David" (2 Kings 12:21). But it is also called "the city of Judah" (2 Chron. 25:28). Shishak, king of Egypt (ca. 950–929 B.C.) seems to have called Jerusalem *Rabbat*, that is, "chief town" or "capital,"[4] and, as we have already noted, in A.D. 135 the Romans renamed the city Aelia Capitolina.

Geographical Setting

"The Jerusalem area" means the site of Jerusalem itself with its valleys, the Hinnom and the Kidron, and also the Mount of Olives to the east. The area is located 36 miles east of the Mediterranean Sea.

The highest point in the area is the Mount of Olives, on the crest of the Palestinian hill country at an altitude of 2,723 feet above sea level. It was known in the Old Testament as Olivet (2 Sam. 15:30, KJV) or the Mount of Olives (Zech. 14:4). Jesus frequently stayed on the mount after an exhaustive day of ministry (Luke 21:37). He would make his way over to the city of Jerusalem by descending the

---

4. G. A. Smith, *Jerusalem* (London: Hodder and Stoughton, 1907), 1: 268.

mount and crossing the Kidron Valley using one of two or three Roman roads, parts of which are in existence today.

The site of Jerusalem itself gives the appearance of a plateau with a fingerlike spur of land projecting to the south on its southeastern side. This quadrilateral plateau is approximately 2,500 feet above sea level, on the same crest of Palestinian hill country as the Mount of Olives. It is bounded on the east by the Kidron Valley, also called the Valley of Jehoshaphat (Joel 3:2, 12). Now known as the Wadi Sitti Maryam (or Valley of Mary) the Kidron separates Jerusalem from the Mount of Olives. On the west and south the city is bounded by the Hinnom Valley (Wadi er-Rababi). These two valleys are easily discernible today. However, a third one, the Tyropoeon, which Josephus (*War* 5.140) called "the Valley of the Cheesemakers" (the name *Tyropoeon* means "cheesemaker"), is not so easily discernible. It runs southward within the Old City complex just to the west of the temple mount (or platform) and to a large extent has been filled up with debris from frequent destructions and rebuildings of the city. What remains of the Tyropoeon Valley today is a shallow depression which is called el-Wad.[5] In ancient times the two main valleys, the Kidron and the Hinnom, were major factors in the defense of Jerusalem, while the Tyropoeon within the city itself divided the area into two parts: the western hill, which is also called the Upper City, and the eastern (or southeastern) hill (or ridge), which is called the Lower City. To the north of the southeastern ridge is a third hill called Moriah (Gen. 22:2; 2 Chron. 3:1). Solomon, Zerubbabel (Ezra 3), and Herod constructed their temples here in the area of the large mound of rock[6] over which the Dome of the Rock, an Islamic memorial, presently stands. This rock seems to have served as the foundation for the altar of burnt offering.[7] North of Moriah there is a fourth hill which Josephus (*War* 5.149) called Bezetha.

On the western side of the Kidron Valley, at the bottom of the slope of the southeastern ridge at a spot below the ancient city of David, which is now called Ophel Hill (cf. 2 Chron 27:3), is the spring in ancient times called Gihon (1 Kings 1:33–45; 2 Chron. 32:30). Farther south at the juncture of the Hinnom and Kidron Valleys is the spring En-rogel (Josh. 15:7; 18:16), now called Bir Ayyub (or Job's Well). Both these springs are used today. South of

5. Jack Finegan, *Light from the Ancient Past* (Princeton: Princeton University Press, 1959), pp. 315–17.
6. The rock is 58 by 51 feet and 4 to 6½ feet high. See Finegan, *Light*, pp. 179–80.
7. See Finegan, *Light*, p. 326, and Josephus, *War* 5.225. Cf. Ezra 3:3: "They set the altar upon its base" (ASV).

En-rogel the Kidron Valley, now joined by the Hinnom, continues down to the Dead Sea. The modern name of that extended valley is Wadi en-Nar.[8]

Geologically Jerusalem and the Mount of Olives, together with Bethlehem and Hebron, lie on the eastern edge of the Cenomanian limestone highlands which, as they run north to south, make up the central ridge of the country. Off to the east and south of Jerusalem and the Mount of Olives and down toward the Dead Sea is a region of soft porous rock material called Senonian chalk. This area is named the Jeshimon, the Wilderness of Judea.[9]

Besides the two springs, Gihon and En-rogel, rainfall provides enough moisture to sustain the Jerusalem area, a situation quite different from the land to the east of the Mount of Olives. It has been observed that this part of Palestine stands at the edge of the rainfall belt with the barren area extending eastward from the Mount of Olives. The western half of Jerusalem is wetter than the eastern half which is closer to the dry Jeshimon wilderness, and often the rain can be seen to stop at the Mount of Olives. Thus the trees in the Garden of Gethsemane may get rain while Bethany on the eastern slope of the Mount of Olives, may not.[10]

Because of a good north-south road running from the Samaria and Ephraim districts along the central ridge and because of the guarantee of at least a minimal supply of spring water and rainfall, it was natural for the Jerusalem area to have been inhabited from very early times. Its defensible flanks on the east, south, and to some extent on the west also contributed to the desirability of the site. In studying the following historical overview it is to be remembered that the inhabited areas of Jerusalem were not constant but expanded and contracted, depending on the interests and needs of the people at the particular time.

Early and Middle Bronze Periods

The archaeological excavations of M. Parker in Jerusalem in 1910 discovered painted ware of the Early Bronze I period, to be dated more specifically to the beginning of the third millennium B.C. In excavations of the southeastern spur of the eastern hill, Early

8. Down nearer the Dead Sea the Mar Saba Monastery clings to the sides of this wadi. See Finegan, *Light*, p. 267.

9. Denis Baly, *The Geography of the Bible*, rev. ed. (New York: Harper & Row, 1974), pp. 6, 83.

10. Denis Baly, *Geographical Companion to the Bible* (London: Lutterworth, 1963), pp. 65–66.

Bronze sherds have been found in the layers overlying the bedrock.[11] All this indicated habitation in Jerusalem prior to Abraham (ca. 1900 B.C.).

The earliest potsherds found west of the Tyropoeon Valley date to Middle Bronze II, a time near that of Abraham and the patriarchs.[12] These sherds were found in brown soil lodged in crevices of bedrock in the necropolis area of the eastern slope of the western hill. This indicates that there was some activity west of the Tyropoeon Valley at the time. In excavating the eastern hill and its slopes, Kathleen Kenyon came upon a solid wall about 8 feet thick, which she estimated to have been built about 1800 B.C. She based her conclusion on the fact that she found only Middle Bronze pottery of that date in the dirt fill between the wall and the bedrock facing.[13] That Abraham did not encounter any opposition when he came to Mount Moriah to offer Isaac (Gen. 22) suggests that the inhabitants of the area were not strong enough or belligerent enough to organize resistance against him.

Pottery from the latter part of the Middle Bronze II period was also found on the western slopes of the Mount of Olives. These pieces included vessels made of alabaster and faience (a fused bluish or greenish glass material) found there by the Franciscan excavations at the site called Dominus Flevit.[14] This evidence points to some Middle Bronze II settlement of the area to the east of the fortified city of Jerusalem. Of interest is the presence here of foreign, imported objects, indicating possible influence of foreign powers at the time.

Late Bronze Age (The Time of the Exodus)

In addition to the biblical record which speaks of Jerusalem and its kings at the time of Joshua's conquest (e.g., Josh. 10:1), the Amarna Letters of Egypt give some account of the early history of Jerusalem. These letters, covering a span from about 1390 to 1360 B.C., include messages from rulers in Syria and Palestine to the Pharaoh Amenophis IV (Akhenaten), whose government was in a weakened state, concerning the threat to peace made by some warlike people called the Habiru (or Hapiru). Jerusalem, among other

11. Mazar, *Jerusalem Revealed*, p. 3.
12. Ibid., p. 40.
13. Kenyon, *Jerusalem*, p. 24. See also Mazar, *Jerusalem Revealed*, p. 3.
14. Mazar, *Jerusalem Revealed*, p. 3.

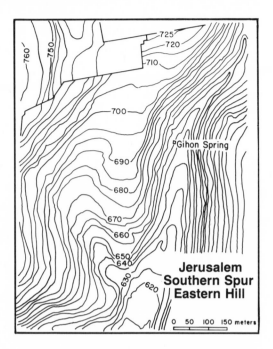

Jerusalem
Southern Spur
Eastern Hill

0   50   100   150 meters

towns, appealed for help.[15] The city was ruled by a certain Abd-Khiba. Six letters in the Amarna group are from the ruler of Jerusalem to the Egyptian king, affirming the loyalty of Jerusalem to Egypt and calling on the Egyptians for help against certain disloyal Canaanite rulers and their warring accomplices, the Habiru. Letters to Egypt from this ruler and other rulers in Canaan suggest that these kings had ties with each other and that Jerusalem was a town of some importance in the fourteenth century B.C.

The Jerusalem of the Late Bronze Age (sixteenth–thirteenth centuries B.C.) basically was still settled on the southeastern hill, as evidenced by stone-filled terraces constructed on the east slopes of that southeastern spur during the fourteenth and thirteenth centuries.[16] The Late Bronze Age sherds and vessels found in the Dominus Flevit excavations on the west slope of the Mount of Olives, together with others found south of Jerusalem, suggest some continued settlement of the area outside the city. Many of these sherds and

15. *Ancient Near Eastern Texts Relating to the Old Testament*, ed. James B. Pritchard, rev. ed. (Princeton: Princeton University Press, 1955), p. 488.
16. Kenyon, *Jerusalem*, plates 29–30.

objects are foreign imports from Cyprus, the Aegean, and Egypt, showing the foreign influence in the land during that period.

It has been suggested that Jerusalem was not Jebusite but Amorite in the Late Bronze Age. For support this view cites the fact that Adoni-zedek, king of Jerusalem, and his confederates are called Amorites in Joshua 10:5. Ezekiel 16:3 also gives some support to this view: "This is what the Sovereign LORD says to Jerusalem: Your ancestry and birth were in the land of the Canaanites; your father was an Amorite and your mother a Hittite." So evidently the Amorites were in control of Jerusalem in the days of Joshua's conquest, although the Hittites as well as the Jebusites were present also (Josh. 15:8). Evidently at some time prior to David's conquest of the city (2 Sam. 5:7–8) the Jebusites had taken control of Jerusalem away from the Amorites, for in Judges 19:10 the city is described as "Jebus (that is, Jerusalem)." Although the Jebusite stronghold was evidently a type of city-state in the midst of surrounding Israel, we should think of it mainly as a small fortified city on the southern spur of the eastern hill, which later was known as the City of David (2 Sam. 5:7).

Davidic and Solomonic Jerusalem

The Jerusalem of David's time consisted of the City of David, that southeastern spur, the area that David took from the Jebusites (2 Sam. 5:7–9). It also presumably included an extension to the north toward the temple mount, the place where Solomon built the supporting terraces and filled in the gap in the wall of the city of David (1 Kings 11:27). It also included the temple mount itself, the site where David purchased the threshing floor of Araunah the Jebusite (2 Sam. 24:16–25) and offered sacrifice. This was the area where Solomon built the temple and his palace. There is no evidence that the settlement extended beyond these limits at the time.

The Monarchy of Judah

Archaeological evidence has shown that during the period of the divided monarchy and the monarchy of Judah alone—that is, from the time of Rehoboam (1 Kings 12) to the Babylonian captivity (2 Kings 24–25)—the city of Jerusalem included the same general area as in the time of the expansion under David and Solomon. The excavations on the eastern ridge of the southeastern spur have produced evidence of continued habitation. Walls and buildings of the eighth and seventh centuries B.C. have been found there, as has evi-

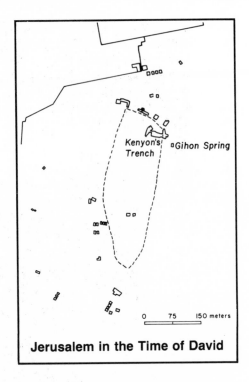

Jerusalem in the Time of David

dence of the massive destruction wrought by Nebuchadnezzar in 586 B.C.[17] Archaeological information about the buildings on the temple mount is not available, since this is a sacred religious site and not open to excavation.

Nevertheless, we do have evidence of expansion to the west of the eastern hill during this period.[18]

Excavations in the Jewish Quarter (the southeastern quarter) of the Old City of Jerusalem in 1969–71 unearthed structural remains indicating some settlement here during the divided monarchy. These include a massive city wall which, from the pottery associated with it, can be dated to the eighth century B.C.

Further, tombs from the eighth and seventh centuries B.C. were found on the lower eastern slopes of the western hill, suggesting that at this date and possibly earlier the kings of Judah were buried here rather than in the royal tombs in the City of David on the eastern hill. Since it was customary to locate cemeteries beyond the borders

17. Ibid., p. 67; plate 53.
18. Yigal Shiloh, *Excavations at the City of David, I, 1978–82* in *Qedem* 19, (Jerusalem: Ahva Press, 1984), pp. 28, 72 (drawing).

The City of David is located on this slope in the Kidron Valley.

of a city, the tombs also suggest that up to this time the central valley (the Tyropoeon) was outside the city proper.[19] From the biblical record it can be postulated that later kings of Judah had their physical remains placed in another necropolis, probably on the eastern side of the Kidron opposite the City of David. Manasseh, for instance, was buried in the garden of Uzza (2 Kings 21:18, cf. 2 Chron. 26:23), which may have been on the eastern slope of the Mount of Olives near the present village of Silwan,[20] where a number of ancient tombs have been found. From this evidence it can be concluded that the necropolis of the kings of Judah was located at first on the eastern slopes of the western hill. When the city expanded into this area, a new necropolis was established on the western slopes of the Mount of Olives.

19. *Encyclopedia of Archaeological Excavations in the Holy Land* (Englewood Cliffs, N.J.: Prentice-Hall, 1976), 2: 597.
20. Mazar, *Jerusalem Revealed*, pp. 8, 40.

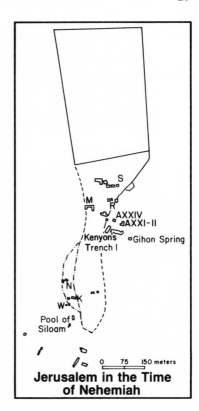

Jerusalem in the Time of Nehemiah

Nehemiah and the Persian Period

When Nehemiah returned from the captivity, he found the walls of the City of David broken down and in disarray (Neh. 2). As the archaeological excavations have shown, he rebuilt these walls, confining himself to the eastern hill from the temple mount southward. The boundaries of his eastern wall ran along the crest of the summit.[21] The conclusion to be drawn is that the western hill at this time was abandoned. There is no solid archaeological evidence regarding Jerusalem's development in the Persian period (539–333/32 B.C.) but the boundaries no doubt continued to be confined to the narrow stretch on the southeastern hill.

21. Kenyon, *Jerusalem*, pp. 107–11.

The Hellenistic and Maccabean Periods

In the earlier part of the Hellenistic period, from about 333/32–
198 B.C., the boundaries of Jerusalem probably continued as they
had been in the time of Nehemiah and in the Persian period. But
after the Seleucids of Syria finally wrested the city from the Ptole-
mies of Egypt in 198 B.C., Jerusalem took on a Hellenistic look. The
new leaders expanded the city again to the western hill, which had
remained unoccupied since the time of Nebuchadnezzar's conquest.
The western hill is what the Hasmoneans came to call the Upper
City. Somewhere in the area of the western hill the Syrians erected
the Akra Fortress (mentioned by Josephus) to overlook the temple
area.[22] At a later time Alexander Jannaeus (104–78 B.C.) built a royal
palace on this site. Thus the city expanded west toward the Citadel
area where Herod the Great's palace was later built.

The city wall was also extended during this period. Running west
from the temple platform, it turned south on the western hill and
then continued east to the region of the Pool of Siloam at the south
end of the eastern hill, where it joined up with the earlier wall of the
Israelite period.[23] It is a moot question whether the Hasmoneans
extended the city north of the Citadel area by building what Josephus calls the second wall. This went to the north and then east
toward the Kidron Valley, turning south to the northwest corner of
the temple compound, where the Antonia Fortress was later constructed. The walled city at this time was the largest it had ever
been.

Herodian Jerusalem

Exactly where all the walls of Jerusalem ran in the Herodian
period (37 B.C.–A.D. 70) is a difficult question which will be discussed
in detail in Chapter 7. However, for the moment we can say that the
walled city included the temple platform and the area west and
slightly to the south of the temple precinct. The southern wall extended south from about the middle of the southern wall of the
temple platform and then continued in a westerly direction past the
present Dung Gate and Zion Gate. Running near the area of what is
traditionally known as David's Tomb, the wall enclosed the northern end of the western hill. Herod the Great's first (north) wall ran

22. Kenyon feels that this is the case (*Jerusalem*, p. 113). Some scholars, however,
think that the Akra fortress was built on the southern spur of the eastern hill; see the
Loeb edition of Josephus (Cambridge, Mass.: Harvard University Press, n.d.), 7: 128–29.
    23. Mazar, *Jerusalem Revealed*, pp. 9–11; Kenyon, *Jerusalem*, p. 109.

east from the Citadel across the Tyropoeon Valley to the west side of the temple platform. Somewhere along this east-west first wall the second wall ran north and then turned east to the Antonia Fortress located at the northwest corner of the temple platform. Herod Agrippa extended the walled city south to include the southern end of the western hill, with the wall running east to meet the wall of the eastern hill at a point south of the Pool of Siloam where the Hinnom Valley meets the Kidron. On the western hill Agrippa also extended the city north to include at least the area from the Jaffa Gate northwest to the New Gate and then northeast over to the Kidron Valley and south to the temple platform, along the line of the present north wall of Jerusalem.[24] Many scholars feel that this was Josephus's third wall. Others, however, argue that the third wall ran farther north, near the grounds of the Albright Institute.

In this period various necropolis areas developed. Early Jewish tombs have been found inside the Church of the Holy Sepulchre and also farther west beyond the old walled city (e.g., Herod's family tombs), also to the north (e.g., the so-called Tombs of the Kings), and to the east in the Kidron Valley and along the western slopes of the Mount of Olives.

Roman and Byzantine Jerusalem

After the destruction of Jerusalem in A.D. 70 the Tenth Roman Legion was left to rule over the ruins. It was not until the second Jewish revolt (132–35) that the Romans decided to undertake a major change in the physical nature of the city. The Emperor Hadrian directed that Jerusalem be rebuilt and renamed Aelia Capitolina. An inscription with this name can be seen over one of the ancient entrances of the Damascus Gate excavated by the British archaeologist J. B. Hennessey in 1964–66.[25] The new Roman city was built over the former Jewish one. Some of the ruins were removed. Fill was added to level out parts of the old city. The main axis of the Roman city was the north-south street that can be seen today running south from the Damascus Gate, which is located in the north wall. Thus the north wall of Aelia Capitolina was approximately the same as the present north wall of the Old City. The eastern hill south of the temple platform was abandoned; the evidence for this is the quarrying which was done there to obtain stone for the new city farther

24. Kenyon, *Jerusalem*, pp. 155–62.

25. J. B. Hennessey, "Preliminary Report on Excavations at the Damascus Gate, 1964–6," *Levant* 2 (1970): 22–27.

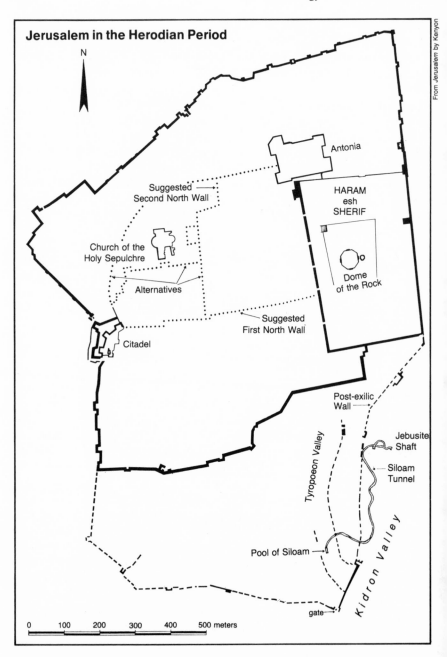

Jerusalem in the Herodian Period

N

Antonia

HARAM
esh
SHERIF

Suggested
Second North Wall

Church of the
Holy Sepulchre

Dome
of the Rock

Alternatives

Suggested
First North Wall

Citadel

Post-exilic
Wall

Jebusite
Shaft

Tyropoeon Valley

Siloam
Tunnel

Pool of Siloam

Kidron Valley

gate

0   100   200   300   400   500 meters

From *Jerusalem* by Kenyon

north. The south wall of the Aelia Capitolina ran east-west from the Kidron on the south side of the temple platform. At about the point of the present al-Aqsa Mosque, the wall turned south with salient (projecting) angles for about 275 feet and then made an angle west along the line of the main south wall of the present Old City over to the slopes of the Hinnom Valley. The wall continued north past the Citadel and then northwest to the point of the present north wall, where it turned northeast to the Damascus Gate.

During the Byzantine period extensive church-building operations were carried on in various locations on the Mount of Olives. In the flurry created by the increase in the number of visitors, the city spilled beyond the southern limits of Aelia Capitolina to include the area enclosed by the southern wall of Herod Agrippa, a wall that ran above the Hinnom Valley toward the Kidron. This wall enclosed the southern end of the western hill, the Pool of Siloam, and the eastern hill along the Kidron south of the Temple platform.[26]

Islamic, Crusader, and Ottoman Jerusalem

During the Islamic, Crusader, and Ottoman periods there was extensive building of Arab and Ottoman structures and church edifices. The boundaries of the city on the north remained the same, but the wall on the south no longer enclosed the eastern hill and the southern end of the western hill. In other words, the walls enclosed virtually the same area that had been enclosed by the walls of Aelia Capitolina. Essentially the same lines were followed in the rebuilding operations of the Ottoman ruler, Suleiman the Magnificent, in 1538–41.[27]

Jerusalem Today

The dimensions of the Old City of Jerusalem are well known. The outline of the present Old City is virtually the same as the boundaries of Aelia Capitolina. Of course, there have been extensions of the city, but the Old City is being preserved as a separate unit.

We have seen that the area encompassed by the city of Jerusalem varied with each of its historical periods. We now turn to examine the evidence of the archaeological remains of each of those periods.

26. Kenyon, *Jerusalem*, pp. 192–93.
27. Ibid., pp. 194–97; Mazar, *Jerusalem Revealed*, p. 96.

The Jerusalem Area
in Pre-Davidic Times

$\mathcal{C}$eramics and tools which have been found in the Jerusalem area indicate that it was inhabited back in the prehistoric periods, including Neolithic (ca. 8000–4000 B.C.). Until recently, however, the earliest literary evidence associating this location with the name *Jerusalem* came from the nineteenth–eighteenth centuries B.C. (the Egyptian Execration Texts). Now it appears that Jerusalem may actually be mentioned in the Ebla tablets, which were recently discovered.[1] These have been dated between 2600 and 2300 B.C.[2]

1. "Of particular interest to students of Syro-Palestinian archaeology, as well as of the Old Testament, is the 3rd millennium documentation at Ebla of cities hitherto epigraphically attested in the 2nd–1st millennia B.C., such as Salem, the city of Melchizedek, Hazor, Lachish, Megiddo, Gaza, Dor, Sinai, Ashtarot, Joppa, etc." (Giovanni Pettinato, "The Royal Archives of Tell Mardikh-Ebla," *Biblical Archaeologist* 39.2 [1976]:46).

2. P. Matthiae, the Italian excavator, argues for the period 2400–2250 B.C. (*Biblical Archaeologist* 39.3 [1976]: 102). The Italian epigrapher Pettinato argues for an earlier date, 2600 B.C., noting two Egyptian cartouches found at Ebla—one of Pepi I of the Sixth Dynasty (twenty-fourth century B.C.) and the other of Khephren of the Fourth Dynasty (twenty-sixth century B.C.) (*Biblical Archaeologist* 41.4 [1978]: 146).

This means that the Jerusalem area was a place of considerable importance at least one thousand and perhaps two thousand years before it became particularly prominent at the time of David.

Prehistoric Times

Prehistoric remains have been found at a site in the upper part of the Valley of Rephaim (also known as Baqa') in the Greek Quarter just to the southwest of the Hinnom Valley. This site was excavated first in 1933 by M. Stekelis and later in 1962 under the direction of B. Arensburg and O. Bar-Yosef. Three strata were uncovered. Stratum 1, an alluvial layer up to six and a half feet thick, contains some prehistoric flint hand axes, flakes, and sherds of various periods; some of the sherds have been dated at least as far back as the Neolithic period. Stratum 2, a gravel layer almost two feet thick, contained many flint hand axes, cores, and flakes; and Stratum 3, which was found between the gravel layer of Stratum 2 and underlying rock, has yielded lentil-shaped inclusions of brown clay. Stekelis and the excavators in 1962 were of the opinion that the materials in Strata 2 and 3 are to be dated to the Abbevillian or early Acheulian periods.[3] R. A. S. Macalister and J. G. Duncan in their report of the 1923–25 excavations on Ophel Hill (i.e., the area of the City of David above the Kidron Valley, including the more or less level sector above the Gihon spring) indicated that they found there evidence of material from the Neolithic period, including pottery fragments with a cord-pattern design.[4]

Early Bronze Age

The evidence for occupation of the Jerusalem area in the Early Bronze Age (ca. 3200–2100 B.C.) is minimal. All we have are ceramic fragments and possible epigraphical evidence for the name *Jerusalem* from the tablets found at Tell Mardikh.

3. *Encyclopedia of Archaeological Excavations in the Holy Land*, 2: 579–80. See also G. A. Barrois, "Valley of Rephaim," *The Interpreter's Dictionary of the Bible*. W. F. Albright, *The Archaeology of Palestine* (Baltimore: Penguin, 1961), pp. 52, 54, dates the Acheulian period from 180,000 to 230,000 years ago and the Abbevillian period before that. But see R. L. Harris, *God's Eternal Creation* (Chicago: Moody, 1971), pp. 62–66, who effectively argues for a considerable lowering of the dates for early man and gives evidence to show that the dating of ancient fossils is quite debatable.
4. R. A. S. Macalister and J. G. Duncan, "Excavations on the Hill of Ophel, Jerusalem," *Palestine Exploration Fund Annual, 1923–1925* (London: Palestine Exploration Fund, 1926), pp. 10, 173.

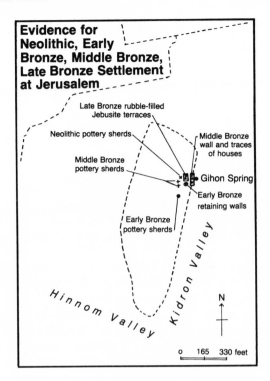

Evidence for Neolithic, Early Bronze, Middle Bronze, Late Bronze Settlement at Jerusalem

Late Bronze rubble-filled Jebusite terraces

Neolithic pottery sherds

Middle Bronze pottery sherds

Middle Bronze wall and traces of houses

Gihon Spring

Early Bronze retaining walls

Early Bronze pottery sherds

Hinnom Valley

Kidron Valley

N

0   165   330 feet

The Parker expedition of 1909–18 found painted pottery of about 3000 B.C. (Early Bronze I) at the lower end of the southeastern ridge of Jerusalem. This pottery displays several of the characteristics typical of the Early Bronze I period: diagonal and wavy lines, cross-hatch design, and cord-eye handles.[5] Macalister and Duncan reported the finds in the Ophel area of Early Bronze pottery fragments with the characteristic ledge, loop, and cord-eye handles.[6] Benjamin Mazar indicated that in the excavations south of the present south Dung Gate in the fill beneath these walls were found pottery sherds from the Early Bronze period, as well as sherds from the Middle Bronze (ca. 2100–1550 B.C.), Late Bronze (ca. 1550–1200 B.C.), and Iron I (1200–1000 B.C.) periods. Further, Kurt Galling has pointed out that forty caves located to the north of Ophel and immediately below the southeast corner of the

5. Benjamin Mazar, *The Mountain of the Lord* (Garden City, N.Y.: Doubleday, 1975), pp. 164–65. The results of the Parker expedition were published by L. H. Vincent. See *Encyclopedia of Archaeological Excavations in the Holy Land*, 2: 583.

6. Macalister and Duncan, "Hill of Ophel," pp. 171–77.

Middle Bronze wall at Ophel excavated by Kenyon.

temple also contain material of the period just subsequent to Early Bronze I (ca. 3200–2850 B.C.).[7]

This points to at least some occupation in the Early Bronze period in this area of Jerusalem, but the evidence is certainly not extensive.[8]

However, Mazar is quite confident that retaining walls discovered on the Ophel Hill on the side of the Kidron Valley show that in the third millennium the sector was occupied and involved at times in elaborate urban development. This occupation continued down through the second millennium B.C.

> Retaining walls on the hill had served to strengthen the terraces upon which the city's houses were built. . . . The finds dating from the

7. Kurt Galling, "Die Necropole von Jerusalem," *Palestinajahrbuch*, vol. 36 (1936) pp. 90–95; Sylvester J. Saller, *The Jebusite Burial Place in the Excavations at Dominus Flevit* (Jerusalem: Franciscan Press, 1964) Part 2, p. 195; J. Simon, *Jerusalem in the Old Testament* (Leiden: E. J. Brill, 1952), p. 195.3.4.

8. Hershel Shanks, "Report from Jerusalem," *Biblical Archaeology Review*, III, 4 (1977): 23. Benjamin Mazar found pottery there from the Early Bronze period.

Bronze Age and the beginning of the Iron Age, including more particularly those discovered in the tombs, attest to continuous occupation during the third and second millennia B.C., and rather elaborate urban development during several periods.[9]

Rahmani states that in an Early Canaanite I (3100–2900 B.C.) tomb cave at Ophel Hill there were found skeletons, food remnants, bones covered with red ochre (symbolic of life force), and painted vessels similar to those found at Mispah, Gezer, and Jericho VI–VII. He concludes that there is some question yet as to whether there existed an early Canaanite settlement at Jerusalem but suggests that pockets of sherds seem to indicate some settlement on Ophel Hill in this period.[10]

Middle and Late Bronze Periods

The Ophel Hill Area

In an early excavation an imported Cypriot milk bowl of Middle Bronze I was found on the southeastern ridge of Jerusalem. Other pottery remains of the Middle and Late Bronze periods were also found by various excavations in debris overlying bedrock on the southeastern spur and its slopes.[11]

In a double cave at the village of Hablet el 'Amud on the eastern slope near the town of Silwan were found disarticulated bones of the Middle Canaanite period heaped in different parts of the cave and pottery of the Jericho type, a pattern Kenyon suggests indicates reburial sites of Nomadic tribes; there were pottery lamps in the wall niches or on the floor.[12]

In addition, Kenyon found on the eastern slope remains of a solid wall about eight feet thick and also remains of an adjacent tower built of rough boulders, a fortification which seems to have been erected in Middle Bronze IIA (1950–1750 B.C.) and which continued in use for some time.

Kenyon indicates that along the Ophel slope there are a few traces of houses from about 1800 B.C. (one hundred to two hundred years after Abraham). This is evidence that in the Middle Bronze period Jerusalem was extended east on terraces down the slope in order to bring the town as near the water supply of Gihon as possible. Concerning this Middle Bronze extension of Jerusalem

9. Mazar, *The Mountain of the Lord*, p. 50.
10. L. Y. Rahmani, "Ancient Jerusalem's Funerary Customs and Tombs, Part Two," *Biblical Archaeologist* 44.4 (1981): 229–30.
11. *Encyclopedia of Archaeological Excavations in the Holy Land*, 2: 583.
12. Rahmani, "Ancient Jerusalem's Funerary Customs," pp. 229–30.

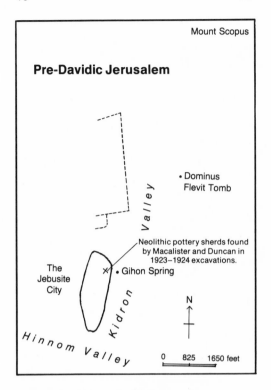

Mount Scopus

Pre-Davidic Jerusalem

• Dominus
  Flevit Tomb

Valley

Neolithic pottery sherds found
by Macalister and Duncan in
1923–1924 excavations.

The
Jebusite   × • Gihon Spring
City

Kidron

N

Hinnom Valley

0   825   1650 feet

Sïlwan, on the slopes of the Kidron Valley.

Kathleen Kenyon discovered the remains of King David's Jerusalem
in this trench on the eastern slope of the Ophel. The trench gives
evidence of Middle Bronze and later period walls.

east and beyond the summit down the slope of the southeastern
ridge, Kenyon states:

> The area so added to the town is uninviting. The present surface slopes
> at an angle of nearly 45°, that of the underlying bedrock at about 25°.
> This would create problems of lay-out for a town. Only a few traces of
> the houses belonging to the earliest defences of c. 1800 B.C. survived.
> They climbed the slope of the hill, following the angle of the rock, and,
> as might be expected, were small and irregularly planned to accommo-
> date themselves to the slope and its irregularities.[13]

On this slope, in a stratum lower than that of the remains of a
massive stone building of the seventh century B.C. (a date determined by the pottery sherds) Kenyon found evidences of an even
more massive wall in the scarp in the natural rock. On the basis of
sherds she found in a fill between the wall and the rock face, she
dated this wall to about 1800 B.C.[14]

Yigal Shiloh found another segment of this wall in his Area E 1
farther to the south of Kenyon's trench A. He calls it the city wall of
the time and also dates it to 1800 B.C. The three phases of this city
wall in Shiloh's Area E 1 included fills, walls, and pavements and

---

13. Kathleen Kenyon, *Jerusalem* (New York: McGraw-Hill, 1967), p. 31.
14. Ibid., p. 24.

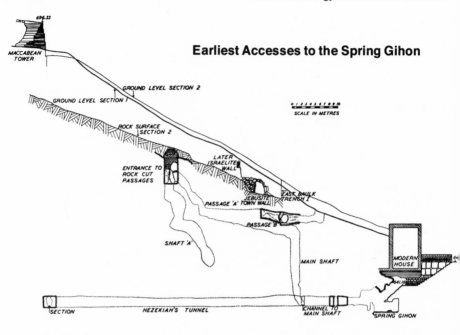

Earliest Accesses to the Spring Gihon

contained pottery dated from the end of Middle Bronze II A and the beginning of Middle Bronze II B.[15]

This early Jebusite wall was positioned about two-thirds of the way down the Ophel slope.[16] If the wall had been built at the bottom of the slope in order to bring the Spring Gihon inside the city, the city would have been left open to attack from the east side of the Kidron Valley. Access to the spring was made available by constructing, from inside the wall, "a stepped entrance twenty-six feet deep and a connecting horizontal slightly oblique tunnel extending east ninety-two feet. At that point now outside the wall and still underground, a shaft forty feet deep was cut to the level of the water flow coming from Gihon seventy-two feet farther east."[17] It was this system that David used in later centuries to gain entrance inside the wall and thus conquer the city (2 Sam. 5:8).

On the slope above the Jebusite wall of 1800 B.C., Kenyon en-

15. Yigal Shiloh, *Excavations at the City of David, I, 1978–82* in *Qedem* 19 (Jerusalem: Ahva Press, 1984), p. 26.

16. Kenyon also notes that this earliest wall had a reentrant angle (i.e., an angle that turned in), suggesting the presence of a tower, possibly a gate tower. See *Digging Up Jerusalem* (London: Ernest Benn, 1974), pp. 83, 86–87; plates 19–20.

17. Kenyon, *Jerusalem*, pp. 24–25; Yigal Shiloh, *Excavations at the City of David, I, 1978–82,* in *Qedem* 19 (Jerusalem: Ahva Press, 1984), pp. 21, 22.

countered huge stone structures, the nucleus of which consisted almost entirely of rubble-filled compartments. These structures were part of a series of terraces built on the east slope of the Ophel hill. Kenyon came to the conclusion that this terrace system is to be attributed to the biblical Jebusites of the Late Bronze Age (fragmentary pottery sherds make a date of the fourteenth–thirteenth centuries B.C. seem certain).

In his Area G, located a little to the left of the top of Kenyon's trench A, Shiloh also found evidence of these terraces, which he discovered did not continue farther south along the slope. In this unique planning technique, used for support purposes, these rock and earth-filled casement type terraces running close to the bedrock and sloping to the north and west, faced south and east. The casemates butted up against one another to form a massive substructure: a two-main terrace system rising to the height of more than thirty-three feet. This system added an artificial surface of 650 square feet to the upper part of the ridge. The terraces in Shiloh's Area G rise abruptly beyond the natural line of the hill, not conforming to the gradient of the eastern slope, but contrasting with terraces normally built on the slope. Terraces farther south in Shiloh's Area E 1 were built on the eastern slope to accommodate eighth- to sixth-century B.C. dwellings. Shiloh argues that the site of this massive structure in Area G, in the upper end of the City of David, was used first as the Canaanite-Jebusite Citadel and then later in the Iron II period as the Citadel of David. Arguing that Ophel is an urban architectural term for citadel or acropolis, a term used for an acropolis area in Jerusalem (Isa. 32:14; Micah 4:8; Neh 3:26, 27; 11:21; 2 Chron. 27:3; 33:14), as well as in Samaria (2 Kings 5:24), and in the Dibon acropolis built by Mesha, etc., Shiloh contends that where Old Testament passages mention Ophel as a location in Jerusalem, they are referring to the Citadel area at this north end of the City of David.[18] The NIV translates this Hebrew word as *citadel* in Isaiah 32:14 and as *stronghold* in Micah 4:8. Both instances refer to this acropolis at the City of David. In connection with this massive terracing in Area G, Shiloh has also helped to further excavate the tremendously large tenth-century B.C. stepped-stone structure (the 1982 exposure being forty-three feet wide, fifty-four feet high, and having fifty-five steps) which in part is integrated with that Late Bronze terracing and in part covers it.[19]

18. Kenyon, *Digging Up Jerusalem*, pp. 94–95; plates 28–29; Shiloh, *ibid*, pp. 16, 26, 55 (figures 17, 18)."Ophel, Mound, hill, only as acropolis," Brown, Driver and Briggs, *A Hebrew and English Lexicon* (Boston: Houghton Mifflin, 1907), p. 779.
19. Shiloh, *ibid*, p. 17.

In her excavation of the Ophel area, Kenyon could find only a little evidence for the western boundary of Middle Bronze–Late Bronze Age Jerusalem. She concluded it ran along the western crest of the ridge. In summary, she says that the Middle Bronze–Late Bronze Jebusite Jerusalem was confined to the top of the eastern ridge and far enough down the eastern slope of that ridge to control the waters of Gihon.[20]

The Dominus Flevit Tomb

Discoveries found in cemeteries of the Middle and Late Bronze periods on the western slope of the Mount of Olives across the Kidron Valley from the northern part of the southeastern ridge point to at least sporadic early settlement outside the relatively small fortified area of Jerusalem.[21] For example, the Dominus Flevit excavations in a Jebusite cemetery unearthed pottery and other remains of the Middle Bronze II, Late Bronze I, and Late Bronze II periods. This Jebusite burial place has a bilobate shape, such as is found also at Fara (identified as bilobate by Flinders Petrie), Gaza, and Lachish. Petrie says that the usual plan of this type of tomb "had a stairway descending from the north and through a narrow doorway on to a ridge from which a step led down into a chamber on either hand. Thus the roof was held up in the middle, yet nearly every chamber had collapsed."[22] Just how the bilobate tomb on the west slope of the Mount of Olives was reached was not clear at the time it was written up by Sylvester Saller (1964), but it can be deduced that since the west end of the tomb is filled with artifacts associated with skeletal remains, the entrance to the tomb would be at the eastern end. "These elements seem to indicate the close relationship of this tomb with those in Southern Palestine and suggest that all should be more or less of the same date, which, however, is not determined by the form but by the contents."[23]

Since the tomb contains many more artifacts than do other tombs in the area, Saller argues that it was used for burials longer than were the others. As to a more precise dating of this Jebusite burial place, W. F. Albright on January 23, 1956, wrote to P. Lemaire:

20. Kenyon, *Digging Up Jerusalem*, pp. 93, 94.
21. Quoted in Saller, *Dominus Flevit*, Pt. 2, p. 7.
22. Ibid.
23. Ibid.

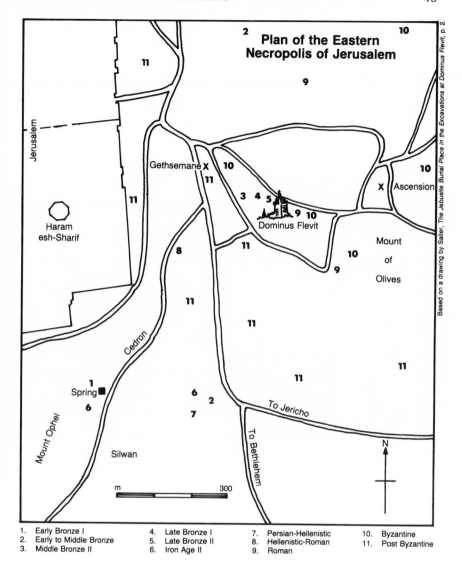

Plan of the Eastern
Necropolis of Jerusalem

Based on a drawing by Saller, *The Jebusite Burial Place in the Excavations at Dominus Flevit,* p. 2.

1. Early Bronze I
2. Early to Middle Bronze
3. Middle Bronze II
4. Late Bronze I
5. Late Bronze II
6. Iron Age II
7. Persian-Hellenistic
8. Hellenistic-Roman
9. Roman
10. Byzantine
11. Post Byzantine

It is very interesting to find a tomb of the outgoing Middle Bronze and the early Late Bronze in this situation. The tomb must have been used intermittently over a considerable interval of time. . . . A number of alabastra and two of the scarabs point to a beginning date no later than the 16th century. The same is true of a few of the vases. . . . I am inclined to think that you have one or more burials in the 16th cen-

tury and others in the Late Bronze. In any case, the pieces you presented cover a period from about 1600 to 1300 B.C.[24]

In more than one instance the Dominus Flevit tomb can be compared to finds at Jericho and other sites. Materials from Jericho that
fall within the second millennium B.C. give clues to the dates of
similar materials found in the Dominus Flevit tomb. Saller notes
that Albright led the way in revising the Jericho chronology: "As a
result of his experiences at Tell Beit Mirsim he was able to assert
that '[John] Garstang is entirely correct in stressing the resem-
blances between the Jericho pottery and the 'Thotmes III' stratum
at Bethshan as well as that of C1, but most of this material should
be dated in the fourteenth century instead of the fifteenth.' "[25]

In his comparative study Saller sees a close parallel between a
group of small painted jars from Dominus Flevit and similar jars
found in tombs 5 and 13 at Jericho by Garstang. Also, it is to be
noted that in dealing with jars from Jericho which resemble those
from Dominus Flevit, Kenyon dated them from the initial date of
about 1400 B.C. to a terminal date of after 1350 B.C.

Parallels to the Dominus Flevit tomb are also found in and
around Jerusalem. For example, in materials from another tomb in
Jerusalem, which are dated Late Bronze II, Ruth Amiran has found
parallels to the pottery from Dominus Flevit.[26] Other parallels are
found in the tomb at Naḥlat Aḥim in the northwest section of Jerusalem. The contents of this rock-cut tomb which was found in 1933,
date to the middle of Late Bronze II—that is, to the fourteenth
century B.C.[27] The Cypriot pottery of the Late Bronze period which
was found there helps us to determine the period of the Dominus
Flevit pottery and "to fix the terminus ad quem of our tomb. It also
seems to indicate that the city of the 14th C. B.C. was not limited to
Ophel Hill in the neighborhood of the spring but had suburbs extending quite far to the northwest."[28] A tomb to the south of Jerusalem, on the site of the United Nations Headquarters (formerly the
residence of the British high commissioner), may point to another
Late Bronze II[29] suburb.

24. Ibid., p. 3.
25. Ibid., p. 28.
26. Ruth Amiran, *Eretz-Israel* 6 (1960): 25–37 (Hebrew); 77 (English summary).
27. Saller, *Dominus Flevit*, Pt. 2, pp. 196–97.
28. Ibid.; D. C. Baramki, "An Ancient Cistern in the Grounds of Government
House, Jerusalem," *The Quarterly of the Department of Antiquities in Palestine*, 4
(1935): 165–67.
29. Saller, *Dominus Flevit*, Pt. 2, pp. 7–8.

Cylindrical Juglet

Of the artifacts found in the Dominus Flevit tomb, Saller takes particular note of a cylindrical juglet. Similar objects have been found at Fara, Gaza, and Lachish. He observes that this juglet is characteristic of the Hyksos period and that this tomb contained other Hyksos artifacts. For that reason he surmises that it could have been a Hyksos burial place. However, since the tomb also contained objects of a time when the Hyksos were no longer in Palestine but the Jebusites were still there, this leads to the conclusion that this tomb on the western slopes of the Mount of Olives was a Jebusite burial place.[30] Other cylindrical and related juglets from the tomb help to determine that it was used as a burial site from about the end of the Middle Bronze Age down to the Late Bronze II period. For comparison we turn to a tomb in Amman.[31] Several cylindrical juglets found there share peculiarities with the Dominus Flevit juglet. These peculiarities are difficult to match elsewhere—for example, the flat raised base, which is not common in Palestine (though it does occur to a limited degree at Ras Shamra).[32] We may conclude, then, that the Dominus Flevit tomb chronologically overlaps the tomb in Amman, which has been dated to about 1700–1400 B.C.

Small Painted Jars and Bowls

Other artifacts found in the Jebusite tomb complex also point to the Middle and Late Bronze periods. Such artifacts include small painted jars with metopes (panels) which can be compared to metopes of Mycenaean vases from the Late Bronze II period. Most of the larger jars have a small flat base and date to the Middle Bronze Age.[33] The very large quantity of bowls found in the tomb complex (based on complete and fragmentary remains, scholars estimate over one thousand bowls; the fragments alone number three thousand) includes a variety of forms. There are carinated bowls (having sharp curves on their sides), bowls with straight or curved sides, and miniature bowls. The bowls have trumpet-disk, ring, flat, and rounded bases. Saller concludes that the large quantity points to a long period of use; the general lack of variety points to stability:

30. Ibid., pp. 7–8, 105.
31. Saller, *Dominus Flevit*, Pt. 2, p. 105.
32. Ibid.
33. Ibid., pp. 29, 31.

Small painted and unpainted jars from Dominus Flevit tomb.

Our detailed studies indicated that each type of bowl found in our tomb was found also in many other places in Palestine and that each type was in use for many centuries. Our group of bowls, therefore, serves as an important link between our tomb and many other tombs, between Jerusalem and many other places, and that for a long time without important changes.[34]

Jugs

The Jebusite burial place also yielded a good many jugs, some of them with a shoulder handle, which is characteristic of the Middle and Late Bronze Ages. The *Gallery Book of the Palestine Archaeological Museum* notes that the shoulder handle is found only during the Middle Bronze period (2100–1600 B.C.) and the transition to the Late Bronze period (1600–1500 B.C.)[35] Among the variety found at Dominus Flevit are jugs with a short neck or no neck at all, jugs with handles from

34. Ibid., p. 73.
35. *Gallery Book of the Palestinian Archaeological Museum for the Stone and Bronze Ages*, p. 63, no. 866; Saller, *Dominus Flevit*, Pt. 2, p. 78. In an unpublished paper entitled "Introduction to Ancient Pottery," James A. Sauer attributes the shoulder handle to Middle Bronze II.

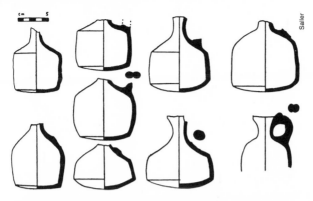

Cylindrical and related juglets from Dominus Flevit tomb.

the rim or the neck to the shoulder, biconical and carinated jugs. One in particular closely resembles a jug found at Jericho which Kenyon calls a carinated jar. "A terminal date somewhat after 1350 . . . seems to be required, while an initial date round about 1400 is suggested by the absence of exclusively fifteenth century forms."[36]

The decoration of biconical jugs from the Dominus Flevit tomb is paralleled in similar jugs discovered at Hazor, whose date is projected as Late Bronze II.[37] Jugs with flat bottoms seem to span the entire period in which the Dominus Flevit tomb was used for burials, while disk-base jugs, both plain and decorated, fall into the Late Bronze I period and the first half-century of Late Bronze II.[38]

Dippers[39]

Dippers with pointed bases and dippers with rounded bases have been found in the Dominus Flevit tomb. Those with pointed bases initially are from the Middle Bronze II period and seem to have

36. Saller, *Dominus Flevit*, Pt. 2, p. 84; Yigael Yadin, Yohanan Aharoni, Ruth Amiran, Trude Dothan, Immanuel Dunayevsky, Jean Perrot, and S. Angress, *Hazor II, An Account of the Second Season of Excavations, 1956* (Jerusalem: Magnes Press, Hebrew University, 1960), p. 149; plate CXXXIV, 8–11.

37. Ibid., p. 84.

38. Ibid., pp. 86–8; cf. Olga Tufnell, et al., *Lachish IV (Tell ed-Duweir) the Bronze Age* (London: Oxford University Press, 1958), p. 216.

39. In Jericho Kenyon found dippers which she dated as early as her first phase of Middle Bronze II (shortly after 1850 B.C.) and as late as her fifth phase (*Archaeology in the Holy Land* [London: Ernst Benn, 1960], pp. 170, 177). Harding says the tomb at Amman which can be used for comparison with Dominus Flevit is Middle Bronze, but Isserlin believes that part of the evidence from the tomb of Amman should be dated to Late Bronze I ("Four Tomb Groups from Jordan").

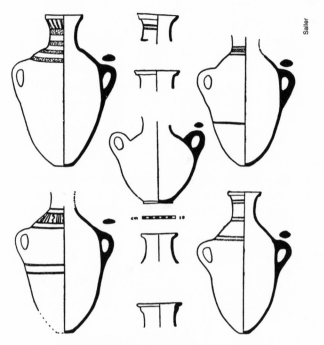

Large jars from Dominus Flevit tomb.

been in use down into the later part of Late Bronze. The dippers with rounded bases overlap in part those with pointed bases. The fact that in temples II and III at Lachish (1400–1223 B.C.) dippers with rounded bases eventually supplanted dippers with pointed bases suggests that the former may have been in use at Dominus Flevit down into the Late Bronze II period as well.[40]

Ring-Base Ware

In the Dominus Flevit tomb were found a number of pottery examples of the ring-base type, both genuine and imitation. These vessels have a ring at the base which is internally arched or inverted in the center. The form and decoration of this group are paralleled in places such as Lachish and Hazor and Jericho.[41] The change from

40. Saller, *Dominus Flevit*, Pt. 2, pp. 124–25; cf. Olga Tufnell, Charles H. Inge, Lankester Harding, *Lachish II (Tell ed-Duweir), The Fosse Temple* (London: Oxford University Press, 1940), plate L II B, cols. II and III; Tufnell et al., *Lachish IV*, plate 78, nos. 795–800.

41. There were found sixteen jugs, thirty-three juglets, a mug, a jug with handles attached to the rim, and four bowls (Saller, *Dominus Flevit*, Pt. 2, p. 129, 137).

true ring-base ware to imitations is said to have come into use in Lachish no earlier than the time of Amenhotep III (1411–1375 B.C.), and the Hazor imitations belong to Late Bronze II.[42] There are also close parallels in form characteristics in examples found at Jericho, pointing to a close relationship with Dominus Flevit. All of this evidence "would make a date late in the fourteenth century B.C. possible also for our jugs. The group would help to fix the terminus ad quem for the use of our Jebusite burial place."[43]

Goblets or Pedestal Vases

Some of the earliest ware from the Jebusite burial place consists of goblets or pedestal vases. There are about eight in all, including one virtually whole, five nearly whole, and some fragments. A date toward the end of Middle Bronze II has been given to this ware.[44]

Lamps

The Dominus Flevit tomb yielded more than three hundred clay lamps, many of which were partially broken; fifty-three, however, were complete or almost so. They were all of the saucer type, and are to be dated generally from the Middle Bronze I period to the first half of Late Bronze II. Most of the lamps had rounded bottoms; twenty-seven had flat bottoms. The lamps had a spout which was formed by pinching the rim of the sides together. Seldom was a straight channel produced in this manner. The Dominus Flevit lamps do not have a broad, flat rim like the F- and G-class lamps of Lachish which are dated to the thirteenth century B.C.[45] Hence the lamps of Dominus Flevit are to be considered earlier. It is on the basis of comparison with similar lamps from a tomb at Megiddo that we conclude the Dominus Flevit lamps came into use in Middle Bronze I and continued throughout Middle Bronze II into Late

---

42. Saller, *Dominus Flevit*, Pt. 2, p. 137.
43. Ibid.
44. Ibid., pp. 138–41.
45. Lamps like those at Dominus Flevit are first in evidence at Megiddo in Stratum XIV (1850–1800, Middle Bronze I; see G. Loud, *Megiddo II*, plate 47.2). The flat base first appeared in Stratum XI (1700–1650; Geoffrey M. Shipton, *Notes on the Megiddo Pottery of Strata VI–XX* [Chicago: University of Chicago Press, 1939], paragraph 85). Only infrequently is this type of base found in Late Bronze II (P. L. O. Guy and Robert M. Engberg, *Megiddo Tombs* [Chicago: University of Chicago Press, 1938], p. 156). In Stratum VIII at Megiddo (1479–1350) lamps with a squeezed lip were found; this constituted very strong evidence for the beginning of the Late Bronze Age. Only rarely did Dominus Flevit have lamps with squeezed lips. Saller, *Dominus Flevit*, Pt. 2, pp. 142–48.

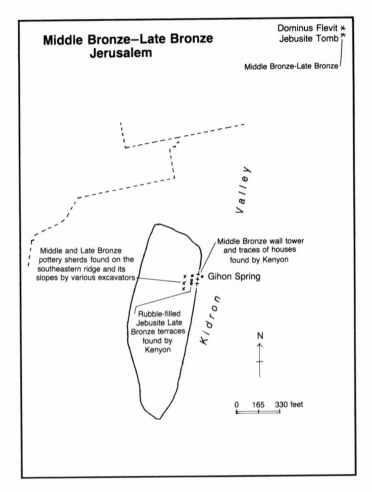

Bronze I.[46] Lamps with a turned-back rim came into use only in Late Bronze II.

Miscellaneous Pottery Objects[47]

Miscellaneous clay objects included flasks (lentoid and handle-less), cooking pots, a vessel with a strainer on its side wall opening into an external spout, a bowl with three looped legs, a cup or

46. "Peculiar to our collection of lamps is that fact that not one has the turned-back rim, said to be peculiar to Late Bronze II. According to the evidence from Lachish it seems the turned-back rim came into use in the latter part of Late Bronze II when our tomb was no longer in use" (Saller, *Dominus Flevit*, Pt. 2, p. 148).

47. Ibid., pp. 149–50.

goblet (red ware), chalices, a fragment of a female figurine, phallic symbols, Mycenaean vases, a zoomorphic vase representing a bull, a rattle, painted sherds, and incised ornaments.

Dating for the lentoid flasks can be projected by comparison with similar flasks found in the Fosse Temple at Lachish. "It is clear that the [lentoid] form was just coming into fashion towards the end of the fourteenth century and that the best decorated are contemporary with the rise of flared bowls after 1300 B.C. . . . Everywhere these flasks came into use in Late Bronze II. They serve to mark the terminus ad quem of our deposit."[48]

Two horn-shaped, round clay objects suggest that those who used Dominus Flevit as a burial site were involved in a phallic cult. The two objects in question, about 2½ inches in length and from 1 inch to 1⅛ inches in diameter, consist of an ashy gray to black ware with brown slip.

A Mycenaean three-handled vase is to be dated to the fourteenth century B.C. Close parallels have been found at Lachish. Another vase found, also with three handles, is a local imitation of the Greek Mycenaean ware. The zoomorphic vase, 8¾ inches long and about 4⅜ inches in diameter, was shaped like a bull, with its horns turned out, flat ears, pellets for eyes, and an open muzzle through which the liquid could be poured out. The ware was gray with a white slip. The Palestine Archaeological Museum has on display similar Cypriot vases from the Late Bronze period, and there are close parallels from Hazor dated to Late Bronze II, as well as from Stratum VIII (1479–1350 B.C.) and Stratum V (1050–1000 B.C.) at Megiddo. There is a possible parallel of a bull vase found in a Middle Bronze Age tomb at Amman.[49]

Alabaster and Faience Glass

Comparison of the alabaster vases found in the Dominus Flevit tomb with similar vases from other sites suggests that they were imported from Egypt during the Middle Bronze II period. From his study of the alabaster objects found at Dominus Flevit, Ben Dor has

---

48. Ibid., pp. 149–50.
49. Yadin et al., *Hazor II*, p. 156; plate 152.12; Loud, *Megiddo II*; plate 247.4; G. H. May and R. M. Engberg, *Material Remains of the Megiddo Cult* (Chicago: University of Chicago Press, 1938), plate xxxviii, 3016, p. 34; Saller, Dominus Flevit, 2, pp. 156–159. Cf. J. Simon, *Jerusalem in the Old Testament* (Leiden: E. J. Brill, 1952), p. 200, Note 6.

concluded that "they indicate that Jebusite Jerusalem had commercial contacts with Egypt."[50]

Only two pieces of glass, both of them in the form of plaques, were found in the Dominus Flevit tomb. Close parallels found at Tell ed-Duweir, Lachish, and Megiddo are to be dated to 1550–1479 B.C. Faience vessels (five in number) were also found; the faience was made of sand and clay with lime added. Parallels are found at Lachish and Jericho. The date assigned would be Middle Bronze II.

The twenty-eight beads found at Dominus Flevit were made of a glassy paste or, in some cases, of stone. They came in a variety of colors: red, white, blue, brown, and black.[51]

Metal Objects

Of the metal objects found in the Dominus Flevit tomb, there were seventy-five bronze (or copper?) blades, about twenty-four rings (their basic shape still intact), about forty toggle pins (most with preserved eyelet), and three needles. These objects span the entire time the Dominus Flevit tomb was used as a burial site.

Objects Made of Bone

Sixteen bone plaques (or inlays), all but one yellowish in color (the exception is white), were found. Small round perforations in five of them suggest that they were once attached by pegs to wooden boxes which have long since disintegrated. The side of the plaques meant to be seen is smooth and polished. The incised geometric designs consist of lines, circles, and dots, often in a darker color than the original bone.

These bone plaques help us in determining the terminus a quo of the Dominus Flevit tomb. W. F. Albright in his study of such material from Tell Beit Mirsim (Debir), Tell el-'Ajjul (Beth-eglaim), and Gezer has concluded that such plaques suddenly appeared in the eighteenth century B.C. and suddenly disappeared in the fifteenth century B.C. Evidence from Lachish tells the same story. The plaques from Dominus Flevit, all of which are decorated, should be assigned to the Middle Bronze period.

The Dominus Flevit tomb also yielded four bone and two raised-coil stone whorls (an instrument with a hole in the middle through which a rod was placed for use in spinning thread) and three sections of flat whorls (Saller calls them flat spindles). Such instruments seem to have been in use from the Middle Bronze II period to

50. Saller, *Dominus Flevit*, Pt. 2, pp. 163–69.
51. Saller, *Dominus Flevit*, Pt. 2, pp. 168–77.

the Iron I period.[52] In practice "two whorls were placed with the flat sides against one another between two cylindrical rods, wood or ivory, in such a way that a (copper) pin passed through the holes in the whorls into the cylindrical rods. This gave the whorls an independent rotating motion, together or separately."[53]

Scarabs

Six scarabs and one scaraboid (a piece somewhat resembling the scarab) found at the Dominus Flevit tomb were identified by P. Lemaire as Hyksos in type. A seventh scarab was found after Lemaire's study. Although Saller feels that these scarabs cannot be fixed as to date, he does make the observation that at least "they do not contradict the results reached by a comparative study of the other groups of objects from our tomb, some of which were certainly in use before the Hyksos were driven out of Palestine, whilst others were in use during the Egyptian occupation of the country from the time of Thutmosis III and afterwards."[54]

We have taken up in considerable detail the finds at the Jebusite burial place because Dominus Flevit seems to have been one of the principal burial sites of Jerusalem, located, as was the general practice of ancient Palestinian cities, outside the fortified town. Furthermore, through this study of burials on the west slope of the Mount of Olives we gain further substantial evidence for an early occupation of Jerusalem in the Middle Bronze–Late Bronze periods.

As has been noted, numerous parallels to the materials from the Dominus Flevit tomb can be found in the published results of the excavations at Jericho, Tell Beit Mirsim, Lachish, Megiddo, and Hazor. Furthermore, many parallels are on exhibit at the Israeli Museum in Jerusalem. These parallels fall within the Middle Bronze and Late Bronze periods. Saller remarks that "these then are the only periods and the only dates which we need to consider for our tomb."[55]

Dominus Flevit was used as a burial site for about three hundred years, from the latter part of the Middle Bronze Age into Late Bronze II. This compares with the Dothan tomb, which was also used as a burial site for about three hundred years (ca. 1400–1100 B.C.).

---

52. Saller, *Dominus Flevit*, pt. 2, pp. 178–184. Saller comments (p. 184) that, since no Middle Bronze weaving tools were found in the Middle Bronze tombs at Jericho and no whorls at Middle Bronze Megiddo, sites with which Dominus Flevit can be compared, possibly the Dominus Flevit whorls should be assigned to Late Bronze II.
53. Saller, *Dominus Flevit*, pt. 2, p. 184.
54. Ibid., p. 193.
55. Ibid., p. 6.

In assessing the importance of Dominus Flevit, Saller comments that it is one of the few known burial sites in the eastern section of Jerusalem. Before its discovery the only burial sites in eastern Jerusalem of which archaeologists knew were one (or more) on Ophel, which dates to the Early Bronze Age, and one in Silwan, which dates to the transition period between the Early and Middle Bronze Ages. "Now we have one more from a somewhat later period (end of Middle Bronze and the greater part of the Late Bronze)."[56]

Evidence of Late Bronze Jerusalem

We earlier referred to the fact that there is interesting literary evidence for Jerusalem in the Late Bronze period. The most important extrabiblical source of information about ancient Jerusalem in this period comes from the era when Canaanite city-states owed allegiance to the Eighteenth Dynasty of Egypt. This literary source is the Amarna letters, which come from the royal archives of Amenophis IV (Akhenaten, ca. 1379–1362 B.C.) and his father Amenophis III. These tablets include diplomatic correspondence between kings of western Asia and the Egyptian pharaoh. The majority were written by vassal kings of Canaan to their Egyptian overlord. The letters reveal political intrigue as well as conditions of life and the social structure in Palestine during the Late Bronze Age.

The ruler of Jerusalem at this time, Abd-Khiba (alternative transliterations include Abdi-Hiba and ARAD-HI-pa, meaning "Servant of Hipa" [a Hurrian goddess]), wrote in Akkadian, the lingua franca of the time. Certain peculiarities of usage indicate that the language spoken in Jerusalem at the time was a West Semitic dialect (Canaanite) closely related to the Hebrew of the Bible. The ruler describes the disturbing situation in Jerusalem and Canaan and requests assistance from the pharaoh in repelling Egypt's enemies, namely, disloyal Canaanite rulers and their allies, the Habiru (Hapiru). He also describes the rebelliousness of certain Nubian troops who were part of the Egyptian garrison in Canaan. In relating how the Nubians broke through the roof of his house in order to rob him, Abd-Khiba may be giving a description of the buildings on the terrace system discovered by Kenyon at Ophel in Jerusalem.

A certain Shuwardat, the ruler of a city in the Shephelah, told the Egyptian pharaoh how dangerous the Habiru were, especially after almost all of his colleagues had deserted; only Abd-Khiba remained to help in the fight against the Habiru. Such ties between local kings

56. Ibid., p. 8.

suggest that Jerusalem was important in the fourteenth century B.C. It is believed that at this period the territory of Jerusalem may have extended over a large area of the southern hill country.[57]

Some of Kenyon's finds can be dated to the Jerusalem of this period. For example, the lower deposits at her site P yielded pottery remains that were entirely of the fourteenth and thirteenth centuries B.C. At this site also "a strip some 8 meters wide, largely occupied by a heavy wall, divided an area which was within the Jebusite town from one which was outside it. One can therefore draw a line across the hill [east-west] on the map at this point with some certainty."[58] Kenyon further argues that a constriction in the southeastern ridge at a point somewhere between her sites H and R or at site R (both located north of Shiloh's area G) figures in the location of the north wall running across the ridge east–west.[59] From this evidence Kenyon maintains that the limits of the town of the Late Bronze Age were restricted, covering only about 10.87 acres. She concludes that at this early period there must have been an entrance gate at a tower down the slope in the early city wall which would give overground access to the Spring Gihon. This gate presumably would have been blocked and hidden when trouble was impending. The route from the summit to the spring must have descended somewhat close to the line of the present path,

> passing just to the south of the tower in the early wall. The tower would therefore fit beautifully as the northern tower of a gateway, the rest of which would lie almost exactly beneath the modern path. One can therefore deduce that here was the water-gate of ancient Jerusalem. It has the further interest that it would have been the way by which Solomon came back into the city after he had been anointed at the Spring Gihon [1 Kings 1:32–40].[60]

We have already observed that for late Bronze Jerusalem of the fourteenth and thirteenth centuries a change occurred in urban planning, especially in the north part of the town. Both Kenyon's and Shiloh's excavations have demonstrated the Late Bronze terrace system issuing into a large platform 650 feet square in Area G in the north part of the city. This terraced platform near the top of the hill,

---

57. Mazar, *Mountain of the Lord*, pp. 47–48; *Encyclopedia of Archaeological Excavations in the Holy Land*, 2: 585.

58. Kenyon, *Jerusalem*, p. 26.

59. Ibid., pp. 26, 27. cf. Shiloh, *Excavations at the City of David, I, 1978–82*, pp. 40–41, figure 3.

60. Ibid., pp. 30–31.

with appropriate defenses, served as the Late Bronze Canaanite-Jebusite Jerusalem citadel or acropolis.

This, then, was the nature of Jebusite Jerusalem and its environs in the Late Bronze Age. The city which David was later to conquer (2 Sam. 5:6–9) was undoubtedly much the same.

The City of David

The ancient site of Jerusalem which David and his army success-fully conquered was defended by natural terrain on all sides except on the north. This Jebusite Jerusalem, confined to the ridge that extended south from the higher point of Mount Moriah, had the Kidron Valley on the east and the Tyropoeon Valley on the west. This was a natural site on which to build a town since it provided access to the Spring Gihon, located in the Kidron Valley, just oppo-site the town of Silwan.

David's antagonists, the Jebusites, had inhabited the area at least as early as the nineteenth century B.C. This tribe was related to the Hittites (cf. Uriah the Hittite, 2 Sam. 11)[1] and had come into control of the site of Jerusalem (see Judg. 19:10–12) following the Amorites, who previously controlled the area (Josh. 10:3–5; cf. Ezek. 16:3).

The archaeological evidence for the remains of David's city is scant, although the evidence that remains clearly suggests that

---

1. Compare the use of the word *Araunah* or *The Araunah* (Hebrew in 2 Sam. 24:16), which is a Hurrian word, *ewrine*, "lord," found also in Hittite and used in Ugaritic as a personal name referring to a ruler. In both 2 Sam. 24:16 and 1 Chron. 21:15, Araunah or Ornah is called a Jebusite.

59

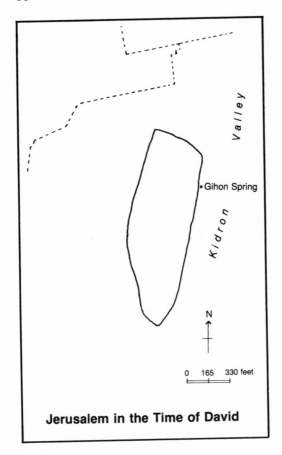

Jerusalem in the Time of David

David continued to live within the confines of the Jerusalem established by the Jebusites and Amorites. This area included (1) the
narrow southeastern ridge, the city wall of which on the west followed the scarp at the top of the western valley and (2) the terraces
built up on the eastern slope of the ridge. On the north this city wall
was identified by Kenyon's excavation as crossing the ridge where
there is a constriction; it then ran north-south along the western
side of the ridge, continuing to the southern tip. On the east the wall
ran north-south slightly in advance of a scarp in the natural rock
(fragmentary remains of massive rough wadi boulders showed this)
at a point about two-thirds of the way down the slope, at least at the
northern end of the site near Gihon.[2] Kenyon reports that it took a
whole season of work getting through the stone tumble to get to this

2. See Kenyon's Sites H, M, and R, *Jerusalem* (New York: McGraw-Hill, 1967), p.
29, figure 5.

Jebusite east city wall. She noted that the excavations down the east slope proved that this wall was at the eastern limits of the town and that it continued as the town wall in David's time and on until the beginning of the seventh century B.C.[3] An important part of the Jebusite Jerusalem which David took over was the shaft to the Spring Gihon, which is referred to in 2 Samuel 5:8. Kenyon aptly comments:

> It is clear that there must have been means of access to the spring from within the walls, for the spring lies so low in the valley that a town wall enclosing it would have been commanded by the slope on the opposite side. Therefore, safe access in times of war required a tunnel leading to a shaft coming up inside the town. Such watershafts are familiar in Palestine, the best known being that of Megiddo.[4]

Other such water shafts are at Hazor, Gezer, and Gibeon.

Early in this century Father L. H. Vincent made a study of the maze of tunnels connected with the Spring Gihon, including the famous Siloam tunnel. He was able to identify the earliest tunnel, originally found by Charles Warren, which consisted of a water channel at the foot of a vertical shaft at the head of which a sloping passage led to steps to the surface at a spot almost due west of the spring. The devious direction of the passage with its sharp angle was presumably made to reduce the steepness of the ascent. In this same tunnel section there is evidence of failure in a first attempt to sink a shaft, the failure no doubt being due to the hardness of the rock at that point.

In recent (1978–82) excavations at the City of David, Yigal Shiloh renewed the study of the Gihon water system: Warren's shaft (referred to above), the Siloam channel, and Hezekiah's tunnel. What concerns us here is Warren's shaft which was used at the time of David. Earlier we described the physical dimensions of the shaft. Shiloh found that some features of the shaft sytem, such as the lower end of the horizontal tunnel, the cave near the end of the horizontal tunnel, the vertical shaft, and the additional "trial shaft" were employed in the shaft system because they were part of natural Karst Clefts' tunnels and shafts. It was easier to use the natural rock features. Some of these features, such as the cave and its opening, were outside (east) of the earlier Jebusite wall found by Kenyon in her Trench A. Any openings to the shaft here would not have protected the city dwellers seeking water in time of siege. But, as indicated by Shiloh as well as Kenyon, there was an entrance to the system farther up the slope, well within the Jebusite wall.[5]

3. Ibid., p. 24.
4. Ibid., p. 22.
5. See the sketch of the shaft in Kenyon, *Jerusalem*, pp. 20–21.

Yigal Shiloh's excavations at the City of David.

It is true that the location of this major entrance to the shaft would have exposed the dwellers to missiles projected from the east by an enemy; but the entrance may well have been camouflaged and then connected by a covered passage to the inner part of the city and up to the citadel on the ridge, something like the covered stone passage seen at the Mycenaean city of Tiryns in the Argolid in the Greek Peloponnesus. Shiloh exposed a vaulted passage (although of a later building phase) near the shaft's main entrance.[6] No doubt this was the shaft system that the attacking Israelites, under Joab, discovered and by which Joab and his men ascended into the city (2 Sam. 5:7–8; 1 Chron. 11:6).[7]

6. Shiloh, *Excavations at the City of David, I*, pp. 21–23; figures 30–32; Kenyon, *Digging Up Jerusalem*, p. 86, figure 17.

7. The text of 2 Samuel 5:8 presents some problems of interpretation. In addition to Vincent's view that entrance was gained through the perpendicular shaft, there is that of J. Braslavi, who regards the Hebrew word *sinnor* (translated in the KJV as "gutter" and in the NIV as "water shaft" or possibly "scaling hooks") as an actual water conduit that conducted the Gihon Spring water from its source to a natural pool below this horizontal water tunnel where the water could be drawn. Access could be made also through such a pool. See Benjamin Mazar, *The Mountain of the Lord* (Garden City, New York: Doubleday, 1975), p. 168.

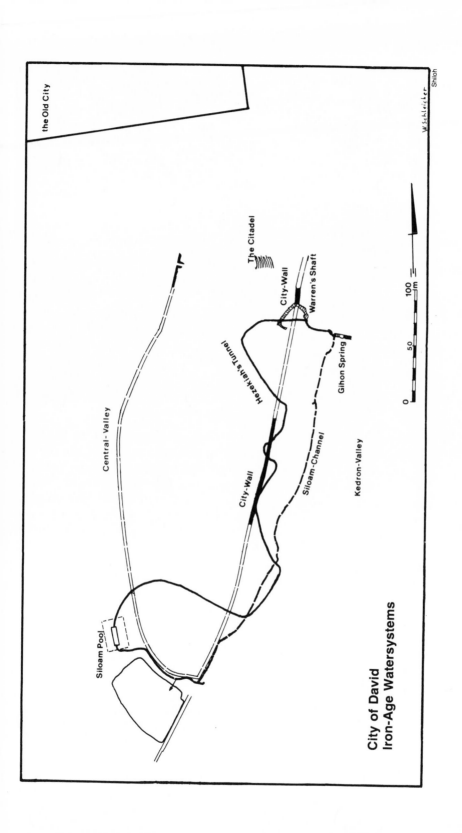

City of David
Iron-Age Watersystems

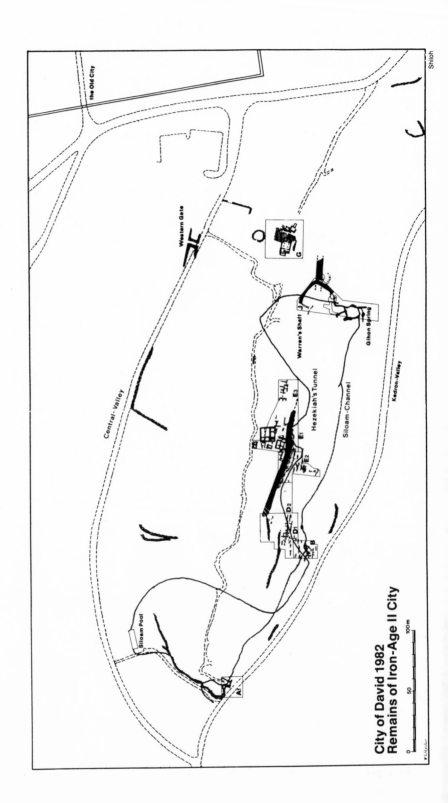

City of David 1982
Remains of Iron-Age II City

the Old City

Shiloh

Western Gate

Central-Valley

Warren's Shaft

Gihon Spring

Hezekiah's Tunnel

Siloam-Channel

Kedron-Valley

Siloam Pool

G

E3

E1

E2

D2

D1

B

A1

0   50   100m

According to 2 Samuel 5:11 (see also 1 Chron. 14:1) King Hiram of Tyre and his artisans built a palace for David, but there are no archaeological remains of such a structure. No doubt David's palace was built on the summit of the southeastern ridge, but it must have been destroyed in one of the later collapses of the fragile terrace walls. We would gather that David's residence, though described as a palace of cedar (2 Sam. 7:2), at best would not have been constructed on the scale of Solomon's palace, since the restricted area on the crest of the ridge, even at the citadel area of 650 square feet discovered by Shiloh, would not have allowed for such an extensive and elaborate building. The mention of 2 Samuel 5:11 of Tyrian masons and carpenters suggests a lack of building techniques among the Israelites, and points up their need to call on foreign craftsmen.

Biblical and archaeological evidence points to David's taking over Jebusite Jerusalem but does not suggest that he extended the limits of the city. In one biblical passage, however, there is indication that he repaired the conquered city (1 Chron. 11:8). This no doubt included repairing the town walls.

In addition to David's general repair of the city, there is a particular reference to his building the city "even from Millo round about" (1 Chron. 11:8a, KJV; cf. 2 Sam. 5:9b). Millo is also mentioned in connection with the building activities of Solomon and others (1 Kings 9:15; 2 Chron. 32:5). This term, which is from a Semitic root meaning "filling," "filling of earth," "earthwork," has received a variety of interpretations:

1. The filling in of a breach in a wall.
2. The filling of the Tyropoeon Valley to join the eastern ridge to the western one.
3. The filling of a transverse ravine limiting the town's expansion to the north.
4. A tower solidly filled with stone.

Both Kenyon and Mazar[8] argue for the view that the term *Millo* refers to stone-filled terraces, specifically the Jerusalem terraces supported by the retaining walls located along the eastern slope of the southeastern ridge. The NIV's translation of 2 Samuel 5:9 describes the activity graphically: "He [David] built up the area around it [the city] from the supporting terraces inward [i.e., to the

---

8. Kathleen Kenyon, *Digging Up Jerusalem* (London: Ernest Benn, 1974), pp. 100–101; Mazar, *The Mountain of the Lord*, pp. 171–73.

west]." After his capture of Jerusalem, the Jebus city, David would naturally have had to repair these terraces damaged in the assault and thus help guarantee proper support for his palace, the house of cedar (2 Sam. 5:11) built at the Citadel near the ridge of the hill. Later Solomon also had to build (or rebuild) these supporting terraces and also repair the breach in the north wall of the City of David (1 Kings 11:27), due to the expansion of the city to include the area of the temple. Mazar contends that later in biblical history, the term *Millo* is replaced by the word *Ophel* (from the Hebrew root, "to rise") referring to a type of (raised) fortress or citadel such as the Ophel at Jerusalem (2 Chron. 27:3; 33:14) and at Samaria and Dibon.[9]

In summary, then, we find that David's Jerusalem has basically vanished. Yet we can piece together from the archaeological evidence available enough to plot the following general features of the city as it stood at that time. It was confined to the southeastern ridge below Mount Moriah (2 Chron. 3:1). It covered the crest of that ridge, running north–south on the western edge of the crest. On the east slope of the ridge another wall positioned two-thirds of the way down the slope also ran north–south. Along this east slope were built stone-and rubble-filled terraces buttressed up against one another. On the top of the ridge houses were built, including David's rather modest palace. Also, stairs and a shaft were cut into the rock on the east slope of the ridge, somehow connecting the water supply of the Spring Gihon with the relatively small walled city.

The Jerusalem of David's time does not compare with the expanded and embellished city of Solomon's reign. With his simple shepherd background David did not have in mind such a grandiose Jerusalem for himself; this he envisaged and planned that his son, Solomon, should have. This he made possible by providing a large quantity of iron, bronze, and cedar logs (1 Chron. 22:3, 4) as well as a great amount of gold and silver (1 Chron. 22:14).

9. Mazar, ibid. 173.

4

The City of Solomon

According to biblical evidence King Solomon inherited the Jerusalem of his father, David (1 Kings 2:12). It is also clear that Solomon, not David, was given the task of building the first temple at Jerusalem (2 Sam. 7:29; 1 Kings 5:1–5), although David had prepared materials for it and had dedicated them to the Lord (2 Chron. 5:1). First Kings 5 does not clearly tell us where Solomon built the temple, but 2 Chronicles 3:1 indicates that it was on Mount Moriah, where David was told to build an altar to the Lord (2 Sam. 24:18); the place where the threshing floor of Araunah was located, which David bought to end the plague (2 Sam. 24:19–25). This place was undoubtedly "one of the mountains" in the region of Moriah, where Abraham was called to offer up Isaac (Gen. 22:2). The high point in the Jerusalem area that would qualify as "one of these mountains" is Moriah, with its large rock now housed in the Dome of the Rock. This site is located just west of the Kidron Valley opposite the Garden of Gethsemane and north of the City of David.

All of the Solomonic structures built north of the southeastern ridge have disappeared or are unavailable for excavation. Those structures in the area between the temple mount and the City of

Dome of the Rock.

David have suffered the ravages of conquest or of quarrying. Any remains of the Solomonic temple that might have been left after the destruction by Nebuchadnezzar are buried somewhere within the temple platform itself; the religious sanctity of the present Haram esh-Sherif with its Dome of the Rock forbids investigation of what might be buried there.

Solid tradition has persisted that the site of Solomon's temple mentioned in 2 Chronicles 3:1 is the correct location. This temple, of course, continued in use down to the time of the Babylonian captivity when Nebuchadnezzar made his final conquest of Jerusalem in 586 B.C. After the captivity, the postexilic temple constructed under Zerubbabel and Ezra, which Ezra calls "the house of God in Jerusalem," was built on this same site (Ezra 3:8). In turn, the temple of Herod the Great was built in the same location. It is to be assumed that any surviving remains of Solomon's temple and possibly other temple area buildings, as well as any surviving structures of the postexilic temple, were incorporated into the expanded platform Herod built to support his magnificent temple (Matt. 24:1–2; John 2:20) and its splendid colonnade (John 10:23). The tradition continued strong, for this same sacred site in succeeding centuries became the place where the Muslim Dome of the Rock, the memorial to Abraham, was located.

The present south wall of the temple platform is about 750 feet north of the northern limits of the old City of David, which had been located on the ridge south of Mount Moriah. It is logical to assume that after David's time Solomon extended the City of David north to

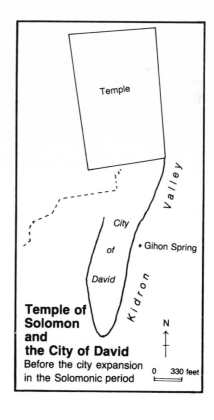

Temple

Valley

City

of

• Gihon Spring

David

Kidron

Temple of Solomon and the City of David
Before the city expansion in the Solomonic period

N

0   330 feet

join it with the temple area. Kenyon's sites H (to the north of the City of David), M (a little to the west and north of Site H), and R and S (farther north of the northern limits of David's City) evidence sufficient space for considerable building. Although meager, there is some archaeological evidence for such building in this space between the temple platform and the City of David. Kenyon says of her Site H,

> [at this site] occupation levels have been found that could belong to the tenth and ninth centuries BC, to the time of Solomon and his successors. . . . The evidence that there was nothing earlier in this area shows that the town only expanded here at this stage. . . . There certainly was a wall here, along the eastern edge of Site H, of the casemate type of construction, consisting of an inner and outer wall joined by cross walls, that was common from the time of Solomon onwards.[1]

It is difficult to determine the extent of building activities in this area since, due to extensive quarrying here, so few remains of buildings have survived. The area just south of the temple complex and north of David's city seems through quarrying to have been stripped almost clean of building structures. It is still interesting to speculate that this is the place where Solomon built his palace and the palace for his wife, Pharaoh's daughter, an area which could be called the Royal Quarter. This view can be argued for the following reasons. First, it would seem, according to the testimony of Josephus (I, 401), that the platform for Solomon's temple was only half the size of that built by Herod the Great. Thus it was too small comfortably to contain all of Solomon's official buildings.

The evidence from Josephus (*Ant.* V, 330ff; *War* 5, 184ff) and the Mishna tractate Middoth do not give us accurate information regarding the size of Herod's temple platform. Hollis gives the measurements of the present Haram esh-Sharif platform as follows: south wall, 929 feet; north wall, 1041 feet; east wall 1556 feet; and west wall, 1596 feet. Schick's figures are in basic agreement, and Finegan seems to follow the measurements of Hollis and Schick in calculating the measurement of Herod's temple platform.[2] Presuming that the present-day platform is about the same size as the

---

1. Kathleen Kenyon, *Jerusalem* (New York: McGraw Hill, 1967), p. 56; See figure 6, p. 57.
2. Judged by the Herodian stone masonry found by excavation on the southwest, south and southeast sides of the present temple platform. About Herod's platform Kenyon says, "This platform is bigger than its predecessor, so the original angles may well have been situated further up the hill, and thus the width of the town area may have been less."

George A. Turner

Model of Royal Portico at Holy Land Hotel, Jerusalem.

Herodian platform (the Herodian stone masonry visible on the west, south, and southeast sides bears testimony to this) we can project that the Herodian platform averaged about 985 feet from east to west and 1576 feet from north to south. This estimate is the best that we can do with the information available today.

On this platform (with further enlargement even today) the Dome of the Rock and al-Aqsa Mosque buildings are comfortably spaced. Positing Solomon's temple platform at half the size of the Herodian platform, one can see the difficulty Solomon would have had in trying to position his several buildings, some of them quite large, on this considerably smaller structure. For example, the temple, including the portico (or entrance), was about 105 feet long and 30 feet wide (1 Kings 6:2, 3), using the measurement of 1 foot, 6 inches to the cubit; the Hall of the Forest of Lebanon (part of Solomon's palace, 1 Kings 7:2) was about 150 feet long and 75 feet wide; the colonnade was about 75 feet long and 45 feet wide. This does not include the other buildings (the dimensions of which are not specified), such as the throne hall (or Hall of Justice), Solomon's private quarters, and the nearby palace for Solomon's wife (1 Kings 7:1–8). To put all of this[3] on a platform approximately 490 by 780 feet would be almost impossible.

The second reason for arguing that the Solomonic palaces and other buildings were placed in the area south of the temple platform is based on the heathen background and status of Solomon's wife,

3. All of these sacred and palatial buildings are compositely referred to in 1 Kings 9:15 as "the LORD's temple" and "his [Solomon's] own palace."

the daughter of Pharaoh.[4] According to 1 Kings 7:8–9, Solomon built a palace for her, a palace which seems to have been physically located not far from Solomon's palace quarters, since its construction is mentioned together with the building of the other royal buildings. There are parallels in building 1723 at Megiddo and in Syria, where the quarters of the wife of the king or governor are a part of the same complex of buildings as those of the king himself. Such close proximity of Solomon's palace to that of his Egyptian wife would have been helpful in fostering diplomatic relations. However, if his wife's palace had been built on the temple platform, she would not have been able to live there because she was a foreigner and of a heathen religion. Second Chronicles 8:11 states that Pharaoh's daughter was not to live in the palace of King David because the holy ark of the Lord had been housed there. More pertinent still for Solomon was the fact that the ark of the covenant had been brought into Solomon's temple and placed in the inner sanctuary (2 Chron. 5:7); certainly Pharaoh's daughter would not have been allowed to live in the same area in which the ark and the temple were located.

In the third place, the complex of buildings described in 1 Kings 7 suggests a sizable royal quarter which would be better accommodated in the area to the south of the platform between the temple platform and David's City. These public and private buildings of Solomon not only could not have been easily placed on the temple platform, but also they would not have fit within David's small city.

Ancient models of such expanded administrative quarters have come to light through archaeological excavations at Samaria, Megiddo, and Hazor. At Samaria the remains of Omri's new city (880 or 882 B.C.) show that the whole summit of the hill was occupied by palaces and administrative buildings. There is also evidence of large administrative headquarters at the Megiddo and Hazor of Solomon's time.

In summary, then, it appears Solomon constructed his magnificent temple on the platform built around the threshing floor that David purchased (2 Sam. 24:18–25; 2 Chron. 3:1). He then built up the area between the platform and the City of David by constructing in that area his palace which, for easy accessibility, he probably located as near as possible to the temple. In addition, he built

4. There is no indication in Scripture (1 Kings 3:1; 7:8; 9:16, 24) that Pharaoh's daughter, Solomon's wife, converted to Yahwism. In light of the statement in 1 Kings 11:1 that Solomon loved many strange and foreign women who led him into idolatry, it is to be assumed that Pharaoh's daughter also remained in her heathen condition, along with the other heathen wives Solomon had married.

nearby the palace for his Egyptian wife, the daughter of Pharaoh. He also constructed other buildings, including his own quarters and court, and what is called the "great courtyard" (1 Kings 7:9, 12). Drawing on Phoenicia and Syria for examples of comparable palaces of the tenth and ninth centuries, we can gain some idea of the architectural plan.[5] From 1 Kings 7 we can infer that the public passed through the colonnade, which evidently consisted of a portico with a roofed entrance supported by columns, and then entered Solomon's audience hall, or Hall of Justice, in which his throne was located. From this audience hall Solomon after his royal functions would retire to the courtyard and to his private quarters nearby. All this would agree well with the *bit-hilani* type of plan seen in the palaces at Sendshirli. Kenyon explains that "the *bit-hilani* type of plan is characterized by entrances on the long side of rooms; an interpretation of such lines would suggest that a wide portico, with an entrance supported on pillars, approached the long side of Solomon's audience chamber at one end of which was his throne."[6] Building 1723 at Megiddo, one of Solomon's own constructions in which he followed a common Syrian plan, is said to be a governor's residence. It followed the *bit-hilani* plan on a smaller scale than Solomon's Jerusalem structure. A colonnaded porch led into the long side of a main room, from which a doorway led to an open court flanked by a number of residential rooms.

Finally, however, it is not clear how the palace of Pharaoh's daughter related to all of this. We can only assume that it was placed somewhere near Solomon's palace.

Architecture of the Temple and Other Buildings

Since the basic archaeological evidence for Solomon's temple was destroyed by Nebuchadnezzar's conquest or in part covered up within the platform area of Herod the Great, we are left with the biblical evidence set forth in 1 Kings 6–7 and 2 Chronicles 3–4, and with parallels found in the Near East. From the biblical evidence we gather that Solomon's temple was a rectangular building with inside measurements of about 90 feet by 30 feet, and 45 feet high. It was oriented east and west. An entrance hall or portico (Hebrew *ulam* or *elam*)[7] approximately 30 feet wide, 15 feet deep

---

5. See Kathleen Kenyon, *Royal Cities of the Old Testament* (New York: Schocken Books, 1971), pp. 50–51.

6. Ibid., p. 51.

7. The Assyrian word is *ellamu*, "that which is in front." See André Parrot, *The Temple of Jerusalem* (London: SCM Press, 1957), p. 26.

(1 Kings 6:3), and 180 feet high (2 Chron. 3:4) was attached at the east end. This was built either flush with or projecting out from the main part of the building.[8]

There were tiers of ancillary rooms built against the outside walls on the sides and back of the temple, with each story about 7½ feet high. Each room in the lowest story was about 7½ feet wide, in the middle story about 9 feet wide, and in the top story about 10½ feet wide. "He made offset ledges around the outside of the temple so that nothing would be inserted into the temple walls" (1 Kings 6:6b). These ancillary rooms were probably priests' quarters and a place for storing religious equipment.

West of the entrance hall of the temple there was a central nave called the Holy Place (NIV "main hall"; Hebrew *hekal*), a room about 60 feet long, 30 feet wide, and 45 feet high (1 Kings 6:17). Its entrance to the east was framed with olive wood, in which were set two folding doors made of pine and decorated with carved figures of winged creatures (cherubim), palm trees, and flowers, all covered with gold (1 Kings 6:33–35). A stone capital, similar to a Greek architectural type, was found at Megiddo and associated with a temple of Solomonic date. The suggestion has been made that in the temple this type of capital was placed on a tall pilaster; five such pilasters were evenly positioned on each side of the main hall to give the room a sense of height.[9]

First Kings 6:4 says that "he made narrow clerestory windows in the temple."[10] These presumably were only on the side walls of the main hall (the Holy Place) since the small inner room (the Most Holy Place) did not have windows. It is thought that these clerestory windows consisted of recessed frames narrowing to the outside in the thick (ca. 7½ feet) side walls. This device, together with bars on the windows, could have kept out all but the smallest birds attracted by the aroma of the sacrifices (cf. Ps. 84:3). The plan for these windows is based on the design seen on an ivory plaque from Babylonia which shows a woman (a goddess of fertility?) looking through a window recessed and equipped with bars. This plaque is virtually duplicated in ivory carvings found at Megiddo at archaeological levels of the time of Ahab. First Kings 22:39 (KJV) speaks of Ahab's ivory palace. Since pieces of ivory inlay were found in the

8. We favor the view that it was flush with the main part of the building. See the Howland-Garber model reconstruction of Solomon's Temple, *Archaeology* 5. 3 (1952): 165–72; also Parrot, *The Temple of Jerusalem*, p. 24.

9. See the Howland-Garber model.

10. The Good News Bible translates 1 Kings 6:4: "The walls of the Temple had openings in them, narrower on the outside than on the inside."

excavation of the palace ruins at Samaria, the biblical statement can be taken to mean that Ahab's palace was inlaid with ivory. It is logical to think that Solomon and Hiram of Tyre used these and other Near Eastern patterns.

For examples of pivots on which the doors of Solomon's temple swung, we can examine stone door sockets which are found in many archaeological excavations in the Near East—for example, at Heshbon, Jordan, and Raddana, Israel. For large doors, metal-tipped pivots set in stone door sockets were used in Egypt and Mesopotamia from earliest times. Under such sockets were deposited valuable items and records. Sometimes these stone sockets carried an inscription of dedication as seen on the stone socket from the Gimilsin Temple at Ur in Mesopotamia; other times the inscription might be an exorcism. The stone socket presumed for Solomon's temple could have served as the "cornerstone" receptacle for the structure, with any important documents stored underneath.

Although 1 Kings and 2 Chronicles do not indicate that the floor level of the Most Holy Place was elevated above that of the floor of the Holy Place, such a feature seen in a palace chapel excavated at Tell Tainat in northern Syria suggests that the same feature could have been built into Solomon's temple. Compare the temple described in Ezekiel 41:8 (NIV) as having a "raised base." Known Canaanite temples had the same feature. Since Solomon seems to have incorporated other features known to have been used in the temples of his day, it may well be that he used this construction technique as well.

West of the Holy Place was the Most Holy Place (Hebrew, *debir*[11]), a room of cube dimensions, about 30 feet long, wide, and high. At the entrance to the Most Holy Place was a double door made of olive wood carved with winged creatures, palm trees, and flowers, all covered with gold (1 Kings 6:31, 32), as were all the floors, walls, and ceilings of the Most Holy Place (1 Kings 6:20, 30). According to the Good News Bible translation of 1 Kings 6:31, there was a pointed arch[12] above the double-doored entrance. In the Most Holy Place stood the winged cherubim and the ark of the covenant, containing the two tables of the Law. Solomon, upon completion of the work on the temple, brought the ark and cherubim into the newly

11. The KJV translates it "the oracle" and the NIV "the inner sanctuary." Actually the Hebrew text of 1 Kings 6:16 gives a composite expression, literally translated "an inner sanctuary, the Holy of Holies," and the Hebrew *debir* is equivalent to the Hebrew *qodesh haqodashim*, "the Holy of Holies, the Most Holy Place."

12. There was a pointed arch at the much earlier (ca. 1400 B.C.) famous Lion Gate at Mycenae in Greece.

constructed house for the Lord (1 Kings 6:19; 7:51–8:9; 2 Chron. 5:1–10). This followed the pattern set when the same ark and cherubim were placed by David and his predecessors in the Most Holy Place in the tabernacle (Exod. 37:1–9; 2 Sam. 6:14).

The inside walls and ceiling of the temple were lined with cedar, and the floor was covered with pine (1 Kings 6:15); the interior walls were carved with intricate designs. It has been estimated that around all the walls of the Holy Place was a carved wainscoting, reaching a height of about 7½ feet from the floor, with designs of winged creatures, palm trees, and flowers (1 Kings 6:29; 2 Chron. 3:7).[13] The whole interior was covered with gold (1 Kings 6:21, 22),[14] and gold chains hung across the entrance to the Most Holy Place (1 Kings 6:21).

The fact that 1 Kings 6:7 states that the temple was erected without the sound of a hammer, chisel, or any other iron tool, and that many parts of the temple were made of wood, makes the suggestion plausible that a prefabrication of some sort was used, possibly that called "pallet" prefabrication. A pallet in this sense is a large self-supporting piece so constructed that it may be covered with boards and used as a floor, ceiling, or wall panel. These could have been manufactured outside the temple area, carried into the structure and put in place silently.[15] An ancient example of building prefabrication!

Just to the east of the temple building and its entrance hall was the bronze altar of burnt sacrifice, about 30 feet square and 15 feet high (2 Chron. 4:1). This altar may well have stood on the highest point of the rock which is now housed in the Dome of the Rock. Also to the east in front of the temple were located the immense bronze basin set on twelve bronze oxen and other large portable basins. The buildings and accompanying structures and equipment were surrounded by inner and outer courts. "And he built the inner courtyard of three courses of dressed stone and one course of trimmed cedar beams" (1 Kings 6:36).

As splendid as Solomon's temple was, as described in 1 Kings 6–7 and 2 Chronicles 3–4, it is to be remembered that it comprises only a small part of the whole complex of buildings Solomon built in this area of Mount Moriah. Solomon's own palace buildings, made of

13. Howland-Garber model, *Archaeology*, pp. 165–72.
14. Some, including G. E. Wright, have interpreted the Hebrew word translated "overlay" or "covered" (1 Kings 6:21, 28, 30) to be more adequately rendered "inlay." According to this view the floor was inlaid with gold, as were the carved figures on the walls.
15. Howland-Garber model, *Archaeology*, pp. 165–72.

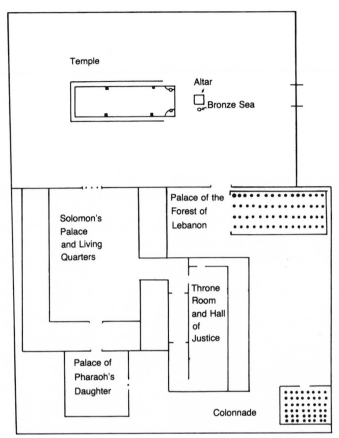

Proposed Layout for King Solomon's Buildings

high-grade stones (1 Kings 7:9) and timbers from the forest of Lebanon (1 Kings 7:2), were a complex (1 Kings 7:1–8) considerably larger than the temple he had built for the Lord (cf. 1 Kings 6:2).[16] It is hard to project Solomon's thinking as we consider this great difference. It could be that he was comparing the size of his temple to

16. Not counting the additional halls and courts, that part of Solomon's palace called the Palace of the Forest of Lebanon was about 150 feet long, 75 feet wide, and 45 feet high, compared with the temple's dimensions, including its entrance hall, of about 105 feet by 30 feet. Not counting the tiers of auxiliary side rooms, the square footage of the temple was about 3,150, compared with the Palace of the Forest of Lebanon's square footage of about 11,250. If one adds to this the colonnade of the palace (about 75 feet long and 45 feet wide), one gets an additional square footage of about 3,375, for a total of about 14,625.

the relatively small size of the tabernacle in the wilderness (45 feet long by 15 feet wide, Exod. 26:36), and even then his temple was only about twice as large.

Solomon's palace included a structure called the Palace of the Forest of Lebanon (1 Kings 7:2–3). This featured forty-five columns in three rows (or four rows[17]) of fifteen columns each, supporting trimmed cedar beams, which in turn supported a cedar roof. Behind or between the columns on each of the two side walls were three rows of windows (1 Kings 7:4–5) possibly narrowed from the inside to the outside wall, if the temple construction was used as a pattern (1 Kings 6:4). The palace had added to it a colonnade, about 75 feet long and 45 feet wide, in front of which was (attached?) some kind of covered porch supported by columns (1 Kings 7:6). The biblical record gives us no other details about this complex of buildings.

In addition, Solomon also built his throne hall, called the Hall of Justice, but all we know about it is that it was paneled with cedar from the floor to the rafters (1 Kings 7:7). In 1 Kings 7:8 only passing reference is made to Solomon's own quarters located somewhere behind the Hall of Justice. All that is said about these quarters is that they were made like the other buildings, meaning that they were made of high-grade stone from foundation to eaves (1 Kings 7:9) and that their walls were lined with cedar panels (1 Kings 7:7). For a similar arrangement one might compare the later structures built at the Persian capital of Persepolis.

Besides his palace Solomon also built a "house for Pharaoh's daughter" (1 Kings 7:8; 2 Chron. 8:11). About this we know only that Scripture indicates that this house was constructed of the same materials and made in a similar way to the other buildings: foundations made of high-grade stones, stone walls topped with cedar beams, and walls covered with cedar panels.

We do not discover from Scripture anything regarding the level of architectural and aesthetic finesse that was used in the ornamentation of these buildings. One clue, however, can be found in the statements that Solomon acquired the services of the craftsmen of Hiram, King of Tyre (1 Kings 5:1–11; 2 Chron. 2:1–16). In addition, the comparable archaeological remains of the Tyrian work done at other sites suggest that the work was on a high level of excellence.

17. The Hebrew text of 1 Kings 7:2 says there were four rows of cedar columns with cedar beams upon the columns. The Septuagint (3 Kings 7:39) says there were three rows of columns, so a transcriptional error in the number may have occurred in the text here. If four is correct, we do not know the location of this fourth row of columns in the palace.

Casemate wall at Hazor.

Kenyon says:

All the archaeological evidence from Palestine goes to show that the Israelites themselves lacked any skill as masons and craftsmen. Evidence of the skill of the Phoenicians in working stone from the second millennium onwards comes from sites such as Ras Shamra and Byblos and from the remains of Tyre itself, though most of the latter have to be studied below the waters of the Mediterranean. Evidence of their skill as craftsmen in ivory and bronze comes from a wide area stretching from North Syria to Cyprus. Still more revealing in relation to Jerusalem is the evidence from Samaria. . . . Excavation has shown that the masonry of the buildings of Omri and Ahab is Phoenician. The masonry is quite exquisite, the heavy walls bold and forceful, the interior walls with stones dressed to a beautifully tooled smooth face and fitted together with minute precision. We can imagine that the walls of Solomon's Temple and palace of stones were of the same fine masonry, and that the platform was constructed of stones with the bolder type of dressing.[18]

In addition to the biblical statements about Phoenician craftsmen employed to build the temple and palace, a structure that has been excavated at Jerusalem also gives evidence of fine architectural work.

Kenyon found in square XVIII of her City of David excavations a group of fallen ashlar blocks like those Shiloh found at the northern edge of his Area G. Kenyon also found there a single palmette "Proto Aeolic or Ionic" pilaster capital. These blocks are similar to those blocks cut with smooth surfaces found at Omri's palace at Samaria and similar capitals are found at Israel's capital too.[19] The location of these architectural pieces in the northern end of the City of David down the slope of the Citadel area suggests an important structure was built above them, possibly one of the buildings of Solomon's palace complex.

The kind and style of masonry used for the Solomonic temple must have been similar to that described above: large limestone blocks of ashlar construction, 12 to 15 feet in length and about 1½ feet high. Reisner, in his reports of the Harvard excavations at Samaria, 1908–10, describes the Phoenician-type masonry used at Jerusalem: "The great limestone blocks used in the Temple walls and raised basement, many twelve and fifteen feet in length, were of uniform tier height (approximately one and a half feet). They were laid in the style of masonry current in that time, as is clear from the excavations at Megiddo and Samaria."[20]

Equipment and Special Features of the Temple and Other Buildings

There is considerable biblical evidence pointing to extensive equipment and special features provided for the temple and its environs. These features include the two free-standing bronze columns called Jakin and Boaz located at the east end of the temple. These columns may have represented a type of memorial structure called *massebah* ("pillar"), similar in function but not in material to the memorial stone set up by Jacob and Laban to indicate a covenant

18. Kenyon, *Jerusalem*, pp. 58–59.
19. Ibid., p. 59.
20. Howland-Garber model, *Archaeology*, pp. 165–172.

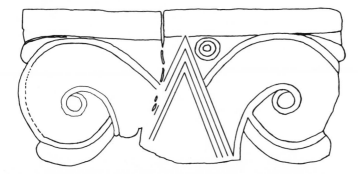

Proto-Ionic pilaster capital, also called proto-aeolic, from an eighth–ninth century B.C. public building. This type of capital, found in the Ophel in Jerusalem, was an important feature of royal architecture.

agreement between them (Gen. 31:45). The stone positioned in front of the Middle Bronze temple at Shechem is a *massebah*.[21]

The columns were each about 27 feet high and 18 feet in circumference and were capped with bronze capitals shaped like lilies— each about 7½ feet high and decorated with a network of two sets of interwoven chains from which two rows of 200 bronze pomegranates hung from each capital (1 Kings 7:15–22; 2 Chron. 3:17; 4:12–13). A suggested design for the capitals can be seen in an incense burner represented on a colored wall painting found at Megiddo.

The text of 1 Kings 7:15 indicates that each of the two columns was a single casting of bronze. Archaeological evidence is lacking regarding the making of such large free-standing castings. However, there is evidence of castings of metal pieces, such as the bronze doorplate exhibited at the Oriental Institute, Chicago, meant to be fastened to a wooden wall or column. It could be that Solomon's bronze columns were made of cylindrical cast copper bands that were slipped over a wooden core. The appearance would then be that of a single bronze casting, and this kind of construction would fit with what skilled workers in Solomon's time were able to do. The two cherubim in the Most Holy Place (1 Kings 6:23–28) were made in this way: the core of wood was overlaid, in this case with gold.

We are not told anything about bases for Solomon's two bronze columns. However, there is archaeological evidence of stone bases, including the elaborately carved column base from the palace at

21. George Ernest Wright, *Shechem, The Biography of a Biblical City* (New York: McGraw-Hill, 1965), p. 119. Compare the menhir columns found in Central Moab at such places as Ader; see J. Maxwell Miller and Jack M. Pinkerton, 1979 Archaeological Survey of Central and Southern Moab, Emory University, unpublished.

Tell Tainat in northern Syria, now housed in the Oriental Institute Museum, Chicago. It may be that bases for Solomon's columns were made of stone and of similar design.

The two bronze columns stood before the temple (2 Chron. 3:17) in or at the entrance hall of the Holy Place (1 Kings 7:21); the one called Jakin was on the right (or south side) and the other called Boaz was on the left (north side). In Hebrew, Jakin probably means "he (God) establishes" and Boaz, "in him (God) is strength." The columns stood in front of the temple until the Babylonians in 586 B.C. broke them up and carried the pieces off to Babylon (2 Kings 25:13). The tradition about them, however, continued on, as seen on a fragment of glass found in the catacombs of Rome. In the museum at Beirut a parallel for them may be seen represented on a small shrine found near Tyre; on it are depicted two free-standing columns in front of what must be a representation of the Tyrian temple of Melqart.

As we have seen, the interior temple walls were covered with cedar panels, the floor was covered with pine, and the whole was overlaid with fine gold. Solomon also adorned the temple with beautiful precious stones (2 Chron. 3:6). We are told that the king obtained the gold and precious stones from the land of Parvaim.[22] Judging from the record of 2 Chronicles 3:8 that Solomon used twenty-three tons of gold to cover the inside of the Most Holy Place, the total quantity of gold used for the temple and other buildings must have been enormous.

The biblical record indicates that Solomon made many pieces of ceremonial equipment for the temple. In the Most Holy Place stood the two winged creatures, the cherubim, hovering over the ark of the covenant. They were carved of olive wood, each about 15 feet high, each wing having a span of about 7½ feet; thus each cherubim's 15-foot wingspan enabled their inner wings to touch each other in the center of the room, and their outer wings to touch the side walls. They were covered with gold. Standing in the Most Holy Place, they faced the Holy Place (2 Chron. 3:13). These matched in beauty the ark of the covenant which was also placed in the Most Holy Place.[23] The ark of the covenant was made of acacia wood, measured 3¾ feet long and 2¼ feet wide, and high, and was covered with gold inside and out; it had a gold molding around it, gold rings

22. This may be identified with Sak el-Farwein in Yemanah, or Farwa in Yemen; or it could be an alternate form of Sephar (Gen. 10:30), a site which is unknown.

23. Mention is made that Solomon had the tabernacle and all of its equipment taken to the temple (1 Kings 8:4; 2 Chron. 5:5), but we do not know what all this included nor where the things were put. Presumably the sacrificial equipment was used at the altar. What happened to the golden altar, the table of the consecrated bread, the seven-branched lampstand, and the tabernacle curtain, we do not know.

attached to it, and gold-covered acacia poles made to be inserted in the rings to carry it (Exod. 37:1–5). The cherubim stood on the top of the ark, 3¾ feet long and 2¼ feet wide (Exod. 37:6). When it was carried into the temple, the ark contained only the two stone tablets of the Law (1 Kings 8:9; 2 Chron. 5:10).

Several conjectures have been made as to the appearance of the ark of the covenant. One is that it was shaped like a throne, based on the implications of 2 Samuel 6:2, which speaks of the ark as "called by the name, the name of the Lord Almighty, who is enthroned between the cherubim that are on the ark" (see 1 Sam. 4:4; 1 Chron. 13:6). The throne suggestion is also based on the evidence of a throne dedicated to Astarte, which was excavated in Phoenicia and is now housed in the museum at Beirut. The throne there represents the empty seat of a god, with cherubim on either side. Another suggestion posits that the ark was "a small scale model of a shrine or altar, similar to the pottery models found during excavations at Megiddo."[24] These suggestions cannot be proved. The ark was at least a suitable receptacle to contain the two tables of the Law. Representing the justice and holiness of God, it was fittingly positioned in the place where Jehovah dwelt.

Just inside the entrance to the Most Holy Place, in front of the ark (Exod. 40:5), the altar of incense was positioned.[25] It too was covered with gold (1 Kings 6:22).

24. Parrot, *The Temple of Jerusalem*, p. 36.
25. Where it was placed is debated, whether in the Most Holy Place (1 Kings 6:22, NIV) or just outside the Most Holy Place, near the curtain, as the KJV may suggest. All that Exodus 40:5 says is, "Place the gold altar of incense in front of the Ark of the Testimony"; Exodus 30:6 stipulates "Put the altar in front of the curtain that is before the Ark of the Testimony." Keil and Delitzsch comment on Exodus 30:6 as follows: "Its [the gold altar's] place was to be in front of the curtain, which concealed the Ark of the Covenant (XXXV. 31), . . . so that although it really stood in the holy place before the candlestick on the south side and the table on the north (XXVI 35, XI, 22, 24), it was placed in the closest relation to the *capporeth* [the atonement cover], and for this reason is not only connected with the most holy place in 1 Kings VI. 22 but is reckoned in Heb. IX. 4 as part of the furniture of the most holy place" (C. F. Keil and F. Delitzsch, *Biblical Commentary on the Old Testament: The Pentateuch*, [Grand Rapids: Eerdmans, 1956], 2: 208). Josephus (*War* V. 215–18) also thinks that the altar of incense was connected to the Holy Place. Compare Hebrews 9:3–4 which says, "The Most Holy Place . . . had the golden altar of incense." The Greek participle *echousa* translated "had" here can carry the idea of "possess" in the sense of belonging to, or having as one's own (cf. Arndt, Gingrich and Danker, *A Greek-English Lexicon of the New Testament* [Chicago: University of Chicago Press, 1979], *echo*); it thus conveys the same idea found in 1 Kings 6:22 that the gold altar of incense really belonged to the Most Holy Place, although it may have actually been placed outside the Most Holy Place, in front of the inner or second curtain (cf. Heb. 9:3).

The curtain that hung at the entrance to the Most Holy Place was made of fine linen and other material dyed blue, purple, and crimson with designs of the cherubim worked into it (2 Chron. 3:14). Whether the curtain was hung inside or outside the gold-covered double doors at the entrance of the Most Holy Place we are not told. Herod's temple may have had the same arrangements (double doors and a curtain at the entrance of the Most Holy Place); if so, the reference to the tearing of the curtain of the temple from top to bottom (Matt. 27:15) suggests that it could be seen by the priests from the Holy Place, meaning that it was outside the double doors to the Most Holy Place. In summary, then, the arrangement of the items, starting from the Holy Place, would be as follows; first the curtain, then the double doors, and then the gold chain placed across the entrance to the Most Holy Place (1 Kings 6:21).

In the tabernacle the Holy Place had one lampstand (seven-branched) and one table for the consecrated bread (Exod. 37:10–24). According to 1 Kings 7:48, Solomon had one golden table made for the consecrated bread. Did he take the table that was used in the tabernacle and refinish it with a new layer of gold, or did he make a new one? We cannot be certain. In addition, 2 Chronicles 4:7–8 tells us that Solomon made ten tables (presumably also of gold; 1 Kings 6:21–22), five for each side of the Holy Place. Since the 2 Chronicles passage does not say that these ten tables were for the consecrated bread, it is to be understood that they were used with the gold lampstands also made for the Holy Place, five to be placed on the south side and five on the north (1 Kings 7:49; 2 Chron. 4:7). Solomon also made lamps for the lampstands, as well as tongs, lamp snuffers (or wick trimmers), cups (to hold the oil), bowls (possibly for carrying the bread, or other utensils, or sprinkling bowls), dishes (or ladles) for incense, and pans (or censors) used for carrying live coals, all made of gold (1 Kings 7:49–50; 2 Chron. 4:20–21). Unfortunately, 1 Kings and 2 Chronicles do not give us any evidence as to the appearance of the ten lampstands, but archaeology suggests for them a model found at Megiddo, consisting of a metal stand with tripod vase, each foot presenting an inverted Proto-Ionic capital. Others like it have been found in the Near East, some of them dating from as early as the twelfth century B.C. Although we have no evidence that Solomon used the seven-branched lampstand model of the tabernacle for each of his ten gold lampstands, it is conceivable that he may have used seven-spouted gold lamps on his ten lampstands. Clay lamps, in bowl shape to hold the oil and with seven pinched "spouts" to hold the wicks, are commonly found in Iron I age sites in the Near East. Such a lamp was also uncovered at

Dothan in tomb finds dating from ca. 1400 to 1100 B.C. That Solomon made his gold lamps following this model is quite possible. In 1 Kings 7:49 it is said that Solomon made gold flowers (or floral work) as a part of the furnishings of the Holy Place. What these were for, beyond aesthetic effect, we do not know. He even made the hinges (or sockets) of the doors of the Most Holy Place and those of the outer doors of the temple out of gold,[26] according to 1 Kings 7:50.

Solomon also made a bronze altar, about 30 feet square and about 15 feet high (2 Chron. 4:1). This stood to the east before the temple. It was probably connected somehow with the rock, the threshing floor of Araunah (2 Sam. 24:18–25), and no doubt was inside the inner priestly courtyard which had a bronze-covered door between it and an outer courtyard (2 Chron. 4:9). We would gather that the bronze altar was placed symmetrically toward the northeast corner of the temple, since 1 Kings 7:39 and 2 Chronicles 4:10 state that Solomon placed the immense bronze basin (or sea) which he built near the southeast corner of the temple.

According to 1 Kings 7:23–26 and 2 Chronicles 4:2–5, this immense bronze bowl was about 7½ feet deep, about 15 feet in diameter, and about 45 feet in circumference, with sides 3 inches thick, evidently made of a cast copper-tin alloy.[27] All around the outer edge of the rim of the basin, which curved outward like the petals of a lily (1 Kings 7:26; 2 Chron. 4:5), were two rows of decoration in the form of bronze gourds which had been cast all of one piece with the rest of the basin (1 Kings 7:24; 2 Chron. 4:3). The basin rested on the backs of twelve bronze bulls, presumably also cast, which faced outward, three facing in each of the four directions (1 Kings 7:25; 2 Chron. 4:4). This huge basin is said to have held between 10,000 and 15,000 gallons.[28] Some experts have suggested that the bulls symbolized fecundity and power, and W. F. Albright has suggested that the arrangement of three bulls in each of four directions sym-

---

26. Gold-plated, possibly, for durability.

27. Solomon had a bronze foundry in the Jordan Valley between Succoth and Zarethan where all such bronze objects were cast (1 Kings 7:45–47; 2 Chron. 4:17–18). The Jordan Valley presented ideal conditions for such casting: the earth there was suitable for molds, water was abundant, and the wind was available to operate the draught furnaces. See Parrot, *The Temple of Jerusalem*, p. 51.

28. Two thousand baths, or 11,500 gallons (1 Kings 7:26) and three thousand baths or 17,500 gallons (2 Chron. 4:5). Keil and Delitzsch remark that the Chronicles number "has risen from the confusion of [Heb] *g* (3) with [Heb] *b* (2); since according to the calculation of Thenius, the capacity of the vessel, from the dimensions given could not exceed 2000 baths" (Keil and Delitzsch, *Biblical Commentary on the Old Testament: Kings*, p. 104).

bolized "the round of seasons through the year."[29] The priests serving at the temple were to use the water of this large basin for washing (2 Chron. 4:6).[30] This great basin, as well as the ten smaller basins on carts, remained in their places until the time of King Ahaz (736–716 B.C.). Ahaz took apart the bronze carts and removed the basins that were on them; he removed the bronze oxen (no doubt to use the metal for tribute) and placed the basin on a stone pavement (2 Kings 16:17).

Parrot feels that the best archaeological discovery to be compared with Solomon's immense basin is the large basin of Amanthus found on Cyprus and now housed in the Louvre. He describes it as "hewn from a single block of fairly soft limestone, it measures 2 meters 20 centimeters [ca. 7 feet] in diameter and 1 meter 85 centimeters [ca. 6 feet] in height. Four imitation handles are carved on the edge of the basin, each with the figure of a bull within it."[31]

Solomon had his craftsman Huram cast ten bronze movable stands, or carts, for the temple service (1 Kings 7:37). Each cart was about 6 feet long, about 6 feet wide, and about 4½ feet high. It was made of square side panels set in frames, with figures of lions, bulls, and cherubim on the panels and on the attached uprights as well. On the frames above and below the figures were wreaths of hammered work, and at the four corners were bronze supports decorated with wreaths on each side. On the inside of the cart was a circular frame about 1½ feet deep for holding a bronze basin. This whole structure was carried on four bronze wheels with bronze axles attached to the cart. The wheels (like chariot wheels made of cast metal) were under or beneath the panels and were about 2¼ feet in diameter. Four handles projected from each corner of the cart, and at the top there was a circular band about 9 inches deep. The supports and panels, decorated with cherubim, lions, palm trees, and surrounding wreaths (1 Kings 7:27–37), were attached to the top of each cart.

The craftsman Huram also made ten basins for the carts. Each

29. But Parrot has noted that this suggestion cannot be accepted "because in the East there are actually only two [seasons]: summer and winter. This is correctly indicated in Gen. 8:22" (*The Temple of Jerusalem*, p. 47 n.).

30. It has been proposed that the bronze basin might suggest "either a sacred lake of Egyptian temples or the Babylonian *apsu*—the mass of 'waters beneath the earth' (cf. Exod. 20:4). . . . As is well known, the bull in the Canaanite world was the type of fertility, and the four groups of three were so placed for the purpose of orientation" (Parrot, *The Temple of Jerusalem*, pp. 46–47).

31. Ibid., p. 47. There is a large bronze basin exhibited in the Hittite Museum in Ankara, Turkey.

A wheeled basin, similar to the type used in Solomon's temple.

basin, presumably of bronze, was about 6 feet in diameter and held about 230 gallons. Five of the carts and their basins were placed on the south side of the temple, probably near the southeast corner of the temple, and five on the north side (1 Kings 7:38–39; 2 Chron. 4:6). The water from the smaller basins was used to rinse the utensils and the parts of the animals that were burned as sacrifices (2 Chron. 4:6). Archaeological comparisons for the wheeled basins come from Cyprus, where at Enkomi and Larnaka two basins have been found resembling those of Solomon. These are on wheeled stands and show decorations of griffins, vegetation, and spirals. In addition, Huram made pots, shovels, sprinkling bowls, and meat forks out of burnished, or polished bronze; these were to be used in the temple worship (1 Kings 7:40; 2 Chron. 4:11, 16). Since they are listed with the immense bronze basin and the ten smaller portable basins, we assume that these utensils were used by the priests in the sacrifices performed on the bronze altar in front of the temple. Such utensils, which are needed for religious sacrifices, are found in all temples.

Mention has already been made of an inner courtyard of the priests (see 1 Kings 6:36) and also of a large court, an outer court (2 Chron. 4:9; cf. 2 Kings 21:5). Although we are not told the exact position of the outer courtyard, we assume it was located to the east of the court of the priests and possibly around at least the north and south sides of the temple.

We have seen that Solomon's temple was elaborately constructed and adorned. If this was true of the temple, one can imagine how magnificently constructed and furnished were Solomon's palace and other adjoining buildings.

Helpful archaeological finds from the excavated sites of Hazor,

Lachish, and Samaria in Palestine and Nimrud in Mesopotamia shed light on the type of decorative art and equipment used in Solomon's Jerusalem. Examples of Phoenician art derived from Egyptian and Mesopotamian models are seen in the ivory carvings in plaques and also carved, round pieces found in the Samaria excavations. There these decorative pieces adorned the furniture and possibly also the walls of the palace of Omri and Ahab. From the biblical description (1 Kings 7 and 2 Chronicles 4) of the ornate decorations made by the Phoenician craftsmen, including the figures of lions, bulls, and cherubim adorning the furniture of the temple and comparing the winged bull-sphinx figures found at Samaria and also at Nimrud,[32] it is easier to visualize the awe-inspiring, more than life-size cherubim figures guarding, as it were, the ark of the covenant in the equally kingly setting of the Holy of Holies in the temple where God the sovereign ruler met with his people. This king of the temple is vividly depicted in Psalm 18:6–10: "... my God ... from his temple he heard my voice ... he mounted the cherubim and flew; he soared on the wings of the wind" (cf. Ezek. 1:4–28). The Solomonic temple's lavish overlay of gold is paralleled in the extensive use of gold panelling by the rulers at Nimrud and in the evidence, though meager, of the quantities of gold used on the carvings at Samaria by Omri and Ahab.[33]

Archaeological evidence for a lavish amount of religious ceremonial equipment such as that described for Solomon's temple in 1 Kings 6–7 and 2 Chronicles 3–4 is seen elsewhere in the Near East. Examples of quantities of elaborate bowls, sacrificial equipment, lavers, offertory tables, and altars have been found in the excavations of the Late Bronze temples at Lachish and the thirteenth-century B.C. Hazor temple. The temple at Hazor even had large lion orthostats at its entrance. A visual picture of the Solomonic portable lavers can be gained from the wheeled lavers, though smaller, found at Larnaka and Enkomi on Cyprus.[34]

Thus, the written records of 1 Kings and 2 Chronicles and the archaeological evidence from Jerusalem and parallels from Palestine and Mesopotamia have given us a reasonably accurate picture of the extent of Solomon's Jerusalem. They also have given us a picture of the general construction of his temple, palace, and other buildings and of the equipment he provided for his temple worship.

32. Kenyon, *Jerusalem*, p. 61.
33. Ibid.
34. Ibid., p. 60. See also O. Tufnell, C. A. Inge, and L. Harding, Lachish II, *The Fosse Temple* (London, 1940); R. D. Barnett, "The Nimrud Ivories and the Art of the Phoenicians," *Iraq* 2, 1935:179–210.

Jerusalem During the Kingdom of Judah

There are frequent references in the Old Testament to Jerusalem in the period of the kings of Judah, but the archaeological evidence for this period is not plentiful. There are two main reasons for this lack of evidence. First, the Solomonic temple was finally destroyed in 586 B.C., and any of its remains lie buried within the temple platform which Herod the Great later expanded and built up. Second, quarrying by Herod and subsequently by the Romans further denuded the area. Despite this, there is some archaeological evidence that can help us in interpreting the history and culture of this period of the monarchy.

The Kings of Judah: An Overview

The history of Judah and its kings is an erratic one. There were good kings and bad. Some were militarily strong, others weak. Some were good administrators, others marginal.

Solomon died about 930 B.C. (1 Kings 11:41–43). The story of his son Rehoboam's mismanagement of the whole nation, and the account of the revolt of the northern kingdom (Israel) are given in 1 Kings 12:1–20; and 2 Chronicles 10. Following Israel's revolt, Rehoboam and the tribe of Judah went their separate way. Rehoboam ruled Jerusalem for a number of years (930–913),[1] building up the country's defenses (2 Chron. 11:5–12). But he allowed idolatry to increase (1 Kings 14:22–24) and had to face the military attack, defeat, and plunder of the Jerusalem temple and the palace treasures, by Shishak, king of Egypt (1 Kings 14:25–28; 2 Chron. 12:1–11). Rehoboam also engaged in warfare with Jeroboam, king of Israel (1 Kings 14:30; 2 Chron. 12:15).

Rehoboam was succeeded by Abijah (913–910) who continued in the sins of his father and also continued the war with Jeroboam (1 Kings 15:1–8; 2 Chron. 13). Abijah was followed by Asa (910–869), a moral and upright king, who made reforms but still allowed idolatry to continue. Asa even went into league with Benhadad of Damascus to fight for him against Israel. The price he paid for this was forfeiting the remaining silver and gold in the temple and in his palace. Asa was known as a builder (1 Kings 15:9–24; 2 Chron. 14–16).

The next king of Judah, Jehoshaphat (872–849; overlapping coregency with his father, Asa, 872–869), especially in his younger years was a man of sterling character who put his trust in the Lord. The city and kingdom benefitted greatly from these characteristics, and Jerusalem and Judah prospered. However, he did ally himself with the wicked kings of Israel, Ahab and Ahaziah (1 Kings 22:1–50; 2 Chron. 17:1–21:1).

The next kings of Judah, Jehoram (849/8–841) and his son Ahaziah (841), both forsook the way of the Lord and involved themselves in idolatry. Judah suffered militarily under their rule (2 Kings 8:16–29; 9:27; 2 Chron. 21:4–22:9). Athaliah, mother of Ahaziah and daughter of Ahab (2 Kings 8:18, 26; 2 Chron. 21:6; 22:2), usurped the throne through murder in 841 (2 Kings 11:1–3; 2 Chron. 22:10–12). Following Athaliah's overthrow in 835 Joash, Ahaziah's son, ruled well for an extended period (835–796). He instituted religious reform, and Jerusalem and the temple prospered during the first part of his reign (2 Kings 11:4–12:21; 2 Chron. 23–24). Later, however, he turned from the Lord, and Jerusalem suffered attack from Hazael, king of Aram. The temple again was depleted of its

---

1. The dates given here throughout for the kings of Judah are approximate and do not always reflect coregencies. For further information see J. B. Payne, "Chronology of the Old Testament," *The Zondervan Pictorial Encyclopedia of the Bible*, 1:829–45.

gold and sacred objects, and gold was taken from the palace as well (2 Kings 12:18).[2]

The next king, Amaziah (796–767), also started his reign well but later turned to other gods (2 Kings 14:1–20; 2 Chron. 25). Jerusalem suffered military defeat again; in the process the wall of Jerusalem was broken down "from the Ephraim Gate to the Corner Gate—a section about six hundred feet long" (2 Kings 14:13; 2 Chron. 25:23), and there was further pillage of the gold and silver and other articles in the temple (2 Chron. 25:24).

Azariah (also known as Uzziah) who reigned for a long period of fifty-two years (790–740/39; he was coregent with his father, Amaziah from 790–767), served the Lord the first part of his reign, was blessed of God, developed military power, and became a great builder. Among other things he built and fortified "towers in Jerusalem at the Corner Gate, at the Valley Gate, and at the angle of the wall" (2 Chron. 26:9). Later, in pride, he turned from the Lord (2 Kings 15:1–7; 2 Chron. 26:19–22).

Next in line was Jotham,[3] (750–735; he was co-regent with his father, Azariah, from 750–740), who also tried to follow the God of Israel. His kingdom prospered; he too was an active builder, rebuilding "the Upper Gate of the temple of the Lord" and doing "extensive work on the wall at the hill of Ophel" (2 Kings 15:35; 2 Chron. 27:3–4).

Ahaz, the following king, did not follow the God of Israel and soon was besieged by the kings of Aram and Israel and others (2 Kings 16; 2 Chron. 28). Taking silver and gold from the temple and palace, he appealed to the king of Assyria for help. When pressured by Assyria, he turned to idol worship. From the temple he "took away the side panels and removed the basins from the movable stands. He removed the Sea [the large basin] from the bronze bulls that supported it and set it on a stone base. He took away the Sabbath canopy that had been built at the temple and removed the royal entryway outside the temple of the LORD, in deference to the King of Assyria" (2 Kings 16:17–18). Further, he "gathered together the furnishings from the temple of God[4] and took them away" (2 Chron. 28:24). Again the temple was devastated.

Hezekiah's reign (715–686) was one of the highlights of the kingdom of Judah. He restored the true worship of the Lord at the

2. Objects of silver and gold such as these were no doubt replenished by the kings from time to time.
3. For a discussion of the complicated chronologies of Jotham, Ahaz, and Hezekiah see Harold G. Stigers, "The Interphased Chronology of Jotham, Ahaz, Hezekiah, and Hoshea," *Journal of the Evangelical Theological Society* 9 (1966): 81–90.
4. Which may have included more than noted above.

temple, and he won military victory over the Assyrian Sennacherib (2 Kings 18–20; 2 Chron. 29–32).

According to 2 Kings 21:1–18 and 2 Chronicles 33:1–20, Manasseh, next in line, ruled for fifty-five years (697–642; he was coregent with his father, Hezekiah, from 697–686). He turned the nation to the worship of Baal and other idolatry and defiled God's temple by installing an Asherah pole (a carved image) and by building heathen altars in the courts. For this defection from the Lord he was defeated by the Assyrians. After he repented, his kingdom was restored. Then he "rebuilt the outer wall of the City of David, west of the Gihon spring in the valley, as far as the entrance of the Fish Gate and encircling the hill of Ophel; he also made it much higher" (2 Chron. 33:14).

Amon (642–640) also did evil in the eyes of the Lord. Some of his own officials conspired against him and killed him (2 Kings 21:19–26; 2 Chron. 33:21–25). His son Josiah in his long reign (640–609) ruled righteously and renewed the worship of the true God (2 Kings 22:1–23:28; 2 Chron. 34–35). He met death, however, in an unnecessary battle at Megiddo when he encountered Neco, king of Egypt, who was on his way to fight at Carchemish on the Euphrates. The next king, Jehoahaz (or Shallum, Jer. 22:11), reigned for only three months; he was conquered by Neco of Egypt (2 Kings 23:30–34; 2 Chron. 36:1–4), who then made Josiah's son, Eliakim, king and named him Jehoiakim. The latter reigned eleven years (609–598) and finally succumbed to Nebuchadnezzar, who took him bound to Babylon (2 Kings 23:36–24:7; 2 Chron. 36:5–8).

Jehoiachin, the next king, reigned for three months (598–597); he was known for his wickedness. He also was taken captive to Babylon by Nebuchadnezzar, who promptly "removed all the treasures from the temple of the LORD and from the royal palace, and took away all the gold articles that Solomon king of Israel had made for the temple of the LORD" (2 Kings 24:13; 2 Chron. 36:7). Zedekiah (also known as Mattaniah), the last king to reign (597–685) before the final fall of Jerusalem, was also famous for his wickedness. Following the siege of Jerusalem by Nebuchadnezzar, Zedekiah was blinded and taken captive to Babylon. The temple and all important buildings in Jerusalem were burned, and the wall of Jerusalem broken down. All remaining items in the temple were plundered (2 Kings 24:18–25:21; 2 Chron. 36:11–21).

The Babylonians broke up the bronze pillars, the movable stands and the bronze Sea that were at the temple of the LORD and they carried the bronze to Babylon. They also took away the pots, shovels, wick trimmers, ladles and all the bronze articles used in the temple service. The commander of the imperial guard took away the censers and sprinkling bowls—all that were made of gold or silver. The bronze from the two pillars, the Sea and the movable stands, which Solomon had made for the temple of the LORD, was more than could be weighed (2 Kings 25:13–16).

Thus, from the literary evidence, we find that the Jerusalem temple, palace, and other buildings were plundered a number of times. Finally this religious and royal center was burned and the walls were broken down. We now turn to archaeology for further evidence regarding the prosperity and the ultimate destruction of Jerusalem and its environs.

The City of David in the Ninth and Eighth Centuries

The first and best archaeological evidence for ninth- and eighth-century B.C. Jerusalem comes from the area to the east of the town wall of the City of David. Kenyon says, "After the identification of the position of the early wall at the east end of the main trench on the eastern slope, an effort was made to pick up its line in the area marked AXXI–XXII on the plan."[5] She did not find the wall continuing here. But later she excavated some distance to the west-north-west in Square AXXIV (about 85 feet north of the west end of Trench I).[6] Working through 31 feet of stony wash, she came upon foundations of a circular building, which would be dated to the seventh century B.C. Its walls had sockets for timber pieces; a viable interpretation held that the building served as a granary and had a raised platform for protection against moisture and rodents (such granaries were found later in Roman Britain). Under the circular building Kenyon found a structure consisting of rectangular rooms built on bedrock. The rooms contained pottery sherds, including a large number of Iron II storage jars, pointing to a date ± 800 B.C. Because of the quantity of storage jar sherds, the conclusion was drawn that the structure contained storerooms. At the southwest corner of the structure a flight of fine ashlar stairs led to an upper terrace.[7] One find in this building was outstanding. In a niche (or cupboard) in one of the walls was a bronze bucket 6 inches high and 5 inches in diameter and with an iron handle. Inside the bucket was

---

5. Kathleen Kenyon, *Jerusalem* (New York: McGraw-Hill, 1967) pp. 63–64.
6. See Kenyon, *Digging Up Jerusalem* (London: Ernest Benn, 1974), p. 146, figure 26.
7. Ibid., p. 132; see also Ruth Amiran, *Ancient Pottery of the Holy Land* (Jerusalem: Massada Press, 1969), pp. 238–47.

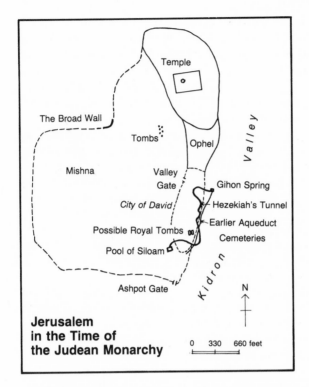

Jerusalem
in the Time of
the Judean Monarchy

a smaller bronze bucket with a bronze handle, and inside that bucket was a bronze jug.[8] Such bronze objects have been found in other countries but are unique for Palestine of this period. Many small animal bones, identified as belonging to the mouse family, were found within the buckets, suggesting that these animals must have crawled into the bucket to get at the grain. The buckets, then, must have been for domestic use. Storage jars found in the adjoining room support this idea.

Although not producing evidence of the wall of the kingdom of Judah, Kenyon's squares AXXI and AXXII did yield some outstanding finds. In excavating these squares which were 9 feet farther down the east slope than her AXXIV,[9] Kenyon came onto another rock scarp against which a walled enclosure was constructed. The walls, 3¼ feet wide, surrounded a 6¼ feet broad area. A hollowed-out cave was found at the foot of the scarp. The walled-in area was only 20 inches from the scarp and the entrance to the cave. The walls

8. Kenyon, *Digging up Jerusalem*, pp. 133–34, plates 49–51.
9. See Kenyon, *Jerusalem*, p. 109, figure 11, for the projected line of the wall north of the trench, which then veers up the hill to the west-northwest.

and this intervening space were covered with a fill of mud plaster.[10] Further excavation in this area of AXIX–XXI determined that the cave, really a shallow recess in the rock, was not used as a tomb in ancient times, although a number of pottery vessels, many of them intact, were associated with it. The pottery deposit can best be interpreted as a *favissa*, the prime example of which are the pits encircling the Late Bronze temple at Lachish.[11]

Further excavation to the north of the shallow *favissa* cave in an area 31 feet by 33½ feet revealed two levels of structures: one was on an upper-level bedrock terrace and the other was at the foot of the scarp into which a cave had been dug. Walls ran across the front of the cave. To the right of the cave and in front of the scarp a small room was found, only 11 feet from north to south, containing two oblong monoliths standing 5½ feet high. Since the room was so small and needed no roof supports, it did not seem that the monoliths were used for that purpose. Rather, Kenyon viewed them as masseboth columns, serving as cult objects.

Historically, the massebah stone might be set up to seal a legal agreement (Gen. 31:45, 51–53), used as a memorial stone for the dead (Gen. 35:19–20), or used as a symbol of the ratification of a covenant (Exod. 24:4). Because of heathen associations with such stones, however, the Lord denounces their use.[12] In Deuteronomy 16:21–22, the Lord says: "Do not set up any wooden Asherah pole beside the altar you build to the LORD your God, and do not erect a sacred stone, for these the LORD your God hates." In the time of the kingdom of Judah, toward the close of this monarchy, Josiah smashed the sacred stones in the high places built just to the east of Jerusalem (2 Kings 23:13–14). These masseboth[13] were no doubt connected with the Canaanite religion and were thought of as lifegiving, all of which Jeremiah condemns (Jer. 2:27). There were masseboth obelisks in Heliopolis in Egypt, and the Israelites were warned against worshiping such sacred stones (Deut. 16:22). But despite such warnings, Absalom set up a "pillar . . . in the King's Valley, as a monument to himself" (2 Sam. 18:18). It is possible that the two pillars found in Kenyon's excavation at the City of David were part of a religious cult center.[14]

10. Kenyon, *Digging Up Jerusalem*, pp. 135–36, Plate 54; Kenyon, *Jerusalem*, p. 64.
11. Ibid., p. 138.
12. See Carl F. Graesser, "Standing Stones in Ancient Palestine," *Biblical Archaeologist*, 35.2 (1972): 34–63.
13. Cf. Brown, Driver, and Briggs, *A Hebrew and English Lexicon* (Boston: Houghton Mifflin, 1907), p. 663, "Massebah."
14. *Illustrated Bible Dictionary*, J. D. Douglas, ed., Vol. I (Sydney, Australia: Hodder and Stoughton, 1980), p. 428, "Egypt"; Kenyon, *Digging Up Jerusalem*, p. 142.

This interpretation is supported by further structures found here. There was a doorway (later blocked) in the west wall of the masse-both room, but it must have been symbolic rather than functional, since the doorway was only one foot from the rock scarp. The door-way seems to have been connected with the structure just above the stairway, on the higher terrace above the scarp. The structure above the stairway had two stone courses preserved, but was only about 1¼ feet square. This proves the area too small for a room. According to Kenyon, this upper level could be interpreted as an altar. Wor-shipers approached the two masseboth, which represented the pres-ence of the heathen deities. The people brought their offerings in pottery vessels and, leaning through the doorway, poured their offerings at the foot of the altar elevated on the "high place." Fol-lowing the offering ceremony, the pottery vessels thus used were then discarded in the *favissa* cave to the left.

Further structures were excavated in square AXXV just to the south where earlier the cache of pottery was found in AXIX–XXI. A number of buildings were located here against a scarp containing the wall which extended the Davidic-Solomonic town to the north. In this building complex a carefully cobbled floor was excavated; at the back of the complex was a cave, 26½ feet deep and 13¾ feet wide. To the rear of the cave a wall with a window in it divided the cave into two parts. The cave's form suggests possible original use as an Iron Age tomb.

Inside the cave a quantity of vessels was found, some 1300 ob-jects. With the lack of human remains, the evidence for Kenyon pointed again to a *favissa* depository. The finds included a large number of pottery objects, mainly of domestic ware, including jugs, bowls, cooking pots, and lamps (for lighting the religious sanctu-ary). Also included was a fine incense burner, covered with a well-burnished red slip. In addition a large group of pottery miniatures were found, representing furniture and human and animal figures—a number being of horses, some with a disk on the forehead. There were 429 miniatures and many fragments. Of the human figures most were female pillar figurines with the splayed stump and prominent breasts, characteristic of fertility idols in western Asia from as far back as Neolithic Jericho of the seventh millennium B.C. All these finds are to be dated to about 700 B.C.

This evidence certainly points to this sector as being a religious cult center. The horse figurines with disk on the forehead add cre-dence to such an interpretation. For example, later, in about 620 B.C., Josiah addressed himself to Judah's practice of this heathen cult: "Josiah removed from the entrance to the temple of the LORD the horses that the kings of Judah had dedicated to the sun. They were in the court near the room of an official named Nathan-Melech. Josiah then burned the chariots dedicated to the sun" (2 Kings 23:11). The clay horses with disks may well have been miniatures of those horses at the temple's entrance, which the people were using in their worship in this shrine. Second Kings 23:13 also speaks of Ashtoreth, the vile fertility goddess of the Sidonians whose high place Josiah destroyed. Ashtoreth figurines with accentuated breasts are well-known finds in the Middle East.

It would seem that this fertility and sun cult worship, taking place just a few hundred feet from the temple where the true worship of God was to take place, continued from 700 B.C. until at least the time when Josiah tried to root out these and other heathen religious practices. Josiah not only instituted religious reform; by these acts the king also showed his resistance to the power of Assyria, which insisted that kingdoms under its jurisdiction worship its gods. Assyria would surely look with disfavor on the desecration of its worship of the horses of the sun.

As archaeological objects have demonstrated,[15] Egypt too used the sun disk symbol to indicate divinity. Josiah, by his attack on Neco of Egypt, may have wanted to show his resistance not only to the power but also to the heathen religious influence Egypt exerted on Israel.

Shiloh doesn't say why he disagrees with Kenyon's interpretation that the structures deep in her Trench A down the eastern slope were cultic in nature.[16] He describes a "cultic corner" in Area E 1 where he found a cult stand which he dates to the tenth century B.C.

Generally Shiloh's conclusions for the period of the monarchy based on his archaeological finds agree with those of Kenyon. He stresses that in the tenth century B.C. the stepped-stone structure (his Stratum 14 in Area G) was built over the supporting walls and terraces of the fourteenth-thirteenth centuries B.C. (Stratum 16) as the support for a superstructure rising near the top of the hill at the north end of the City of David.[17] Shiloh found little evidence of activity in the ninth century (except for a layer of pottery in Area E 1), but found considerable evidence of building activity in the eighth century which he thinks probably points to the work of Hezekiah (Isa. 22:9–11; 2 Chron. 32:3–5, 30).

Shiloh summarizes that he and Kenyon have exposed 360 feet of

15. Shiloh, *Excavations at the City of David, I, 1978–82*, p. 28b.
16. Ibid., p. 27a.
17. Ibid., p. 28a.

Area G, City of David, in Archaeological Park, Jerusalem.

3. series of Hellenistic and Early Roman fortifications
4. step-stone structure, tenth century B.C.
5. house of Aḥiel with pillars
8. retaining walls and stone fill, fourteenth–thirteenth century B.C.

the fortified city wall on the east slope (Kenyon: 65 feet in her Trench A; Shiloh: 295 feet, a little south of Kenyon's trench). The evidence shows that the Israelites of the Iron II period utilized parts of the fourteenth–thirteenth (Stratum 18) fortified structures in their wall building, and took advantage of the natural rock scarp which is found in the middle of the slope and on which the wall was built. Shiloh observes that this Iron II fortification wall was extended to the southern end of the City of David, giving credence to the position that the city of Jerusalem expanded beyond its original dimensions.[18] Shiloh states that the evidence in his Area E points to renewed activity in building the city wall in the eighth century (Stratum 12) of the period, and at the same time there was activity in rebuilding a residential area on a series of terraces and supporting walls which were integrated into the external walls of the dwellings. These served as a buttress for still further terraces built above them. Excavation in Area D 1 and E 2 on the eastern slope revealed simple dwellings built on terraces.

Kenyon's wall NA,[19] low on the eastern slope of the southeastern ridge, also gives evidence of Jerusalem in the period of the later monarchy of Judah. Kenyon assigns this rather substantial wall to Hezekiah, as evidence of his attempt to stop the advance of the Assyrians (2 Chron. 32:5). However, Dan Bahat argues that this wall is to be attributed to Manasseh.[20] Located as it is, low on the eastern slope, it fits the description of Manasseh's activities related in 2 Chronicles 33:14, which states that Manasseh "built the outer wall of the City of David, west of the Gihon Spring in the valley." Whichever view is held, the wall does give evidence of defense activity at Jerusalem in the later period of the monarchy.

We have already observed (chapter 3) that the Gihon water system consisted of three segments. Warren's shaft was earliest, at the time of David, tenth century B.C. The Siloam channel, contemporary or slightly later, about 1315 feet long, located on the west edge of the Kidron Valley, consisted of both a rock-covered channel and a rock-cut tunnel. (Shiloh revealed segments [395 feet] of this channel in his areas J, B, and A 1.) Openings on the valley side of this channel provided irrigation in the valley. Other openings made water available for the reservoirs both on the slope and in the lower

18. Ibid., p. 28b.
19. Kenyon, *Digging Up Jerusalem*, pp. 150–51, figures 15 and 25.
20. Dan Bahat, "The Wall of Manasseh in Jerusalem," *Israel Exploration Journal*, 31 (1981): 235–36.

end of the valley at the southern end of the City of David. But the channel was vulnerable to the enemy. The third segment of the system was Hezekiah's tunnel.

Hezekiah's Tunnel

One of the outstanding engineering feats of this period was the construction of Hezekiah's tunnel, which ran south in a zigzag pattern from the Spring Gihon, low on the eastern slope of the City of David, to the pool of Siloam. Hezekiah's reign, like that of many of his predecessors, was beset by pressure and military action from foreign powers. In 701 B.C. Sennacherib, King of Assyria, began his siege of fortified cities of Judah. To defend Jerusalem, Hezekiah

> consulted with his officials and military staff about blocking off the water from the springs outside the city, and they helped him. A large force of men assembled, and they blocked all the springs and the stream that flowed through the land. "Why should the kings of Assyria come and find plenty of water?" they said. Then he worked hard repairing all the broken sections of the wall and building towers on it. He built another wall outside that one and reinforced the supporting terraces of the City of David (2 Chron. 32:3–5).

Second Chronicles 32:30 gives more specific detail about his defense activity. "It was Hezekiah who blocked the upper outlet of the Gihon spring and channeled the water down to the west side of the City of David" (cf. 2 Kings 20:20). Hezekiah's work on the tunnel, the directions it ran, the pool it ran into, and its relation to the actual City of David have caused considerable discussion.

The direct distance from one end of the tunnel (the Spring Gihon) to the other (the Pool of Siloam) is about 1,050 feet, whereas the winding course of the tunnel makes its actual length about 1,750 feet. Shiloh's recent research has shown that the channel at the end of Spring Gihon is only about 1 foot higher than at the end of the tunnel, a gradient of only 0.6°/00.[21] There were also channels running from the Spring Gihon down the western edge of the Kidron Valley,[22] which was an easier way of providing water for the city. Although it was outside the city, this source would seem to have been adequate in the days following David's conquest of the region. One channel (or tunnel), starting from Gihon near the outside

---

21. Shiloh, *Excavations at the City of David, I*, pp. 22–23.
22. This was investigated originally by the Parker expedition (1911) and by Father L. H. Vincent.

Siloam inscription, now in museum, Istanbul.

edge of rock, probably ran into the "Old Pool" of Siloam, which Avigad and Shaheed suggest was most probably the present Birket el-Hamra, located southeast of the Pool of Siloam where the Kidron and Hinnom Valleys join. Mazar says, "It is also evident that the overflow from this pool was used to irrigate the King's Gardens just outside the city limits."[23] This is probably the channel referred to in Isaiah 22:9–11, where the prophet rebukes Hezekiah by saying, "You saw that the city of David had many breaches in its defences; you stored up water in the Lower Pool. . . . You built a reservoir between the two walls for the water of the Old Pool, but you did not look to the one who made it, or have regard for the one who planned it long ago." In other words, although earlier kings had no doubt cut this outer channel, Hezekiah was puffed up about what he had done.

This channel, however, did not provide a protected water supply. Lying outside the city, it was too vulnerable. When Assyria became a dominant power, and especially when the aggressive attitude of Sennacherib toward Palestine became evident, stronger measures to defend the water supply had to be taken. The work on the new tunnel, which was dug through rock, was arduous. The workers evidently used picks and hacked their way, some from one end and

23. Benjamin Mazar, *The Mountain of the Lord* (Garden City, N.Y.: Doubleday, 1975), p. 177. See also the plan showing Solomon's irrigation channel along the eastern scarp, in Naseeb Shaheen, "The Siloam End of Hezekiah's Tunnel," *Palestine Exploration Quarterly*, July–Dec., 1977, p. 109.

some from the other, through the hard and soft strata of rock. The two gangs of diggers met closer to the northern end than the southern.[24] The Siloam inscription,[25] cut in the wall of the tunnel near the tunnel's southern end, tells the story:

> ... when the tunnel was driven through. And this was the way in which it was cut through:—While ... were still ... axes, each man toward his fellow, and while there were still three cubits to be cut through, there was heard the voice of a man calling to his fellow, for there was an overlap in the rock on the right and on the left. And when the tunnel was driven through, the quarrymen hewed the rock, each man toward his fellow, axe against axe; and the water flowed from the spring toward the reservoir for 1,200 cubits, and the height of the rock above the heads of the quarrymen was 100 cubits.[26]

Victor Sasson suggests that the inscription, possibly the work of a foreman, simply signaled the event of breaking through this last segment of rock in the construction of the tunnel.[27]

Thus the tunnel was completed. As to the level of the flow of water, the diggers must have worked by trial and error. At the southern end of the tunnel the height is 13 feet; a little farther north it is as high as 17 feet, much higher than necessary. All this suggests, that when the diggers met in the middle, they found that the southern end of the tunnel was too high for a proper flow of water, and so they had to lower it.

Other questions arise. Why was the tunnel dug in such a circuitous winding route? As it turned out, the diggers, starting from opposite sides, were able to meet in the middle. Could they not, then, have dug in a straighter line throughout? The accompanying sketch shows that much of the tunnel swings outside the steep rock scarp on which the city was built. Why wasn't the route made in a straight line from Gihon to Siloam, so that most of the tunnel would lie under the city and could be drilled into to tap the water supply, especially in time of siege? Arguing from the results of her 1961–67 excavations Kenyon concludes that the Pool of Siloam, into which

24. Kenyon, *Digging Up Jerusalem*, p. 156.

25. The Siloam inscription was removed from the tunnel's wall and is now housed in the Museum of the Ancient Orient in Istanbul.

26. Translation by W. F. Albright, in *Ancient Near Eastern Texts*, ed. James B. Pritchard, (Princeton: Princeton University Press, 1955), p. 321. Albright here comments that the contents and script point to the reign of Hezekiah, a dating confirmed by 2 Kings 20:20 and especially 2 Chron. 32:30.

27. Victor Sasson, "The Siloam Tunnel Inscription," *Palestine Exploration Quarterly*, July–Dec., 1982, pp. 111–17.

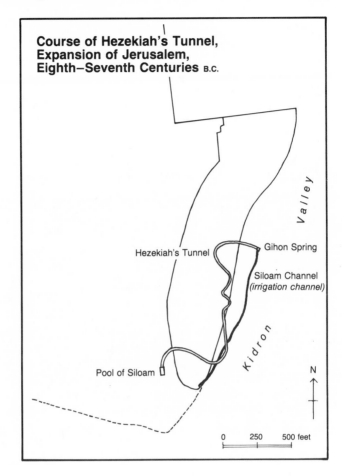

Course of Hezekiah's Tunnel,
Expansion of Jerusalem,
Eighth–Seventh Centuries B.C.

Valley

Hezekiah's Tunnel   Gihon Spring

Siloam Channel
(irrigation channel)

Kidron

Pool of Siloam   N

0   250   500 feet

the southern end of the tunnel channels the water, and the "area of the western ridge adjacent to the Pool of Siloam were not enclosed within the city walls until the first century A.D."[28] How then did Hezekiah protect the city's water supply at the Pool of Siloam? Kenyon says: "one must therefore conclude that the original reservoir was a rock-cut cistern, lying outside the line of the walls defending the eastern ridge, but accessible from within them by a shaft or staircase of the type so familiar at an earlier date in Jerusalem, and also at sites such as Megiddo, Hazor and Gezer."[29] But she admits she has no proof for this interpretation.

In contrast to Kenyon, who believes that the summit of the west-

28. Kenyon, *Digging Up Jerusalem*, pp. 148–58.
29. Ibid., p. 159.

The western hill Israelite broad wall excavated by Avigad.

ern ridge was not inhabited during the monarchy of Judah, Avigad, an Israeli archaeologist, argues that the massive wall (some 23 feet thick) which he discovered in the Jewish Quarter of the Old City in 1970 on the eastern slopes of the western ridge, about 900 feet west of the Wailing Wall, extended south and east and enclosed the Pool of Siloam. Thus, it would provide protection for the water supply. Avigad suggests that Hezekiah built this wall and that this is supported by 2 Chronicles 32:5: "Then he [Hezekiah] worked hard repairing all the broken sections of the wall and building towers on it. He built another wall outside that one and reinforced the supporting terraces of the City of David." The 130 feet of this massive (the remains rise as high as 10 feet) wall Avigad excavated contained two west-turning angles; he used this evidence to support his argument that the wall extended to enclose the Pool of Siloam.[30] An intermediate viewpoint suggests the possibility that Avigad's wall ran south only to include the northern part of the western hill, then curved east to join the southeastern ridge at its northern part only, above Kenyon's site M and Shiloh's area G.[31]

A third view, proposed by David Ussishkin, suggests that Hezekiah's tunnel ended some 360 feet east of the Pool of Siloam at a

30. Mazar, *The Mountain of the Lord*, p. 177.
31. Kenyon, *Digging Up Jerusalem*, p. 148; cf. N. Avigad, *Israel Exploration Journal*, 22, 4 (1972), p. 195, figure 2.

pool located in the valley of the Kidron. Ussishkin believes that the tunnel in Old Testament times did not terminate at the present Pool of Siloam but continued southeast and east to a point on the western edge of the Kidron Valley; then it continued east briefly to a steep slope in the valley at this second pool. Based on this theory, the original length of the Siloam tunnel was 2110 feet instead of the commonly proposed length of 1749 feet. Ussishkin argues that it was because of Empress Eudocia's identification of the present pool as the historical Siloam pool that the ancient pool fell into oblivion.[32]

In his recent excavations in the Kidron Valley south and east of the City of David, David Adan reports a first-century A.D. pool which would take care of the Gihon overflow waters coming from the Pool of Siloam. Adan posits that this pool indicates an earlier one there.[33] It could be argued, however, that Ussishkin's view still puts Hezekiah's pool outside the city walls and on the eastern side of the city in contradiction to the statement of 2 Chronicles 32:30 that Hezekiah "channeled the water down to the west side of the City of David."

Ruth Amiran has suggested that the tunnel followed a winding route because the diggers were following a crack in the rock where the water from Gihon seeped through; as the crack varied, so did the digging. Another view holds that the excavators were attempting to avoid the royal necropolis on the ridge above.

Taking a different approach, Shaheen suggests that the tunnel ran in a circuitous route to enable contact to be made above the tunnel at strategic places in the City of David—(for example, to make use of the Jebusite water shaft at its northern end, 2 Sam. 5:8). Farther south, outside the City of David, the diggers could maintain contact with persons on the surface who could help direct their operation. This explanation would be logical, since the rock above the diggers along the eastern part of the ridge was as little as 18 feet thick, compared to 45 to 155 feet where the tunnel was below parts of the city itself. More than half of the tunnel runs along this thinner ledge of rock.[34]

The majority of scholars, however, agree that today's Pool of Siloam was the pool at the southern end of Hezekiah's tunnel. Accepting this view, one can posit that, besides the water the Jebusite-Davidic-Solomonic City of David used from the shaft system, the

32. David Ussishkin, "Original Length of the Siloam Tunnel in Jerusalem," *Levant*, 8 (1976): 82–95.
33. David Adan (Bayewitz), "The 'Fountain of Siloam' and 'Solomon's Pool' in First Century C.E. Jerusalem," *Israel Exploration Journal* 29, 2,(1979): 92–100.
34. Naseeb Shaheen, "The Sinuous Shape of Hezekiah's Tunnel," *Palestine Exploration Quarterly*, July–Dec., 1979, pp. 105–8; see also figure 1, p. 104.

excess of water from the Gihon was allowed to flow down into the Kidron Valley through an irrigation channel which Solomon or one of the kings of Judah had constructed for the purpose. Actually two channels (or canals) that led from Gihon down the Kidron Valley to the south have been discovered. The second of these channels, called by Wilson the Second Aqueduct, has been traced to its termination at the Old Pool, the Birket el-Hamra. This channel, in part open to the air and in part covered by flat stones and running underground, was to be used for irrigating the western Kidron Valley floor and slope. It may well be referred to in Isaiah's rebuke to King Ahaz and the people for having "rejected the gently flowing waters of Shiloah" (Isa. 8:6). The slow-moving water in this Siloam channel fits Isaiah's reference to gently flowing waters. Weill calculated that the fall of water level in the channel was very slight: less than a quarter of an inch per yard for the first 755 feet and a quarter of an inch per yard for the next 328 feet; only near its termination at the Old Pool does the fall increase to between 1 and 2 inches per yard. This is a drop of just a few feet over the entire course of the channel investigated.[35] Simons has indicated that

> the irrigation of the terraces was effected through a number of aper-
> tures in the eastern wall of the channel, a few decimetres above its
> bottom. Water could be drawn from the canal through these "win-
> dows," sometimes also from a small basin in front, and it could be
> made to flow over the sill of the "windows" by damming up the
> channel at any given point.[36]

It was at a later time, when Hezekiah was being pressed by Sennacherib, that the king of Judah "blocked all the springs and the stream that flowed through the land" (2 Chron. 32:4). This no doubt means he stopped all the exits to Gihon and blocked off all the outlets from the Kidron channel itself to conceal where the water was coming from and to keep the enemy from using any of it. Simon notes that

> Parker [1910] found a section of canal II [the Second Aqueduct,
> Shiloh's Siloam channel] purposely blocked with sand, debris, and big
> stones on top. Ceramic finds showed the obstruction to date from the
> last centuries of the Monarchy. The corridor (III) branching off from

35. R. Weill, *La Cité de David* (Paris: Institut Français L'Archeologie de Beyrouth, Bibliothèque Archeologique et Historique, 1947), pp. 76–77.
36. J. Simons, *Jerusalem in the Old Testament* (Leiden: E. J. Brill, 1952), pp. 175–77.

The Pool of Siloam at the end of Hezekiah's tunnel.

this canal to the south-west and finally linking it to the tunnel of Hezekiah was also blocked.[37]

Having blocked off and concealed the Kidron water channel, Hezekiah then made an alternate route for the excess waters from the Gihon. That alternate route passed through his tunnel, and then the Gihon water was channeled into the new and possibly concealed Pool of Siloam, located about 325 feet north of the exposed pool, Birket el-Hamra. Accepting the results of Avigad's excavation of the broad wall that the western hill and the pool of Siloam were part of the fortified southeast ridge of the eighth-century b.c. Jerusalem, one can see the validity of Shiloh's view that upon completion of Hezekiah's tunnel which channeled the water through the rock ledge to designated reservoirs within the fortified area (e.g., Siloam pool), Jerusalem had now provided adequate protection for its water supply.[38] Any excess from the Pool of Siloam could then flow out through another underground rock-cut channel which Kenyon observed veering off to the east from the Pool of Siloam and descending to the center of the Kidron Valley.[39] The excess water flowing through this channel would have dissipated virtually unnoticed on the valley floor except for the irrigation it provided.

37. Ibid., p. 178.
38. Shiloh, *Excavations at the City of David, I, 1978–82*, p. 24
39. Kenyon, *Digging Up Jerusalem*, p. 158.

En-rogel

Not too far to the east of the Second Aqueduct Channel, at the junction of the Kidron and Hinnom Valleys, is another water source, the spring En-rogel (*Bir Ayub* in Arabic). The lower part of this well consists of large rough-hewn stones to a depth of 31 feet. An upper section is about 40 feet higher than the lower segment. The water comes from a cave at the bottom, and in the rainy winter season overflows the upper part of the well. En-rogel must have been used to help water the gardens in the valley, such as the King's Garden (2 Kings 25:4; Neh. 3:15). Father L. H. Vincent concluded that the lower part of the well is to be dated to the tenth to the eighth centuries B.C., or to the time when Hezekiah blocked all springs outside the walls.

Seventh-Century Expansion

Kenyon's excavations in Square AXXIV showed a considerable extension of the city along the eastern lower slopes, an area which was included within the walls of the City of David in the eighth–seventh centuries B.C. Several biblical passages refer to the rebuilding or repair of the walls (2 Chron. 26:9; 27:3; 33:14). Although there is archaeological evidence that the city extended south along the southeastern ridge, Kenyon argues that the city did not expand to the summit of the western hill in the time of the monarchy of Judah. She claims that her excavations in the southwest corner of the Old City at the Armenian Patriarchate produced no evidence of buildings to support such an expansion, although much Iron II pottery was probably dumped there.[40] However, others have argued that the city did expand to the western hill, based on Avigad's excavations in the Jewish Quarter west of the Wailing Wall on the eastern slope of the western hill. There Avigad found eighth-century B.C. houses built on bedrock and a massive wall 23 feet thick which he dates to the time of Hezekiah and suggests to be a part of a town wall.[41] Kenyon's view is that this wall enclosed an area west of the temple platform and included only the eastern slope of the western hill; the wall then returned to the temple platform not far from the present south wall of the platform.[42] One can, however, posit that Avigad's wall ex-

---

40. Ibid., pp. 147, 160, 161.
41. Mazar, *The Mountain of the Lord*, p. 37; Shaheen, "The Siloam End of Hezekiah's Tunnel," *Palestine Exploration Quarterly*, July–December (1977), p. 108.
42. Kenyon, *Digging Up Jerusalem*, p. 148 and figure 26.

tended south on the western hill and then turned east to connect with the City of David wall somewhat below the Pool of Siloam.

Hillel Geva, in arguing the view that the entire southwestern hill was within the Jerusalem city limits at the end of the Judean monarchy, bases this interpretation on accumulative archaeological evidence: (1) Avigad's wall in the Jewish Quarter; (2) C. N. John's excavations in the Citadel courtyard; (3) Amiran and Eitan's excavations in the same area (where the inner eastern face of their wall showed occupation layers including the Israelite period); (4) the uncovering of eighth–seventh-century B.C. pottery in an area near the present Jerusalem's west wall; and (5) the wall found by Kenyon and Tushingham on bedrock in the southern part of the Armenian Gardens.[43] From the evidence it has been argued that Avigad's wall on the eastern slope of the western hill enclosed an area entirely separate from the walled City of David, an area that has the incorrect name of Mount Zion.[44]

Whichever view one accepts, it seems clear that there was some expansion of the city to the west of the temple platform on the eastern slope of the western hill in the time of the later monarchy of Judah. It may well be that the Mishneh (a term translated "second district") and Maktesh ("mortar," a hollow) were to be located in this area. Second Kings 22:14 and 2 Chronicles 34:22 speak of the prophetess Huldah living in the Mishneh, "the Second District," of Jerusalem, and in Zephaniah 1:10-11 we read about the "New Quarter" (Mishneh) and the "market district" (Maktesh) of Jerusalem. Mazar suggests not only that the Mishneh was located in this expansion to the western hill, but also that it may have been here that King Jehoiakim built his new palace (Jer. 22:13–14).[45] G. A. Smith suggests that the Mishneh and the Maktesh may have been located in "the hollow between the West and the East Hills where the Phoenician merchants and money-dealers had their quarters."[46]

At any rate, we know from Kenyon's excavations that the City of David extended north along the eastern lower slopes of the south-

43. Hillel Geva, "The Western Boundary of Jerusalem at the End of the Monarchy," *Israel Exploration Journal* 29 (1979): 84–91.

44. Shaheen, "The Siloam End of Hezekiah's Tunnel," p. 108 and figure 1.

45. Mazar, *The Mountain of the Lord*, p. 37. An alternate view is that the new palace that Jehoiakim built was the palace on the early eighth–seventh century B.C. royal citadel at Ramat Raḥel, a site halfway between Jerusalem and Bethlehem. Since Jehoiakim reigned for eleven years, he would have had time to build this palace. However, no traces of such a structure have as yet been found.

46. George Adam Smith, *Jerusalem* (London: Hodder and Stoughton, 1908), 2:260.

eastern hill. The houses in the period of the monarchy were constructed on the terraces built originally in the Jebusite Late Bronze period. The excavation at the top of the eastern slope reveals several floors of these eighth–seventh-century houses built on the massive stone fill of the Late Bronze period; those floors, according to the pottery finds, are Iron II, the time of the monarchy of Judah. The terraces were destroyed toward the close of the seventh century and the beginning of the sixth century at the time of the Babylonian destruction. Kenyon says, "The steep erosion slope . . . sheered away the outer edge of the upper terrace and the complete superstructures of the lower terraces, an erosion that took place after the Babylonian destruction of 587 B.C."[47]

These seventh-century houses, built on the terraces on the eastern slope, and the walls, exposed on the north end of the excavation area and preserved only to a maximum height of 6½ feet, were not impressive. The rooms were small and crudely constructed of rough-shaped stones, and their surfaces plastered with mud mortar. Regarding the crude building technique Kenyon says:

> The builders had returned to the ancient Palestinian methods; the excellent building-techniques of the Phoenician masons imported by Solomon were entirely lost when Hiram's technicians returned home. The evidence at Samaria was similar. When the Phoenician masons imported by Omri and Ahab departed, the locals showed no skill at all in copying them, and reverted to the age-old rough masonry of the land.[48]

The general plan of the houses was similar to that found at many sites in the hill country of Judah of that period. A typical example is a one-room domestic structure containing the base of an oven and its clay dome. In the northern part of the excavated area, another room revealed a typically seventh-century plan; the tripartite division included a central nave with two side aisles divided off by piers, usually monoliths (single columns of stone), possibly for roof support. An accompanying staircase, probably used to go to rooms higher up the terrace, suggests that the terraced buildings extended on up to the crest of the ridge.

Artifacts found in these houses excavated by Kenyon consisted of pottery sherds representing bowls, dishes, jugs, and juglets. These were finished with a dark red, buff, or sometimes black slip (i.e., a liquid clay coating) which was then highly burnished on the potter's wheel. Other vessels included lamps, cooking pots, and large stor-

47. Kenyon, *Digging Up Jerusalem*, p. 162.
48. Kenyon, *Jerusalem*, p. 82.

age jars. The figurines were human (mainly fertility cult mother-goddess types) and animal (dogs and horses). There were also a few personal ornaments, including bronze brooches and earrings, bronze bracelets and anklets, and some fragments of pins made of bone. Also found was a cache of at least forty-one well-shaped limestone weights which were used commercially. Twenty-two of these limestone pieces had their weights inscribed on them, sixteen of them in shekel weight (the normal biblical weight reference), two in the *payim* (two-thirds of a shekel) weight, and two in *neseph* (about 85 percent of a shekel). R. B. Y. Scott made a study of the shekel value of these weights which showed that some of the specimens weighed more than the standard in use in Jerusalem at the time. This suggests that when Josiah in his reforms attempted standardization of weights, the copies made for new weight standards from specimens kept in the royal treasury may not have compensated for the reduction in weight through wear; thus some official copies and their duplicates varied from earlier originals.[49]

During his 1978–82 excavations Shiloh gained additional information about residential building and house plans. In Area E he found evidence of a rebuilt eighth-century residential section. The houses were erected on a series of terraces and several houses were bonded to supporting walls or to the Iron II city wall which Shiloh traced there. He found remains of the city wall up to 16 feet wide and 13 feet high. The house walls were covered with thick white plaster; some of the floors were covered with hard gray plaster. Shiloh found that later in the seventh century B.C. modifications were made in the houses in Area E 1: inner walls were removed and floors were raised. An important excavation here was the Ashlar House with its four-room plan. From excavations farther to the north in Area G near Kenyon's site A, it is obvious that during the late seventh and very early sixth centuries B.C. the need to keep up the stepped-stone structure was no longer felt; rather, two new terraces were constructed on which house structures were erected. On the upper terrace, the "House of Aḥiel" (so designated from the name found there on an ostracon) represented the four-room house plan. This house contained two roof-supporting monoliths, thirty-seven Iron III storage jars, a toilet installation, and an incised Hebrew inscription. Another important structure on the upper terrace was the "Burnt Room" which contained carbonized remains of ceiling wood timbers and a monolith to support the beams. On the

49. R. B. Y. Scott, "The Scale Weights from Ophel, 1963–64," *Palestine Exploration Quarterly*, Jan.–June, 1965, pp. 128–39.

lower terrace Shiloh excavated the "House of the Bullae" in which fifty-one clay bullae were found. All of this activity on the southeastern ridge and the spread of the city on the western ridge as indicated by the Avigad "Broad Wall" points to the expansion of Jerusalem in the eighth and particularly the seventh centuries B.C. Such expansion was to be expected following the fall of the northern kingdom in the late eighth century (2 Kings 17) and the ensuing exodus of refugees to Judah and Jerusalem.[50]

Nebuchadnezzar's Destruction

Second Kings 25 records that Nebuchadnezzar's final siege of Jerusalem lasted for eighteen months—a testimony to the strength of the city walls. A sketch of the late Iron II period wall exposed at the base of Kenyon's Area A, Trench 1, bears testimony to the ravages of Nebuchadnezzar's assault. Shiloh's areas D 2, E 1–3, and G also testify to the intensity of the Babylonian attack. There was wholesale destruction of buildings and the burning of anything that could be set on fire.[51]

The pottery in the destruction layers was similar in type to that found at other Iron II period Palestinian sites: Lachish (in the Shephelah), Stratum 6; En Gedi (on the west shore of the Dead Sea), Stratum 5; Arad (northern border of the Negev), Stratum 6; and Ramat Raḥel (between Jerusalem and Bethlehem), Stratum 5. As further evidence of the siege, many weapons were found especially in Area G.[52]

Literary testimony to the massive destruction is given in 2 Kings 25:9–10:

> He [the Babylonian Commander] set fire to the temple of the LORD, the royal palace, and all the houses of Jerusalem. Every important building he burned down. The whole Babylonian army under the commander of the imperial guard broke down the walls around Jerusalem.

There is no opportunity to investigate any remains of Solomon's temple that may have survived the Babylonian destruction, since this area today is a sacred sanctuary.

50. Yigal Shiloh, "The City of David Archaeological Project, the Third Season, 1980," *Biblical Archaeologist* 44, (1981): 162–65; *Excavations of the City of David, I, 1978–82*, pp. 12–14; 18, 19; 28, 29.

51. Shiloh, *Excavations at the City of David, I, 1978–82*, pp. 14, 29.

52. Ibid, p. 29

Thus, climaxed by the Babylonian destruction, the monarchy of Judah came to an end. In 598–597 Jerusalem was captured and sacked but not totally destroyed. In 587–586 the walls were broken down and the city was sacked and burned. Included in the destruction were the Solomonic temple with its upper courtyard (Jer. 36:10); several gates (the New Gate, Jer. 26:10; 36:10; the Upper Gate of Benjamin, Jer. 20:2; and the "third entrance," Jer. 38:14); and the royal palace located lower and to the south, with its "courtyard of the guard" where Jeremiah and other prisoners were kept (Jer. 32:2). Jerusalem was destroyed.

The Mount of Olives

First Kings 11:7–8 tells us that "on a hill east of Jerusalem Solomon built a high place for Chemosh the detestable god of Moab, and for Molech the detestable god of the Ammorites. He did the same for all his foreign wives, who burned incense and offered sacrifices to their gods." This hill is understood to be the Mount of Olives, on the west slopes of which were the Middle-Late Bronze Jebusite tombs, a likely area for worship of heathen gods. This was a logical place for such worship, for Solomon would not have dared to have brought such worship over into the City of David or into the temple.

Such heathen worship places continued on through the monarchy of Judah. Second Kings 23:13 bears testimony to this when it says that Josiah "desecrated the high places that were east of Jerusalem on the south of the Hill of Corruption—the ones Solomon . . . built for Ashtoreth . . . for Chemosh . . . and for Molech." The area described here is the southern part of the Mount of Olives ridge east of Jerusalem, the area located above the modern village of Silwan, across from the City of David. We do not have any archaeological evidence to identify these heathen places of worship, but we gather from the literary evidence that at this period part of the Mount of Olives was used for worship of heathen gods.

Burial Sites in this Period

In addition to the Middle-Late Bronze Jebusite burial site on the west slope of the Mount of Olives tombs have also been found to the south at the village of Silwan. Could these Silwan burials be a part of the royal necropolis used during the period of the monarchy of Judah? Let us review the evidence for such burial sites.

Four locations in the Jerusalem area are possibilities for royal burial sites in the period of the Judean monarchy. The west slopes of the Mount of Olives across from the temple platform; the west slopes of the southern section of the Mount of Olives at the site of the village of Silwan; a site at the southern end of the City of David above the Pool of Siloam; and a site on the lower east slopes of the western hill at the Tyropoeon Valley. There is no validity to the view that the traditional tomb of David located on "Mount Zion" on the western hill was the royal burial place of David, and royal tombs are certainly not to be identified with the tombs in the west part of the Church of the Holy Sepulchre nor with the so-called Tomb of the Kings, which is actually the mausoleum of Queen Helen of Adiabene, and is to be dated later.

The Books of Kings and Chronicles state that David (1 Kings 2:10) and Solomon (1 Kings 11:43) and several of their successors were buried in the City of David, and that Hezekiah was buried "on the hill where the tombs of David's descendants are" (2 Chron. 32:33). Some kings before Hezekiah (e.g., Jehoram and Judah) were buried elsewhere in the City of David, "but not in the tombs of the kings" (2 Chron. 21:20; 24:25), and Uzziah (Azariah) "rested with his fathers and was buried near them in the City of David" (2 Kings 15:7), "in a field for burial that belonged to the kings" (2 Chron. 26:23). Manasseh is said to have "rested with his fathers and was buried in his palace garden, the garden of Uzza" (2 Kings 21:18; 2 Chron. 33:20 says "in his palace"), and his son Amon was buried there likewise (2 Kings 21:26). It is to be noted that the same necropolis could be identified under different names: "the tombs of David" (Neh. 3:16); "the tombs of David's descendants" (2 Chron. 32:33); "with his fathers in the City of Judah" (2 Chron. 25:28); "the tombs of his fathers" (2 Chron. 35:24); "tombs of the kings" (2 Chron. 21:20); and "tombs of the kings of Israel" (2 Chron. 28:27).

We have no archaeological evidence that the west slope of the Mount of Olives across from the temple was a place for such royal burials. There is dispute over whether the rock cuttings in the area above the pool of Siloam excavated by Raymond Weill in 1913–14 constitute the royal tombs of the House of David, as Weill claimed.[53] Mazar reminds us that according to Nehemiah 3:15–16 there were "tombs of David" located near the pool of Siloam and the King's Garden (i.e., somewhere in the southern part of the City of David). Mazar admits that a number of scholars agree with Weill's claim. Definitive investigation of the area has been difficult because of damage caused by later quarrying.[54]

53. In another view Yeivin (1948) claims that early royal tombs are to be located possibly on the north end of Ophel Hill. L. Y. Rahmani, "Ancient Jerusalem's Funerary Customs and Tombs, Part Two," *Biblical Archaeologist*, 44.4, (1981): 232.

54. Mazar, *The Mountain of the Lord*, pp. 183–84.

The rock cuttings discovered by Weill show three or four principal tombs which had been considerably damaged as a result of stone quarrying done in the Roman period (or in the earlier Maccabean or later Byzantine periods). One large tomb, with access through a cut shaft, consisted of a vaulted tunnel 54.4 feet long and 13.2 feet wide, at the end of which was a stone bench with a carved niche probably for the body. Another tomb had a vertical shaft and a burial loculus at one side, which, together with the other tombs, convinced Weill that there was Phoenician influence evidenced here, a fact to be expected since Solomon had brought in Phoenician workers from the north (1 Kings 5).

One of the difficulties of identifying Weill's rock cuttings as the royal tombs is that they would have had to be within the actual City of David, which is contrary to the common ancient city practice. We observe that in towns such as Dothan (north of the city of Samaria) the necropolis was found on the outer edge of the tell, not within the city.[55] Furthermore, it is to be noted that in Nehemiah 3:16, the words "made repairs up to a point opposite the tombs of David" (NIV) might mean that those tombs were opposite, or east, on the Mount of Olives. The Hebrew word used means opposite.[56]

Mazar uncovered another possible royal burial field in the Tyropoeon Valley in the course of his excavations at the southwest corner of the temple platform. This elaborate necropolis is to be dated to the time of the monarchy of Judah. Mazar thinks it was used by the royal family and the upper strata of society. Uzziah was said to be buried "in a field for burial that belonged to the kings," and this could well be that place. The most common type of the Tyropoeon Valley tombs consisted of a square shaft leading into a large burial chamber. Above the chamber was a square or rectangular opening thought to be the "nephesh," the symbol of the spirit of the dead. The opening was covered with stone slabs or gable.[57] These tombs, like those at the City of David, have similarities to those in the Achziv Phoenician Cemetery.[58] One of the tombs contained considerable pottery dating to about the eighth century B.C. Some of the pots were inscribed with personal names in the Hebrew

55. With regard to the date of these tombs located at the south end of the City of David, Rahmani notes that there are two conclusions which may be drawn: (1) these are royal tombs of the time preceding David, of the time of Melchizedek and of the Jebusites; (2) these constitute the tombs of David and of his successors. (L. Y. Rahmani, "Ancient Jerusalem's Funerary Customs and Tombs, Part Two," *Biblical Archaeologist* 44.4 (Fall, 1981):229–35). See Neh. 3:16, Acts 2:29, and Josephus, *Antiquities* 7.15.3; 16.7.1.

56. Brown, Driver, and Briggs, *A Hebrew and English Lexicon*, p. 617, "neged."

57. Mazar, *The Mountain of the Lord*, pp. 186-187.

58. Ibid., p. 187.

script of the time of the monarchy, one name being of particular interest; YŠ'YHW = Isaiah. This cemetery was situated between the City of David to the east and the area of expansion up the eastern slope of the western hill.

Another burial place for Judean kings was called the "palace garden, the Garden of Uzza" (2 Kings 21:18, 26), where Manasseh and his son Amon were buried. This place could well have been that area on the lower slope of the Mount of Olives at the village Silwan where ancient tombs have been found. Mazar claims that the reference to Manasseh's burial site suggests that the royal cemetery had been moved, perhaps because of building activities on the Tyropoeon side of the western hill in this period. Mazar projects that the transfer took place over a period of time and was well in progress before Manasseh died.[59]

The area at Silwan was investigated in 1872 by Clermont-Ganneau, who found tombs carved in rock and tombs of monolithic structure. One monolithic tomb had a roof topped with a pyramidal stone, showing Egyptian influence; the Arabic name for this structure was Tomb of the Daughter of Pharaoh. Above the entrance to a cave tomb were incribed a few lines of archaic Hebrew, which Avigad translates as:

> This [is the burial . . .] of . . . yahu who is over the house. There is no silver and no gold here but his bones and the bones of his handmaiden [slave-wife] with him. Cursed is the one who opens this [tomb]!

It is possible that the date of the tomb and the inscription might fit the high official Shebna of Hezekiah's day (Isa. 22:15–19); Shebna's full name would have been Shebnayahu. Avigad, positing the period involved to be that of the kings of Judah, goes on to argue the case: "Whatever the name of the owner of the tomb, he was without doubt one of the king's ministers, and his sepulcher stands in the midst of the necropolis where persons of rank and high distinction were laid to rest."[60]

Reifenberg also argues that a necropolis of the kingdom of Judah was located in this area and states that "there is no doubt that men of high rank were buried here."[61] Thus we have the distinct possibil-

---

59. Ibid., p. 187.

60. N. Avigad, "The Epitaph of the Royal Steward from Siloam Village," *Israel Exploration Journal* 3 (1953):152.

61. A. Reifenberg, *Journal of the Palestine Oriental Society* 21, (1948): 136; on the other hand Loffreda argues that the Silwan monolithic tomb and some rock-cut tombs are later than the time of the Judean kings, being from the late Hellenistic

ity that kings and members of the court of the later Judean monarchy could have been buried in the Silwan area, across from the City of David.

Rather recently (1975) two cave tombs were uncovered on Mount Zion, both from the period of the monarchy of Judah, specifically the eighth century B.C. One of them had been reused in Hasmonean times. There were Israelite remains, possibly royal, found in a cemetery west of the present city walls, in the region of the Citadel to the southwest corner of the city wall. Here the remains included Israelite II pottery, a "pillar of Astarte," lamps placed near the head of the skeletal remains (to light the way in the netherworld) and a water decanter at the feet.[62]

The common people were buried in the Kidron Valley. Passages such as Jeremiah 26:23 speak of "the burial place of the common people." Jeremiah 31:40 speaks of the valley "where dead bodies and ashes are thrown, and all the terraces out to the Kidron Valley on the east." This reference may suggest the Hinnom Valley at the point where it is joined by the Kidron Valley. Mazar argues that the Hebrew word *shdemōt*, meaning "fields," may carry the connotation of fields for burial, and notes that some interpret *shdemōt* as the equivalent of *sdē-māvet*, fields of the dead. This graveyard, too, would have been outside the City of David.[63]

---

times (S. Loffreda, "The Later Chronology of Some Rock-Cut Tombs of the Silwan Necropolis, Jerusalem," Studii Biblici Franciscani: *Liber Annuus* [Jerusalem: Franciscan Printing Press] 23 (1973): 7–36).

62. Rahmani, "Ancient Jerusalem's Funerary Customs, p. 235.

63. Mazar, *The Mountain of the Lord*, p. 188; tomb remains from the seventh century and beyond have been found in the Hinnom Valley in the St. Andrews excavation (ca. 1982–86).

Jerusalem After the Exile

The Persian Period

When Nebuchadnezzar devastated Jerusalem in 587/586, 2 Kings 25:11 indicates that most of the population were taken into exile. Only the poorest class of people were left to work the vineyards and fields. Judah was pretty well devastated and poverty stricken. Relief came only when Persia conquered Babylon in 538 B.C., at which time Cyrus, the king of Persia, gave the decree for the return of many Jewish exiles to Jerusalem. He sent back with them the gold and silver vessels that had been taken from Solomon's temple (Ezra 1). The rebuilding of the temple was a major priority.

Unfortunately we do not have any archaeological evidence of Zerubbabel's rebuilt temple at Jerusalem. The literary evidence we do have (Ezra 6:3) tells us that this temple was 90 feet high and 90 feet wide. This contrasts greatly with Solomon's temple, which was only 30 feet wide. Only gold and silver vessels taken from the temple by Nebuchadnezzar were returned to Jerusalem. There is no mention of the pillars and the basins of bronze that adorned Solomon's temple.

119

Southeast Jerusalem Wall. In the middle of the picture is a perpendicular straight joint. To the left are Herodian blocks of the temple platform. Heavier, irregular bosses (stones) are on the right.

The ark of the covenant is not mentioned. It may have been lost when Jerusalem was destroyed.

There was at least a shell of the burned temple still existing, according to Jeremiah 41:5, where it is said that following the destruction of Jerusalem persons came to the "house of the Lord" bringing grain offerings and sacrifices. Although rebuilding the temple was begun sometime after 538, the operation was interrupted because of enemy criticism and did not resume until 520, in the time of Darius. It was finally completed in 515. It may be assumed that Zerubbabel used what was left of Solomon's temple walls and platform. Masonry at the so-called straight joint on the east wall of the temple platform, just to the right of the joint, is probably from Zerubbabel's time. This masonry is characterized by large stones with heavy irregular bosses, similar to that found in Phoenicia from the sixth to the fourth centuries B.C.

We have little evidence, literary or archaeological, of other rebuilding in Jerusalem in Zerubbabel's time or, for that matter, during the next sixty years. Obviously there was no rebuilding of the palace, for Jerusalem no longer had a king. From 2 Kings 25:9 we gather that there had been considerable destruction of the houses in Jerusalem as well as of all the important buildings. The returning exiles evidently rebuilt some of the houses in the area. In support of this, Haggai 1:4, 9 states that the exiles were busy taking care of their own paneled houses, while the Lord laments that his temple was still in ruins. Kenyon comments that her excavations at Jerusalem were able to contribute only little to the record for the 140 years following the fall of Jerusalem in 586. The kind of masonry to the right of the straight joint on the east wall of the temple platform is one of the few archaeological evidences pointing to this early part of the period. Archaeology picks up the story only when Nehemiah conducted his restoration at Jerusalem.[1] Nehemiah came to the city in 445 (in the twentieth year of the reign of King Artaxerxes) and began to survey the devastation. Nehemiah 2:11–15 graphically describes it:

> I went to Jerusalem, and after staying there three days I set out during the night with a few men. I had not told anyone what my God had put in my heart to do for Jerusalem. There were no mounts with me except the one I was riding on. By night I went out through the Valley Gate toward the Jackal Well and the Dung Gate, examining the walls of Jerusalem, which had been broken down, and its gates, which had been destroyed by fire. Then I moved on toward the Fountain Gate and the King's Pool, but there was not enough room for my mount to get through; so I went up the valley by night, examining the wall. Finally, I turned back and reentered through the Valley Gate.

In this account there are two things that stand out as certain. The King's Pool is no doubt the Pool of Siloam, into which the water of Hezekiah's tunnel ran; the pool was located near the southern end of the eastern ridge. Having reached the pool he "went up the valley" (presumably the Kidron Valley), but as he tried to make his way he was hindered by the debris. This fits well the picture given by archaeology that the eastern ridge was in shambles and filled with rubble. Evidence of the rubble was everywhere, both in Kenyon's Trench 1 and Shiloh's areas E 1 and G (Stratum 9). The pottery of the period was found in parts of Shiloh's excavation areas, supporting walls, and gravel dumps in D 1 and 2, probably evidence of Nehemiah's rebuilding on the slope higher up.[2] Nehemiah realized the scope of the project (Neh. 2:17) and must have centered his rebuilding efforts on the east side near the top of the ridge.

Nehemiah 2:17–20 recounts how Nehemiah had persuaded the people to rebuild the walls of Jerusalem. Chapter 3 tells how the

---

1. Kathleen Kenyon, *Digging Up Jerusalem* (London: Ernest Benn, 1974), pp. 180–81; Shiloh, *Excavations at the City of David, I, 1978–82*, p. 29
2. Kenyon, *Digging Up Jerusalem*, p. 182.

Kathleen Kenyon excavated this section of Nehemiah's wall (upper right) on the hill of Ophel.

Levant

people proceeded in their work of repairing the walls and rebuilding the various gates and towers: the Sheep Gate (vv. 1, 32); the Tower of the Hundred (v. 1); the Tower of Hananel (v. 1); the Fish Gate (v. 3); the Jeshanah (or Old) Gate (v. 6); the Broad Wall (v. 8); the Tower of the Ovens (v. 11); the Valley Gate (v. 13); the Dung Gate (vv. 13, 14); the Fountain Gate (v. 15); the wall of the Pool of Siloam, "by the King's Garden, as far as the steps going down from the City of David" (v. 15); the area "opposite the tombs of David, as far as the artificial pool and the House of the Heroes" (v. 16); the area "facing the ascent to the armory as far as the angle" (v. 19); Azariah's house (v. 24); the area opposite the angle and the tower projecting from the upper palace near the court of the guard (v. 25); the area "opposite the Water Gate toward the east and the projecting tower" (v. 26); the wall of Ophel (v. 27); the area "above the Horse Gate in front of the priests' houses" (v. 28); the East Gate (v. 29); the area "as far as the house of the temple servants and the merchants, opposite the Inspection Gate, and as far as the room above the corner" (v. 31); and back to the Sheep Gate (v. 32). Nehemiah 3 seems to describe the repair of the circuit of the damaged wall starting and ending with the Sheep Gate, which was located at the northeast corner of the walled area of Jerusalem.

It is possible to identify archaeologically only a few of these points enumerated by Nehemiah. One of the easiest is the King's Pool—that is, the Pool of Siloam—by the King's Garden, presumably in the lower part of the Kidron Valley, which was watered by the overflow from the Pool of Siloam. The Fountain Gate would suggest a region near the Pool of Siloam where there was an entrance to the pool.[3] The Dung Gate is to be located presumably below, or south of, the Pool of Siloam and Fountain Gate; this was a gate through which refuse was taken to the Hinnom Valley.[4] It also may possibly be identified as the Gate of Tophet, where in the Hinnom Valley in the reign of Manasseh (2 Kings 21:6; 2 Chron. 33:6) the rite of infant sacrifice was performed, a rite that was abolished in the reforms of

3. This gate was identified by F. J. Bliss and A. C. Dickie in a location near the step cut into the rock; its lower sill was seen as belonging to the time of the later kings of Judah (Bliss and Dickie, *Excavations at Jerusalem* [London: Palestine Exploration Fund, 1898], pp. 327–28). Mazar points out that opinions differ as to whether this is the gate that led to En-rogel, or whether its name came from the outlet of Hezekiah's tunnel at Siloam. He notes that it may have been called the Lower Gihon in contrast to the upper outlet of the Gihon Spring mentioned in 2 Chron. 32:30 (Mazar, *The Mountain of the Lord* [Garden City, N. Y.: Doubleday, 1975], p. 195).

4. Bliss and Dickie found such a gate at the south end of the City of David, below the Pool of Siloam and further below the Old Pool (*Excavations at Jerusalem*, pp. 322–23, 325–26).

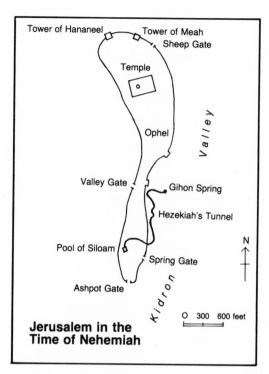

Jerusalem in the
Time of Nehemiah

Josiah (2 Kings 23:10).[5] The "steps going down from the City of David" and the point "opposite the tombs of David" suggest the region near the Gihon Spring. "The upper palace near the court of the guard" would presumably be somewhere near the hill of Ophel. The Inspection Gate may have been somewhere in the vicinity of the

---

5. So argues Mazar, who says that the Hebrew text of Nehemiah 3:13 reads "Gate of $Š^h$pt." He goes on to say: "It may therefore be worth determining etymologically whether the name does not derive from the root $Š^h$Pt in the sense of 'hearth'. Compare it in this connection with the Hebrew MŠ^{h}PTAYM. . . . The term $Š^h$Pt may be derived from the archaic ṬPT conceived as a by-form of 'Tophet' as suggested by some scholars. Indeed, many sources point to the Tophet or 'place of burning,' in the valley of Hinnom, south of the City of David, where the popular rite of infant sacrifice to Molekh was observed in the days of King Manasseh. . . . Jeremiah voices his protest against this barbarous custom by saying: 'And they have built the high place of Tophet, which is in the valley of the son of Hinnom, to burn their sons and their daughters in the fire; which I did not command, nor did it come into my mind' (7:31). He proclaims: 'Therefore, behold, the days are coming, says the Lord, when it will no more be called Tophet, or the valley of the son of Hinnom, but the valley of Slaughter' " (*The Mountain of the Lord*, pp. 194–95).

temple and the temple platform, if the term *inspection* had anything to do with the inspection of the animals to be used for sacrifice.[6] All of these identification points we are assuming to be in the region south of the temple and along the east side of the walled area. But aside from the King's Pool, the Pool of Siloam, we have no archaeological evidence.

We are uncertain about the location of the other sites mentioned. It could be that the Valley Gate was located on the opposite side (or western side) of the Gihon Spring; that is, on the western side of the City of David on the slope of the Tyropoeon Valley. It was here that J. W. Crowfoot excavated a gate about 12 feet wide constructed between two towers, a gate that seems to have been in use during the Iron II period and down into the Persian and Hellenistic periods, a conclusion determined by the Iron II pottery and hoard of coins of Alexander Jannaeus (103–76 B.C.) found there. This may be the Valley Gate that Nehemiah rebuilt. The Broad Wall mentioned in Nehemiah 3:8 may well refer to that wall excavated by Avigad in the Jewish Quarter on the western hill, but only as a point of reference since this wall and area were not used in the post-exilic period (including Nehemiah's time).

The Water Gate is presumably the one in the eastern wall leading to the Spring Gihon. Nehemiah 3:26 describes it as being "toward the east." Mazar notes that in Nehemiah's time Gihon no longer served as an important source of water, but still "the site retained its hallowed associations with the past,"[7] evidenced by the people's gathering before the Water Gate to hear Ezra read the law of the Lord (Neh. 8:1–16). Nehemiah 12:37 mentions the house of David as being in the vicinity of the Fountain Gate and the Water Gate. This may well have been the site of David's former palace. Mazar comments that this verse suggests the possibility "that the Water Gate had already been abandoned in Nehemiah's time, when the new city wall was built higher up on the crest of the ridge." The pottery finds there dated to the Persian period confirm that the wall belongs to this period.[8]

---

6. The Hebrew word here, *mip‹kad*, means muster, appointed place. In one instance it is connected with sacrificial animals, in the prescription where the bull for the sin offering is to be burned "in the designated part of the temple area outside the sanctuary" (Ezek. 43:21).

7. Mazar, *The Mountain of the Lord*, p. 195. At this time there was more dependence on cisterns, since lime mortar was efficiently used to line them; also aqueducts may have been in use to bring water from the southwest. See Kenyon, *Digging Up Jerusalem*, pp. 182–83.

8. Ibid., p. 198.

The "great projecting tower" may possibly be connected with the large structure found by R. A. S. Macalister in 1923–25 on the crest of the ridge, but it is difficult to determine whether it was built in Hellenistic or Persian times. The wall of Ophel would seem to refer to the wall in the region between the City of David and the temple platform. Archaeologically it is not clear that the section of untrimmed stones excavated by Warren southeast of the southeast corner of the Herodian temple platform is a portion of that Ophel Wall.[9] The Horse Gate farther to the north may have been a gate that led from the temple platform down to the Kidron Valley. Jeremiah (31:40) indicates that he already knew of it when he says that "all the terraces out to the Kidron Valley on the east as far as the corner of the Horse Gate, will be holy to the LORD." Evidently the East Gate was in the east wall near the temple area, close by "the house of the temple servants and the merchants" and the area of the goldsmiths. This section of houses could have continued north from Ophel along the east side of the temple platform on to the Sheep Gate, which was evidently located near the northeast corner of the temple complex close to the Bethesda Pool (John 5:2). Sheep Gate may have been a later name for the gate known as the Benjamin Gate (Jer. 37:13).

West of the Sheep Gate were the Tower of the Hundred and the Tower of Hananel, which were located somewhere along the north wall of the city, north of the temple platform. The location of the Fish Gate is problematic. Since the Fish Gate is mentioned after the Tower of the Hundred and the Town of Hananel located on the north wall, we conclude that the Fish Gate of Nehemiah's time was somewhere in the same vicinity. It may have led out to the road leading to Beth Horon, Aijalon, and the coastal plain.[10] A Fish Gate is mentioned in the time of Manasseh (2 Chron. 33:14; Zeph. 1:10). The reference in 2 Chronicles 33:14 to the area "west of the Gihon spring in the valley" may refer to what was later called the Tyropoeon Valley, while "as far as the entrance of the Fish Gate" may refer to an entrance in that outer wall somewhere on the west or northwest corner of the Tyropoeon Valley, west of the temple itself.[11] We assume that the Jeshanah Gate (or Old Gate, KJV) was somewhere south of the Fish Gate and north of the Valley Gate, just west of the temple. There is, however, no archaeological evidence to prove it.

9. Ibid., pp. 198–99.
10. Ibid., p. 199.
11. Ibid., p. 192, for Mazar's location of the Sheep Gate, the Tower of Meah (Tower of the Hundred), and the Tower of Hananel. The Fish Gate would be somewhere south and west of the tower of Hananel.

The Jeshanah Gate may have been so named because this gate in Persian times led out to the town of Jeshanah on the border between Judah and Samaria. Another interpretation would make it a corruption of Mishneh (the quarter), which in that case would put the gate west of the temple, leading to the Mishneh section of the city located on the eastern slopes of the western hill. The Tower of the Ovens was presumably west of the temple, somewhere between the Jeshanah Gate and Broad Wall and the Valley Gate.

There is no archaeological or literary evidence pointing to the location of the rest of the sites; the artificial pool and House of the Heroes, the armory and the angle; the corner and the tower projecting from the upper palace. We can only assume that they were somewhere along the city's east wall, since they are mentioned in this context in Nehemiah's counterclockwise enumeration of important locations.

In addition to the archaeological certainty of the Pool of Siloam, Hezekiah's tunnel, the Spring Gihon, and the remains of the great destruction on the eastern slope of the eastern ridge of Jerusalem, there is the evidence of a wall of Nehemiah's time. Kenyon found it running along the crest of the eastern ridge; a series of debris layers contained pottery sherds from the fifth–fourth centuries B.C. In interpreting this wall as built by Nehemiah, Kenyon reports that the wall "was solidly built, c 2.75 metres thick, but its finish was rough, as might be expected in work executed so rapidly."[12] Although Kenyon had at first believed that Nehemiah only replaced the earlier Davidic-Solomonic walls which had been destroyed by Nebuchadnezzar in 586, the excavations of 1961–67 demonstrated that this was not the case. Kenyon's evidence points to Nehemiah finding the earlier walls and terraces on the eastern slope of David's City in a shambles. So Nehemiah built his wall on the crest of the eastern ridge. Also in area G of his 1980 City of David excavations on the southeastern ridge Shiloh identified a Hellenistic earthen glacis sealing the eastern slope, and also several walls and fills as belonging to the time of the rebuilding of Jerusalem in the Persian period.[13]

Kenyon and Shiloh agree that Nehemiah's western wall ran north and south along the eastern side of the western scarp of the summit of the southeast ridge. We have no knowledge of other buildings and structures built in the Persian period in Jerusalem, although it is

---

12. Kenyon, *Jerusalem*, p. 111; see *Digging Up Jerusalem*, pp. 183, 184, 191, plates 76, 77, 79.

13. Yigal Shiloh, "The City of David Archaeological Project, the Third Season—1980," *Biblical Archaeologist* 44.3 (1981):164–65; Shiloh, *Excavations at the City of David, 1978–82*, p. 29.

known that various structures were built in Judah in the Persian period.

> In various parts of the country, massive buildings which have been identified as residences or adminstrative headquarters of the Persian period have been brought to light. There is no evidence as to where these stood in Jerusalem, and in fact very few objects or pottery that can be ascribed to the period have been found.[14]

The ruins of the administrative residence at Lachish, a structure to be dated to the Persian period, give an example of such buildings.[15]

Whether one can properly estimate the population of Jerusalem of Nehemiah's time to be about 10,000 persons, as Mazar has done,[16] is questioned by some. It is true that there are a considerable number of men enumerated in Nehemiah 11–12, and it is true that according to Nehemiah 11:1, "the leaders of the people settled in Jerusalem, and the rest of the people cast lots to bring one out of every ten to live in Jerusalem," but one cannot be certain as to how many persons actually lived in Nehemiah's Jerusalem.

The Hellenistic and Maccabean Periods

The Hellenistic and Maccabean periods overlap. Strictly speaking, the major phase of the Hellenistic period in Palestine runs from 333 B.C. (the beginning of the conquest of Alexander the Great) down to about 168 B.C. when, following the dominance of the Egyptian Ptolemaic empire (ca. 300–200 B.C.) and that of the Syrian Seleucid Empire (ca. 200–168 B.C.), the Jews under Judas Maccabeus revolted. This Maccabean latter period is also known as the Hasmonean period, named for the ruling family (the father's name was Mattathias Asmoneus) which through the high priesthood, dominated the Jewish people of this time both politically and religiously. This period continued on down to 63 B.C. when Rome, under the military campaign of the Roman general Pompey, conquered Palestine. Archaeologically speaking, the whole period from the beginning of Alexander's con-

---

14. Kenyon, *Jerusalem*, p. 112. See also Shiloh, *Excavations*, p. 29.

15. See "Lachish," *Encyclopedia of Archaeological Excavations in the Holy Land*, 3: 745–46.

16. Mazar estimates that Nehemiah 11 enumerates 3,044 men, including 1,648 servants of the temple (priests, Levites, and gatekeepers) and 1,396 other citizens of Judah and Benjamin. He estimates there would be 12,000 other family members (women and children), totaling 15,000. If 5,000 of these lived outside the walls, then the population inside Jerusalem would be 10,000 (*The Mountain of the Lord*, p. 200).

quest to the military triumph of Pompey is generally known as the Hellenistic (or Greek) period. The meaning of the archaeological evidence will be enhanced by a brief review of the historical background of the period. Following Alexander's death in 323, his kingdom was divided between four of his generals, two of whom became dominant in Palestine affairs. To the south and west was Ptolemy, who became king, or pharaoh, in Egypt. The other, Seleucus, reigned over Syria to the north and also Mesopotamia. In the ensuing struggles between the Ptolemaic and Seleucid regimes, Egypt dominated Palestine in the third century B.C., but lost its position when Antiochus, ruler of Syria, assumed control over Palestine and Jerusalem following the battle of Panias in 198 B.C. The ensuing Syrian rule was tolerable until Antiochus IV Epiphanes gained power in 175 B.C. This Syrian king injected himself into the struggle between Hellenizing Jews on the one hand and the Orthodox Jews on the other. The former were willing to compromise their religious beliefs by adopting some of the Hellenistic religious and secular customs, while the latter adhered strictly to the law of the Old Testament. Antiochus sided with the Hellenizing element, and in 169 attacked Jerusalem, destroying its walls and establishing a Syrian fortress Akra ("in the lower city," Jos. *Ant.* 12, 25) to help dominate the city. In 167 he abolished the worship of the Jewish God and set up at Jerusalem the cult of the Olympian Zeus.

The revolt of the Orthodox Jews was led by the Hasmonean family, first by the father of the clan, Mattathias, and then by his son, Judas Maccabaeus who established Maccabean rule over Jerusalem and then over Judah. The Maccabean Hasmoneans strengthened their power and after the death of Judas Maccabaeus other sons of Mattathias led the country. One son, Simon, in 142 wrested the Akra fortress from the Syrians (Jos. *Ant.* 13, 215). Simon was followed by John Hyrcanus (134–104), Alexander Jannaeus (107–76), and his widow, Salome Alexandra (76–67). Salome's warring sons, Aristobulus II and Hyrcanus II, were eventually conquered by Pompey, and Jerusalem fell to the Romans.

The Jerusalem area is better represented archaeologically in the Hellenistic and Maccabean periods than it is in the Persian. Although not abundant, this archaeological evidence is important. The area of habitation is concentrated in the "Upper City," the western hill, and on the southeastern ridge of the City of David and the temple area. The large quantities of Rhodian stamped handles of Hellenistic amphorae found in the "Lower City" area of the City of David, by Macalister, Crowfoot, Kenyon, and most recently by Shiloh (who found over 350) help date the material. Thus concentration of finds in the "Lower City" compared with the scarcity of artifacts found in the "Upper City" (Armenian and Jewish Quarters, and the Citadel) of this period suggests the importance of the "Lower City" at this time. It is true, however, that finding the remains of a building to the west outside the City of David, at the foot of Mount Zion (Shiloh's Area H) indicates population movement in the direction of the western hill in the Hasmonean period.

Shiloh also found architectural remains of the Hasmonean period, the end of the second century B.C., on the summit and east slope of the City of David. Shiloh uncovered more of a new city wall system (in areas A1 and D1), the "First Wall," parts of which had been uncovered earlier by Clermont Ganneau, Guthe, Macalaster, Crowfoot, Weill, and Kenyon. Down the east slope Shiloh found evidence of additional building activity, consisting of supporting walls and terraces at the middle of the slope (areas D and E). This system was connected with the earlier north-south Canaanite-Israelite wall on which the Hasmoneans constructed a narrow wall. Toward the north at the top of the ridge in area G Shiloh uncovered further evidence of the "First Wall" and its square tower. These structures were integrated into the tenth-century B.C. stepped-stone structure and possibly parts of Nehemiah's summit wall. The square tower was built over the sixth-century B.C. Iron Age ruins and the rubble fill of the Persian period. An earth-gravel glacis was applied to the stepped-stone structure.[17] Being of the Maccabean-Hasmonean period, the tower and surrounding structure could have been constructed by Jonathan who ordered the walls to be built higher (1 Macc. 12:36); or by Simon Maccabeus who worked on completing the walls of Jerusalem (1 Macc. 13:10); or even by John Hyrcanus who also constructed city walls (1 Macc. 16:23). This need for rebuilding and buttressing may well fit the report in 1 Maccabees 12:37, "They gathered together to rebuild the city. Part of the wall over the eastern ravine had fallen."

In addition to the material above there is some further evidence which points to the presence of Ptolemaic influence over Palestine. This is seen in the third-century coins with the imprint YRŠLM (Jerusalem). Also to be noted are "The few recently discovered silver coins bearing the legend YHDH (יהדה = pronounced Yehûda) and the portrait of Ptolemy I, dated around 300 B.C., i.e., the beginning of the hellenistic period; they are of unknown provenance."[18]

The archaeological evidence becomes clearer in the time of the

---

17. Shiloh, *Excavations at the City of David, 1978–82*, pp. 4–6, 8, 10, 11, 15, 29, 30.
18. Mazar, *The Mountain of the Lord*, p. 202.

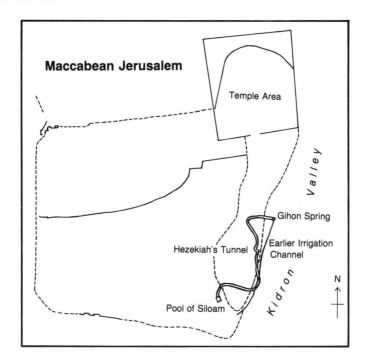

Maccabean revolt. Identifying the specific location of the Fortress Akra is a problem. According to Josephus, (*Ant.* 12, 252) the Akra rose above the temple itself. His exact words are: "He [Antiochus Epiphanes] burned the finest parts of the city, and pulling down the walls, built the Akra [citadel] in the lower city; for it was high enough to overlook the temple, and it was for this reason that he fortified it with high walls and towers, and stationed a Macedonian garrison therein."

The key words are "the lower city" and "overlook the temple." From this description some experts, such as Schürer and Ralph Marcus, argue that the Akra was thus located south of the temple on the southeastern ridge, in contrast to the earlier citadel of Persian times located to the north of the temple. The latter was rebuilt by the Hasmoneans, and later still by Herod the Great who named it the Antonia. But there are problems with this interpretation. The southeastern ridge is at a considerably lower elevation (about 2300 feet) than the rock on the temple platform which rises to about 2425 feet. The Syrians would have had to build the walls and towers of the Akra fortress enormously high for them to overlook the temple. Furthermore, it would have been more practical for the Syrians to have built the Akra closer to the temple (like the Antonia) for easier access.

Another view proposes that the Akra was built to the west of the temple platform just across the Tyropoeon Valley on the slopes of the north end of the western hill. This would be at, or near, the site of the present Citadel near the Jaffa Gate in the area excavated by Avigad. So argue Kenyon and Avi-Yonah.[19] But this again would put the Akra a considerable distance from the temple it was supposed to guard.

Still another theory would place the Akra slightly southeast of the temple site itself in the area which Herod the Great added to the temple platform. This view holds that such an Akra location would have had some connection with the east wall of the temple compound, north of the "straight joint," the wall material of the Persian period (or Hasmonean period, according to Mazar).

Since archaeological confirmation is lacking, and since we do have the statements of Josephus which suggest that the Akra was located near the temple, it would be best to adopt the view of Mazar that the Syrian Akra was located on both sides of the present Herodian south wall near the Huldah Gates.[20] At this point the Akra would have been close enough to the temple to guard it and on a site not lower than the temple, making it possible for its walls to be high enough to overlook the temple, just as Josephus suggests. As a matter of fact Josephus (*War* 5, 137, 138) states that later (by the first century A.D.) the second, or lower hill itself (in comparison to the higher western hill, with its upper city), "a hog's back" was called Akra. The artifact finds in the area point to the same conclusion. The Hellenistic coins, pottery and Rhodian jar handles of the third–second centuries B.C. found in 1927 by J. W. Crowfoot on the western slope of Ophel Hill support the idea of Syrian domination of this section of Jerusalem at this time.[21]

But this western slope of the southeastern hill gives evidence of Maccabean-Hasmonean activity as well. Kenyon, through her investigations along this western slope, sees some evidence of Hasmonean expansion here, but she denies a general population expansion in this period to the western hill (as we will discuss below). She bases this conclusion on excavations along the west side of the southeastern hill. On her sites K and N to the north of the Pool of Siloam she found a Maccabean terrace built on a massive wall with substantial foundations indicating some additions to the town in

19. Kenyon, *Jerusalem*, p. 113; *Encyclopedia of Archaeological Excavations in the Holy Land*, 2:603
20. Mazar, *The Mountain of the Lord*, p. 216.
21. Ibid.

this direction. She also uncovered remains of an important public building (second–early first century B.C.) A gate discovered earlier farther north and slightly northeast by Crowfoot she concludes was in use in the late second–first century B.C. This conclusion is based on a group of coins of Alexander Jannaeus (103–76 B.C.) found there. The Maccabean-Hasmonean wall she projects as going farther north to her site M. Here at the east end of the site she found a tenth-century B.C. fill which was cut by a wall of the first century B.C. Below and to the west of this were second–first century B.C. Maccabean-Hasmonean walls.[22] In summary, then, the Hasmonean wall on the west slope of the southeastern hill ran north near the Pool of Siloam and then northwest for about 328 feet in an expanding bulge. Then it extended north and continued northeast to Crowfoot's gate and Kenyon's site M.

In addition to the problem of locating the Akra, there is also uncertainty about the location of the Hasmonean palace. There are a few items found in the Jewish Quarter of Jerusalem on the western hill that are thought to belong to the palace: an Ionic capital, with its scroll-like ornaments and its simple but delicate Attic base, and some other architectural fragments. Josephus says, "The palace had been erected long before by the sons of the Asamonaios [the Hasmoneans] and being situated on a lofty site, afforded a most delightful view to any who chose to survey the city from it" (*Ant.* 20.190). This "lofty site" can surely be identified as the northern part of the western hill where it reaches a height of well above 2425 feet. In his *Jewish War* (2.344) Josephus is more specific when he speaks of "the roof of the palace of the Hasmoneans, which stood above the Xystos on the opposite side of the upper town; the Xystos was connected with the Temple by a bridge." This seems to point to the structure being located to the west of Wilson's Arch just north of the present-day Wailing Wall across the Tyropoeon Valley. Such an interpretation places the Xystos (perhaps a gymnasium) on the eastern slopes of the western hill. "Above the Xystos" must mean that the Hasmonean palace was higher up on the western hill, in the northeastern section of the present-day Jewish Quarter.

It is possible, too, that the Maccabeans and Hasmoneans carried on other building activities in the region of the present-day Citadel. Kenyon believes that evidence points to the fact that buildings of Herod the Great located there were built on the fortifications of the Maccabeans.[23] C. N. Johns, who excavated at the Citadel, found four

22. Kenyon, *Digging Up Jerusalem*, pp. 193–95.
23. Ibid., p. 195.

building phases in the fortification in this region. The first one (the lowest) he dated to the time of Jonathan Maccabeus (ca. 153–143 B.C.); Kenyon, however, suggests that this may be only the rough foundations of the second building stage. At any rate, the second building phase can be dated to about 100 B.C. and can thus be attributed to the Hasmoneans, either to John Hyrcanus (134–104) or to Alexander Jannaeus (103–76). The third stage was Herodian, and the fourth Roman.[24]

We have seen that Kenyon allows for some Maccabean-Hasmonean expansion along the west slope of the southeastern hill. But she holds the view that in the Hasmonean period there was no general occupation of the western hill, particularly on the east slope of the western hill and in the Tyropoeon Valley. However, Kenyon does argue that in Maccabean times defense walls were established on the ridge of the western hill, as seen in the Maccabean layers excavated at the Citadel and in the wall segments Bliss and Dickie uncovered in an area to the southeast of the Cenacle on Mount Zion. The stones of this wall of header-stretcher construction[25] had heavy bosses similar to those found in the Maccabean level at the Citadel. Defending the generally unoccupied western hill does make sense to Kenyon, for protection was needed against the catapult (invented in Syracuse about 400 B.C.) and against the torsion projectile machine developed about 350 B.C.

For Kenyon, then, the Maccabean defense line continued south from the Citadel beyond the Cenacle, then east to include Bliss and Dickie's wall segments; then it abruptly turned north in a hypothetical line along the lower east slopes of the western hill to the temple area, leaving out the Tyropoeon Valley and disconnecting the southeastern ridge of the Maccabean period from this system.[26]

Mazar, on the other hand, argues that in the Maccabean-Hasmonean period the fortified city walls, as those at the Citadel, surrounded the expanding city and included both the "Upper City" and the "Lower City" portions. This expansion to the western hill is also suggested by the remains of the Hasmonean building (the pottery obtained there was Hasmonean) that Shiloh found in area H at the foot of the wall to the east of Mount Zion.[27] With this expansion and these defensive walls the whole city—upper and lower including that

24. Ibid., p. 199.
25. In header-stretcher construction rectangular stones laid lengthwise alternate with others laid crosswise.
26. Kenyon, *Digging Up Jerusalem*, pp. 200–201.
27. Mazar, *The Mountain of the Lord*, pp. 203, 204; Shiloh, *Excavations of the City of David, I, 1978–82*, pp. 6, 30.

important religious and public building, the Hasmonean palace, built on the eastern slopes of the western hill which provided such a commanding view of the temple area—was protected from the catapults and torsion projectiles of the enemy. Further archaeological evidence for Hasmonean influence on Jerusalem is to be seen at the straight joint on the east wall of the temple platform, which Kenyon dates to the time of Zerubbabel. Near the corner of the platform, south of the straight joint, the stones are cut in the typical Herodian manner with neat incised cutting around the edge of each stone, leaving a low-profile rectangular boss in the center. The stones to the north of the straight joint exhibit a rough, less finished appearance, with the central boss of the stones protruding unevenly, a characteristic, according to Mazar, of stones cut in the Hasmonean period and also seen in the rectangular stones found in the lower levels of the Citadel.[28]

Pottery representing Maccabean-Hasmonean motifs found in these ruins gives evidence that the Jerusalem of this time basically resisted the influence of the heathen culture that had spread throughout the eastern Mediterranean and Near Eastern world following Alexander's conquest. In contrast to quantities of Hellenistic finds representing this period at Samaria,[29] only a few black-glazed Hellenistic pottery vessels or black-washed copies are found at Jerusalem. There is also an almost total absence of cooking pots based on Hellenistic models. Almost the only exception is the presence of a number of Rhodian stamped jar handles, indicating that the Jews of this period were at least willing to import wine from heathen sources, from Rhodes or from some other pagan islands, such as Thasos.[30]

A considerable quantity of coins representing Hasmonean rulers has been found and help enlighten us as to the power, culture, and religion of that family. Alexander Jannaeus seems to have been the first Hasmonean ruler to stamp his coins. Earlier, however, Antiochus VII had given the Maccabean high priest Simon the right to stamp coins. The coins were usually stamped with flowers, sheaves of wheat, anchors, or cornucopias; in the time of Mattathias Antigonus (40–37 B.C.) they were stamped with the temple's seven-branched candelabrum (menorah).

The inscriptions on the coins are in Hebrew or in Hebrew and

28. Mazar, *The Mountain of the Lord*, p. 203; see also Kenyon, *Digging Up Jerusalem*, pp. 177, 178.
29. Samaria, since the times of Omri and Ahab, had been willing to accommodate and compromise with the heathen world around it.
30. Kenyon, *Jerusalem*, p. 136.

The tomb of James in the Kidron Valley.

Greek, with the Hebrew in the archaic script, such as was used in the days of Hezekiah.[31] Coins with Hebrew inscriptions give the name of the ruler (e.g., Jonathan for Alexander Jannaeus; Yehûda for Aristobulus II). Some identity the ruler's religious position (e.g., high priest) together with the national group, *Heber Hayehudīm* (Community of the Jews). John Hyrcanus II's new title, "Jonathan the High Priest and Head of the *Heber Hayehudīm*," may indicate the new title of ethnarch (i.e., ruler of the nation) given him in 47 B.C. by Julius Caesar as a vassal of Rome. On the bilingual coins the Greek inscriptions give the Greek name. Also on these bilingual coins both the Hebrew and Greek inscriptions stress the ruler's civil position—Jonathan *ha-Melech* (the king); Alexander Basileos (King Alexander).[32]

The Mausoleums in the Kidron Valley

On the lower east slope of the Mount of Olives in the Kidron Valley and opposite the east wall of the present temple platform are tombs or mausoleum complexes popularly but incorrectly called the tombs of Absalom, Jehoshaphat, James, and Zachariah. Except for the tomb of James, these mausoleums can be dated from the last half of the first century B.C. to the beginning of the first century A.D.; therefore they will be discussed in the next chapter.

31. This use of the archaic script on coins continued up to the time of Bar Kochba, A.D. 132–135. The Siloam inscription is in archaic script.
32. Mazar, *The Mountain of the Lord*, pp. 72–73.

The tomb of James features two Doric columns, two corner pilasters, and an adjoining façade which may once have carried pyramidal superstructures, similar to Egyptian funerary structures with pyramid and colonnade. On the basis of its type of architecture this tomb is to be dated to the latter half of the second century B.C., the time of the Maccabeans. The inscription on the entablature above the columns and pilasters can be determined paleographically (from the square Hebrew letters) to belong to the first half of the first century A.D. However, the inscription gives the genealogy of several members of the priestly family of Hezir and may have been inscribed here as much as two or three generations after the tomb was originally cut. "This is the tomb and *nephesh* of Eleazar, Haniah, Jo'azar, Iehudah, Sheme'on, Iohanan, (the) sons of Joseph of 'Obed (and also) of Joseph and Eleazar (the) sons of Haniah, priests (of the family) of the sons of Hezir."

First Chronicles 24:15 lists a Hezir as head of a priestly house, and another Hezir appears in Nehemiah 10:20. The Hezir here was no doubt a descendant of this illustrious priestly family. The reference in the inscription to *nephesh* (meaning life or soul, but on occasion referring to a tomb or sepulchral monument) must mean that some part of the complex was considered the *nephesh*, or sepulchral monument. The porch and sepulchral rooms of the tomb of James are decorated with motifs that show the influence of the Graeco-Oriental art of the time.

The Herodian Era

After the conquest of Palestine by the Roman general Pompey, in 63 B.C., leaders of Rome were struggling for political and military position, enabling the Hasmonean factions to vie for power. In the ensuing struggles Antipater gained favor largely due to his friendship with Julius Caesar and his alliance with the Hasmonean Hyrcanus II who became high priest. Later after Caesar's assassination in 44 B.C., Herod, one of Antipater's sons, became the dominant figure. Herod's influence moved in two directions: he eventually married Mariamne, granddaughter of Hyrcanus II (Josephus, *War* 1, 240–241; *Ant.* 14, 467) to the pleasure of the Jews; and also solidified his position with the Romans. Playing the true diplomat, Herod journeyed to Rome, appealed to, and secured the favor of, both Antony and Octavian. As a result, in 40 B.C. the Roman Senate made him king of Judea. By 37 B.C., with Rome's backing he conquered Judea, and with it Jerusalem. Herod eventually swung his support behind Mark Antony, the rival of Octavian. When Octavian defeated Antony at Actium, Herod cleverly switched his allegiance to the new emperor, Octavian Augustus. Consequently Augustus rewarded

Herod with additions to his territories, so that he became ruler for Rome over all of Palestine.

Herod, an admirer of Greek and Roman culture, set about to spread that culture in his domain. One example of this building activity included the city of Samaria, to which he gave the name Sebaste, the Greek form of the Latin name Augustus. He also built the new town of Caesarea Maritima, at Strato's Tower on the Mediterranean coast. Other important examples of such building showing Roman embellishment can be seen at Herod's palace-fortress at Masada, at the Herodian, and at his villa at Jericho. Herod tried his best to embellish Jerusalem in the same way, but he met opposition, particularly from the Orthodox segment of the Jews. Josephus tells us that Herod built in Jerusalem a theater, an amphitheater, and a hippodrome (*Ant.* 15.268; 18.255; *War* 2.44), but we have no sure archaeological evidence for these structures.[1]

We do have archaeological evidence of Herod the Great's building activities at Jerusalem in three major areas: the temple platform at the site of Solomon's earlier temple; the Antonia fortress at the northwest corner of the temple platform; and his palace at the Citadel. But because of the devastation in the city in the intervening centuries, and particularly in the first and second centuries A.D., the evidence is not as plentiful as we could have hoped for. Kenyon puts it succinctly:

> The city of Herod the Great and Herod Agrippa was brutally destroyed and devastated after the capture of Jerusalem by Titus in A.D. 70, and its ruins still further overturned by the Hadrianic building operations of the second century A.D. Our excavations have shown that with the exception of a few of the public buildings, quite literally scarcely one stone stands on another.[2]

The Temple Area

The most important building project Herod the Great undertook at Jerusalem was his reconstruction of the temple, which he began about 20–19 B.C. The grandeur of this immense project can be gathered from Luke's brief description (21:5–6): "Some of his disciples were remarking about how the temple was adorned with

1. Schick thought he had discovered the theater in Wadi Yasul, 2800 feet south of Jerusalem, but that has been disputed.

2. Kathleen Kenyon, *Digging Up Jerusalem* (London: Ernest Benn, 1974), pp. 236–37.

beautiful stones and with gifts dedicated to God." Josephus says that the work on the temple complex continued beyond the time of Herod the Great until A.D. 62–64 (*Ant.* 20.219). In the New Testament, John 2:20, referring to the time of the early ministry of Jesus (ca. A.D. 27/28), states that the building activity on the temple up to that point had lasted forty-six years. The Talmud (B.T. Shabbat 115a) indicates that there were temple building activities in the day of Rabbi Gamaliel, and further Josephus mentions that the temple construction was completed only in the days of Albinus, the Roman procurator, close to the start of the first Revolt of the Jews (*Ant.* 20.219).[3] We do not have any of the remains of the Herodian temple itself because of the devastating Roman destruction in A.D. 70. Yet there are considerable remains of the temple platform, of the stairway on the south of the platform, and of other architectural and artifactual items which fell from the platform.

Herod the Great increased the size of the Solomonic sacred precinct by doubling the size of the platform.[4] Josephus indicates that the stones of the platform structure were exceedingly large, about 25 cubits long, 8 cubits high, and 12 cubits wide; some were as much as 45 cubits in length,[5] and he describes them as being extremely white in appearance (*Ant.* 15.392; *War* 5.223–24). Such a massive platform was necessary as a foundation on which to build the temple, with its courts and its colonnades. As indicated in chapter 4, the outside measurements of the Haram esh-Sharif platform are: the south wall, 929 feet; the west wall, 1,596 feet; the north wall, 1,041 feet; and the east wall, 1,556 feet—a total of about

3. Benjamin Mazar, "Herodian Jerusalem in the Light of the Excavations South and South-West of the Temple Mount," *Israel Exploration Journal* 28 (1978): 230–32. Actually Herod's secular artisans did not do the rebuilding of the temple itself, since it would have violated Jewish law for them to have worked on it. Josephus says that "the Temple itself was built by the priests in a year and six months" (*Ant.* 15.421).

4. Evidence of Herod's expanding of the platform is seen in the extension about 110 feet south from the straight joint on the east wall of the temple foundation. On the south he extended the platform west across the Tyropoeon Valley and also about 90 feet up the eastern slope of the western hill, to the southwest corner of the present platform. The Herodian masonry, consisting of rectangular stones with flat dressed border surrounding a flat surfaced central boss, can be traced on the west wall from the southwest corner of the platform for a distance of more than 600 feet to Wilson's Arch. On the south side vaulted corridors which are misnamed Solomon's Stables and which show in the lower parts of the piers evidence of Herodian masonry (the upper part of the piers show crusader work), were used to support the upper 42 feet of required height (*Digging Up Jerusalem*, p. 213).

5. The Greek word is πηχυς; a cubit originally indicated the length of the forearm, thus being about 18 inches in length.

thirty-five acres.[6] The height of this platform above the Kidron Valley is vividly described by Josephus:

> And it was a structure more noteworthy than any under the sun. For while the depth of the ravine was great, and no one who bent over to look into it from above could bear to look down to the bottom, the height of the portico [colonnade] standing over it was so very great that if anyone looked down from its rooftop, combining the two elevations, he would become dizzy and his vision would be unable to reach the end of so measureless (or immense) depth (*Ant.* 15.412).

Of course, Josephus speaks in expansive terms. However, the existing Herodian wall at its southeast corner survives today to a height of about 130 feet.

With archaeological evidence thus limited, we must look to Josephus for further description, inadequate as it might be (see *War* 5 and *Ant.* 15). The Jewish historian tells us that the front of the temple and seemingly all of its sides were covered with massive plates of gold "that flashed when the first rays of the sun hit them."[7] Josephus further states that the temple was about 90 feet high, 90 feet long, and 30 feet in width; in the Holy Place were three articles: the lampstand, the table for the loaves of bread, and the altar of incense.[8] The inner sanctuary, the Holy of Holies, some 30 feet square, was curtained off and contained nothing. The priests' chambers along the sides added another 60 feet to the temple's height, making the total height of the building about 150 feet. There were sharp gold spikes on the top of the temple to keep off the birds and golden vines hung down from the entrance. Herod affixed a golden eagle over the great gate, an act which led to riots.[9] Twelve steps led up to the Holy Place from the east.

6. Jack Finegan, *Archaeology of the New Testament: The Life of Jesus and the Beginning of the Early Church* (Princeton: Princeton University Press, 1969), p. 118. Finegan seems to be following the measurements of F. J. Hollis (*The Archaeology of Herod's Temple*, London, 1934), as does Ralph Marcus, Josephus, *Ant.* 15.400, Loeb (Cambridge: Harvard Univ. Press, 1963) p. 193; Simon's figures are slightly less (J. Simon, *Jerusalem in the Old Testament* [Leiden: E. J. Brill, 1952], p. 346).

7. Kenyon's translation (*Digging Up Jerusalem*, p. 208) renders it "the outward face of the Temple in its front," whereas the Loeb translation says, "the exterior of the building . . . on all sides."

8. The lampstand and table, carried off by the Romans after the fall of Jerusalem and exhibited as spoils in the triumphal procession of Vespasian and Titus in Rome, are seen sculptured on the inner side of the Arch of Titus in the Roman Forum.

9. Herod may have affixed the eagle as a symbol of his desire for Hellenization and imitation of pediments in Greek temples. "In the early temples of Zeus the flat surface of the pediment was ornamented with an eagle as a symbol of the god, whence the whole pediment derived its name (ἀετός or ᾿αέτωμα)," (Josephus, *War* 1.650, footnote a, Loeb Edition). ἀετός, meaning eagle, also in architecture meant

The Temple Courts

To the east, in front of the temple itself, was the court of the priests, which was located in that area of the large foundation rock that is to be seen today (presumably a part of the threshing floor of Araunah that David purchased; 2 Sam. 24:18–25). In this court was the altar, which according to Josephus was about 23 feet high and about 75 feet square; it had projections at each corner and was "approached from the south by a gentle sloping acclivity." In an alternate view David Jacobson locates the temple structure farther to the east; he argues that the Herodian temple coincided almost exactly with the Dome of the Rock, that the center of the temple was over the Dome of the Rock, and that the Holy of Holies was just to the west of the rock; he claims that this agrees with Josephus's statement that the temple was built at the top of the mount.[10] Josephus further states that there was a stone wall about 4½ feet high surrounding the temple and the altar. Surrounding the court of the priests on the north, south and east, and on a lower level, was another narrow court;[11] this court was for the men, and entrance by women was forbidden. To the east of the court of the men (also called the court of Israel) was located what was called the first court of the Temple, which women were allowed to enter for worship. Ten gates provided entrance into all of this sacred area of the temple and its courts—four each on the north and the south; and two on the east. The northern gate farthest to the east led into the court of women, a gate through which Josephus says "those of us who are ritually clean used to pass with our wives" (*Ant.* 15.418). The second eastern gate, located west of the court of women and reached by fifteen curved steps, led into the Court of Israel.[12] There is a problem with the identity and location of the gate Josephus calls the gate "of Corinthian bronze" (distinct from the others which were plated with silver and set in gold, *War* 5.201). Either it is to be identified with the Nicanor Gate,[13] leading into the court of Israel,[14] or the Corin-

---

gable or *pediment*, from resemblance to outstretched wings. ἀέτωμαις is equivalent to ἀετός and also meant *gable*.

10. David M. Jacobson, "Ideas Concerning the Plan of Herod's Temple," *Palestine Exploration Quarterly*, Jan.–June, 1980, p. 39.

11. See Finegan's plan, *Archaeology of the New Testament*, p. 117.

12. Benjamin Mazar, *The Mountain of the Lord*, (Garden City, N.Y.: Doubleday, 1975), p. 116.

13. Josephus, *War* 5.201, note d, Loeb Edition; Mazar, *The Mountain of the Lord*, p. 117.

14. Mazar, *The Mountain of the Lord*, pp. 116–17; J. Jeremias, *Jerusalem in the Time of Jesus* (Philadelphia: Fortress Press, 1969), p. 117.

thian bronze-Nicanor Gate was the gate which led into the court of women,[15] or the Nicanor Gate and the Corinthian Gate were separate, the former leading into the court of Israel and the latter into the court of women.[16] Josephus's description is not clear at this point.

A further problem relates to whether or not the Nicanor Gate is to be identified with the Beautiful Gate (Acts 3:2, 10) where the beggar, healed through the ministry of Peter and John, was sitting. Some experts suggest this.[17] It may be that as these two disciples were passing through the court of women in order to enter through the Nicanor Gate into the Court of Israel, they were actually going through this gate located on the west side of the court of women; on the other hand it is more likely that this gate was located on the east side of the court of women, since the beggar's physical handicap would likely have kept him from even entering this court. Further support for this latter view comes from the Christian tradition which states that the Beautiful Gate was the eastern city gate that led from Jerusalem to Gethsemane. This latter view places the Beautiful Gate on the east side of the temple platform somewhere along Solomon's Colonnade.[18]

Josephus says that this Corinthian or Nicanor Gate had two doors, each about 45 feet in height and about 23 feet in width. Beyond these were gate rooms leading into the court of Israel. He says that all the other gates had been plated with silver and gold by Alexander (Alabarch of Alexander, brother of the philosopher Philo). The gate on the east wall of the court of women was very large, some 75 feet high.

All around the temple and its inner courts there extended a forebidding but exquisitely made, stone wall about 4½ feet high. Stone slabs were inserted in it at regular intervals containing inscriptions, some in Greek, some in Latin. These gave warning to Gentiles not to enter the sacred area upon pain of death. Remains of two such stones with the warning message in Greek have been found, one by Charles Clermont-Ganneau in 1871 (now in the museum in Istanbul), and the other a fragment, found in 1935 outside the Lion's (St. Stephen's) Gate.[19] Inside this warning wall there was a wall some 60

15. Josephus, *War* 5.201, note d, Loeb Edition; F. F. Bruce, *The Acts of the Apostles* (Grand Rapids: Eerdmans, 1965), p. 104.

16. Finegan, *Archaeology of the New Testament*, p. 117, shows the Corinthian Gate to be in the east wall of the court of women and the Nicanor Gate in the west wall.

17. Andre Parrot, *The Temple of Jerusalem* (London: SCM Press, 1957), p. 85, Figure XX; Josephus, *War* 5.201, note d, Loeb Edition.

18. Finegan, *Archaeology of the New Testament*, p. 130.

19. Mazar, *The Mountain of the Lord*, p. 114.

feet high enclosing the whole sacred area. Fourteen steps led up to the terrace on which this wall was placed, and beyond this five more steps led up to the gates into the sacred area of the temple and its inner courts.

It has been assumed by most scholars that the temple and its inner courts, oriented on an east-west axis, occupied basically the same location as the present-day Dome of the Rock and its immediate surroundings; the rock was either within the Holy Place or located just to the east of the temple at the site of the brazen altar. Recently, however, Asher Kaufman, basing his arguments on literary sources and air photos (since archaeological excavation cannot be conducted on the temple mount), has theorized that the temple and its inner courts, including the court of the women, were located on an east-west axis more to the north of the Dome of the Rock structure. And he argues that the rock protrusion now covered by the small cupola called the Dome of the Spirits (located some 650 feet north-northwest of the Dome of the Rock) was originally the "foundation stone" which stood in the Holy of Holies of the temple.[20] But archaeologists critical of this theory ask why Herod would not have constructed this temple on the highest available rock on the mount—the one housed in the Dome of the Rock—rather than on a nearby lower point.[21] At any rate, Kaufman does feel that the present raised platform of the Dome of the Rock and its immediate surroundings bears some relation in size and shape to "the physical limits of the Temple."[22]

The Court of the Gentiles where Jesus often taught the people (Solomon's Colonnade; John 10:23) lay outside all this sacred area with its warning wall. No doubt it was here that the blind and lame came to Jesus (Matt. 21:14), since there were certain religious restrictions on those who were physically handicapped entering the inner courts. The blind man of John 9 presumably met Jesus at one of the southern gates of the temple platform, since Jesus at the time was on his way out of the temple grounds (John 8:59); here Jesus healed the man and sent him to the Pool of Siloam, which was south of the temple grounds (John 9:1–7).

20. Asher S. Kaufman, "The Eastern Wall of the Second Temple at Jerusalem Revealed," *Biblical Archaeologist* 44.2 (1981) pp. 108–15.

21. Abraham Rabinovich, "The Temple Puzzle," *The Jerusalem Post Magazine*, March 28, 1980, p. 12.

22. Kaufman argues that the chance exposure in 1970 of an ancient wall off the northeast edge of the Dome of the Rock platform, where the Muslim Council was constructing a water reservoir, helps support this view.

The Colonnades

All around the temple platform Herod constructed colonnades, which were formed in some cases by two rows of roofed columns. Mazar says that except for the Royal Colonnade on the south side, the colonnades were 49 feet wide.[23] According to Josephus (*War* 5.190), the double columned colonnades were composed of single-block (monolith) columns of pure white marble, each about 38 feet high, with ceilings of paneled cedar.

The colonnade on the east side of the temple platform took the name of Solomon. Josephus says that the original wall on the east side of the platform was the work of Solomon (*Ant.* 20.220–21), and the New Testament notes a colonnade in the temple area called "Solomon's colonnade" where Jesus taught (John 10:23). This is one of the colonnades built by Herod.

The southern colonnade, called the Royal Colonnade, a structure Josephus describes as "more noteworthy than any under the sun" (*Ant.* 15.412), had three aisles and four rows of columns—162 in all—with Corinthian capitals and double-molded bases. The fourth row of columns was attached to a wall of stone. The columns were large in circumference (4.6 feet in diameter) and 27 feet high. This colonnade ran along the southern edge of the temple platform from the southeast corner at the Kidron Valley to the Tyropoeon Valley on the west. Mazar reports that several fragments of the columns and Corinthian capitals of the Royal Colonnade, as well as parts of two stone sundials, friezes, panels, and cornices were found in the debris to the south of the platform. These column fragments and their capitals had been reused by later Byzantine and Islamic builders. Two such monolithic columns stand in the inner vestibule of the double Huldah Gate directly under the floor of the al-Aqsa Mosque. Such reuse explains why there was only a comparatively small number of columns found in the debris at the foot of the south wall of the platform.[24]

The question of how these columns and blocks of stone were raised to such heights may be answered by referring to a fresco found in the excavations at Stabia (near Naples), a town which was buried in A.D. 79 under the volcanic ash of Mount Vesuvius. This fresco, though difficult to make out, seems to show an engineer's work yard with a balance machine which may have been used to raise heavy marble.[25]

23. Mazar, *The Mountain of the Lord*, p. 124.
24. Ibid., p. 125.
25. Ibid., p. 121.

The outside aisles of the Royal Colonnade were 30 feet wide, whereas the center aisle was 45 feet wide, the total giving the effect of a Roman basilica. The ceiling of the middle aisle was raised higher than that of the outside ones, evidently making a pitched roof. From Josephus's remarks about "the two elevations" at the point at the southeast corner of the temple platform where one looked down from the rooftop of the Royal Colonnade to the depths of the Kidron Valley, we may gather that the colonnade was double tiered. The ceilings were ornamented with wood carvings. All of this must have been most impressive. Josephus remarks that Herod reconstructed these colonnades from the foundations up (*War* 1.401). The Jewish historian reports that Herod completed this part of the work in eight years, whereas the temple itself, built by the priests, was completed in one and a half years.

The Gates

Josephus mentions a number of gates in the walls of the temple platform. In speaking about the Roman attack in A.D. 70 he mentions a gate in the north wall (*War* 1.537; 6.222) called in the Mishnah the Todi Gate. He also mentions four gates on the west side: "the first led to the palace by a passage over the intervening ravine, two others led to the suburb, and the last led to the other part of the city, from which it was separated by many steps going down to the ravine and from here up again to the hill" (*Ant.* 15.410). The gate which had "many steps going down to the ravine" must refer to the gate near the southwest corner of the temple platform, the remains of which are called Robinson's Arch.

Excavations by Mazar have shown that Robinson's Arch sprang west from the platform about 42 feet to a massive pier built parallel to the west wall (Wailing Wall) of the platform. Further excavation has shown a series of equidistant arches in descending scale toward the south until they reached the level of the excavated Herodian pavement that ran north-south outside and along the west wall of the platform. This series of descending arches was part of a monumental stairway that led from the double gate in the western wall of the Royal Colonnade down to the street below. Mazar says: "A fragment of the doorpost of this gate has been found, as well as a large number of the steps leading to it which have fallen down. Some of the steps are still attached to the original threshold which occupies its ancient site to this day."[26]

The second gate on the west was about 267 feet north of the

---

26. Ibid., p. 132.

Robinson's Arch.

southwest corner of the temple platform and must be one of Josephus's two gates that led to the suburb. This is Barclay's Gate
(named for the person[27] who discovered it in 1848), otherwise known
as the Coponius Gate, thought to be named for the Roman procurator Coponius, A.D. 6–9, who may have underwritten some of its reconstruction and embellishment. At this gate there is a very large
lintel, 25 feet long and over 7 feet high; it is part of the gateway
which is below ground and walled up. Behind it is a passage which
led through stone archways (later turned into reservoirs) up to the
temple courts.[28]

27. Finegan, *Archaeology of the New Testament*, p. 131, and J. Simon, *Jerusalem in
the Old Testament* (Leiden: E. J. Brill, 1952), p. 364, claim that Barclay was an American. Mazar, *The Mountain of the Lord*, p. 133, says he was British.
28. Ibid., p. 133–34; Finegan, *Archaeology of the New Testament*, p. 131.

Herodian stones in the Wailing Wall.

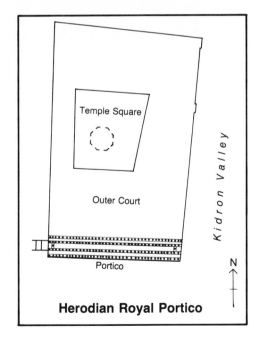

The third gate, Wilson's Arch, is located 325 feet north of the southwestern corner of the temple platform; this must be the second of Josephus's other two gates. It is located just at the north end of the Wailing Wall, and was the beginning arch that carried the viaduct across from the west colonnade of the temple area to the Upper City. This region included the area of the Xystos, that earlier Hellenistic gymnasium which seems to have contained an open-air colonnaded plaza paved with polished flagstones (2 Macc. 4:9); it was used for public assemblies. Josephus says "the Xystos was connected with the Temple by a bridge" (*War* 2.344); this agrees with the projection that this bridge was the viaduct extending from Wilson's Arch. We do not know, however, at what point the Xystos was connected with the viaduct. Above the Xystos, up the western ridge, was the Hasmonean palace. It was rebuilt later. King Agrippa II and his sister Bernice (Acts 25:23) used it. Wilson's Arch is 43 feet wide and has a span of 42 feet. At the present level of the Wailing Wall, the arch is about 70 feet above the bedrock level of the Tyropoeon Valley. The studies of William F. Stinespring in 1963, 1965, and 1966 have shown that Wilson's Arch is architecturally connected with the temple platform and can, therefore, be presumed to have been built by Herod and to have been a part of the bridge that led across to the Xystos.

In earlier Maccabean times there may have been there a smaller bridge, and the large chamber, the so-called Masonic Hall found in the region, may go as far back as Hellenistic times, to the time of Antiochus IV Epiphanes (175 B.C.).[29] Michael Zimmerman reports on recent excavations north and west of the hall under Wilson's Arch, which have uncovered an area of refuse-filled rooms, some of them 40 to 60 feet below ground level in the Tyropoeon Valley; the material dates back to the time of Zerubbabel and onward. Some believe the room known as Masonic Hall was used by the Sanhedrin; it has a lower archway that seems to be made of Herodian ashlars. One part of this room (cruciform) is Crusader in date. Zimmerman also tells of uncovering an underground tunnel, known as the Rabbinical Tunnel, which runs to the north of Wilson's Arch along the western wall. The tunnel is 600 feet long but still falls short of the northwest corner of the temple platform by 225 feet. At Wilson's Arch the floor level of the tunnel is about 60 feet above bedrock, but at its end 600 feet to the north the tunnel is 30 feet below bedrock because the tunnel maintains its level orientation while the bedrock rises. The stonework of the tunnel consists of beautiful, well-preserved Herodi-

---

29. Finegan, *Archaeology of the New Testament*, p. 132.

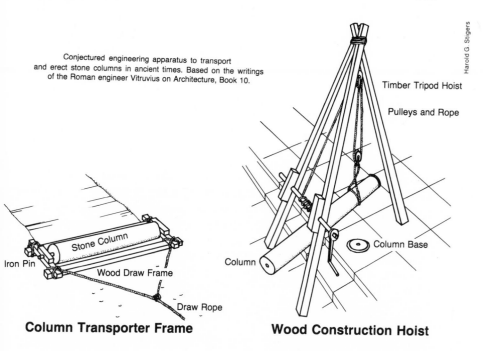

Conjectured engineering apparatus to transport
and erect stone columns in ancient times. Based on the writings
of the Roman engineer Vitruvius on Architecture, Book 10.

Harold G. Stigers

Timber Tripod Hoist

Pulleys and Rope

Stone Column

Iron Pin

Wood Draw Frame

Column

Column Base

Draw Rope

Column Transporter Frame   **Wood Construction Hoist**

an ashlars belonging to the temple retaining wall, and their seams
are almost perfect. Near the beginning of the tunnel, near Wilson's
Arch and at nine courses above bedrock, there is a huge ashlar, 46
feet long, 10 feet high, and 10 feet deep, weighing 415 tons. Also in
the tunnel is a discarded chord stone (i.e., a discarded cut piece of a
round ashlar).[30]

In a 1981 article Murray Stein addresses the question of how
Herod the Great had such large stones moved into place. He argues
that such large stones were cut in the quarry in the round, then
rolled on a pavement to the site, where the chord was cut off on one
side. The stone was rolled over into place; then the chords on each
of the other three sides were cut off, making room for the next
stones to be rolled into place.[31]

Along this west side of the temple platform Mazar found additional evidence of a paved Herodian street, a part of which had been
discovered earlier by F. J. Bliss and A. C. Dickie, who had found this

30. Michael A. Zimmerman, "Tunnel Exposes New Areas of Temple Mount," *Biblical Archaeology Review* 7.3 (1981): 34–41.
31. Murray Stein, "How Herod Moved Gigantic Blocks to Construct the Temple
Mount," *Biblical Archaeology Review* 7.3 (1981): 42–43.

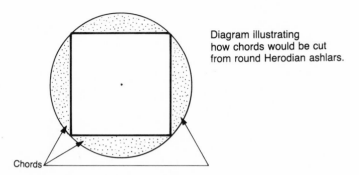

Diagram illustrating
how chords would be cut
from round Herodian ashlars.

Chords

street running farther south to a point near the Pool of Siloam.[32] Mazar states that in the Herodian period this was the main street of Jerusalem, which continued south to the southern gate of the city which opened into the Hinnom Valley. A side branch of this street led to the Pool of Siloam. Going north along this north-south street in the Tyropoeon Valley, just above Robinson's Arch the street branched, one branch going northwest to Damascus Gate and the other north to the Antonia. Mazar believes this street was the artery between the upper market on the northwest and the lower market on the south, and that the southwest corner of the temple mount was the center of daily life. Here at the southwest corner of the temple mount excavators found a large ashlar stone, fallen from the platform above, with a Hebrew inscription reading "to the place of trumpeting." Mazar's interpretation of this is that on the temple platform one of the priests would blow the trumpet announcing the sabbath.[33] Below this paved street there was found, dug in bedrock, an underground channel covered by low vaults; collecting rainwater through side channels on the east and west, this channel directed the water farther south toward the Pool of Siloam and on south of the City of David. This water could have been used to help irrigate the vegetable gardens in the lower Kidron and Hinnom Valleys.[34]

Besides the gate on the north side of the temple platform and four gates on the west side, Josephus says that on the south side and under the Royal Colonnade there were "gates in the middle." These correspond to the two gates about 228 feet apart on the south side of

32. Mazar, *The Mountain of the Lord*, p. 135; F. J. Bliss and A. C. Dickie, *Excavations at Jerusalem* (London: Palestine 'Exploration Fund, 1898), pp. 140, 329.

33. Mazar, "Herodian Jerusalem in the Light of the Excavations South and South-West of the Temple Mount," p. 234.

34. Mazar, *The Mountain of the Lord*, p. 135.

The Triple Gate, also known as the Eastern Huldah Gate.

the temple platform. They are now popularly called the Double Gate (the western Huldah Gate) and the Triple Gate (the eastern Huldah Gate). The gates are now walled up. The Double Gate, or western Huldah[35] Gate, about 43 feet wide, 8½ feet long, and 3 feet thick, has a center pier. This gate was one of the southern entrances into the court of the Gentiles in Herodian times. There is a massive lintel stone above the arch and other large stones along the side, all of which are Herodian. Behind the gate entrance is a double-vaulted vestibule[36] which leads into an ascending passageway under the present al-Aqsa Mosque, coming out to the east of the mosque. Both passageway and vestibule show Herodian masonry.

The Triple Gate, or Eastern Huldah Gate, is about 50 feet wide. It has three portals: a broad central one and two smaller side ones. Extant are a piece of the western door jamb as well as a portion of the paved street which faced its sill. On the south side of the temple platform other parts of this paved street were found. Near the southwestern corner, steps led from the street up to the Double Gate. The

35. The word *Huldah* in Hebrew means weasel or mole (Lev. 11:29), a name perhaps suggested by the tunnel-like passage up to the temple courts. (Finegan, *Archaeology of the New Testament*, p. 128). Huldah also is the name of a prophetess (2 Kings 22:14; 2 Chron. 34:22).

36. In the vestibule are two monolithic columns whose dimensions are similar to the ones in Herod's Royal Colonnade, about 5.9 feet in diameter (Mazar, *The Mountain of the Lord*, p. 141).

The monumental stairway just south of the Double Huldah Gate.

street continued east to the Triple Gate and then descended to the Ophel level of the southeast corner of the platform.[37] At the Triple Gate a deep vault was discovered under this east-west street.[38] The vault served as support for a stairway which led from the lower plaza to the Triple Gate and then into the temple area. The Triple Gate has been walled up since medieval times. It has an inner vestibule, divided by rectangular pillars engaged in the wall, and a rock-hewn passage-way which leads north and northwest until it merges with an abandoned reservoir.[39]

The large monumental stairway just to the south of the Double Gate was excavated. This stairway of thirty steps is 215 feet wide, paved with smoothly trimmed stones, and its foundation steps are cut into the bedrock. From a wide plaza below on the south (where large crowds of pilgrims gathered before entering the temple area) the stairway rose 22 feet to the upper street in front of the Double Gate.[40] Scattered down the stairway were a number of the large

37. Mazar, *The Mountain of the Lord*, p. 140.
38. Ibid., p. 146.
39. This stairway to the Triple Gate was much narrower, as the width of the vaulting there has shown (Mazar, "Herodian Jerusalem in the Light of the Excavations South and South-West of the Temple Mount," p. 236).
40. Mazar, *The Mountain of the Lord*, p. 143.

columns that had fallen from the Herodian Royal Colonnade above.[41] A piece of stone fragment found in front of these gates was identified as belonging to another piece found over one hundred years ago near the Triple Gate. The two pieces preserve part of an inscription which includes the word elders in Hebrew. This may refer to the elders of the Sanhedrin who met, among other places, "at the entrance to the temple mount" (*Sanhedrin* 11. 2), probably at a place near the Triple Gate.[42]

South of the Double Gate Mazar found a subterranean tunnel running north-south toward the Double Gate, containing niches for lamps. The excavator thinks this tunnel is possibly the winding passage described in the Mishnah (*Middoth* 1.9): "He would go out and go along the winding passage that lead below the citadel where lamps were burning here and there, until he reached the Chambers of Immersion." Rabbi Eliezer ben Jacob said: "He used to go out by the winding passages that leads below the Rampart, and so he came to the Tadi Gate." It is to be noted that the Tadi Gate is now in the northern wall of the temple platform.[43]

Mazar in his excavations found another tunnel of fine construction located below the south wall of the temple platform and east of the Triple Gate (about 112 feet west of the southeast corner of the wall). The tunnel, made of Herodian ashlars, is about 69 feet long, with its southern entrance coming through a vaulted chamber in the face of the southern wall; it may have led into the underground system of treasury chambers in the temple. The destroyed building identified east of the Triple Gate is represented by ornamental architectural fragments, together with pieces of a monumental, yet undeciphered, Hebrew inscription. Mazar suggests that this building may have been the seat of the Beth-din, one of the three courts of the temple, located "at the gate of the Temple Mount" (Mishnah, *Sanhedrin* 11.2).[44]

Another gate, the Single Gate, on the south wall is to be seen east of the Triple Gate and not far from the southeast corner of the platform, which is the highest point of the Temple (Luke 4:9). Warren found this area of the temple platform to be on an average 106 feet above the lowest courses of the structure. Such a platform needed supporting substructures, and the south part of the temple area is supported by massive vaulted structures under which there is a 69-foot tunnel, 3 feet wide and 11.5 feet high. This passage,

41. Ibid., p. 149.
42. Ibid., pp. 146, 148.
43. Mazar, "Herodian Jerusalem in the Light of the Excavations South and South-West of the Temple Mount," p. 236.
44. Ibid., pp. 127–28.

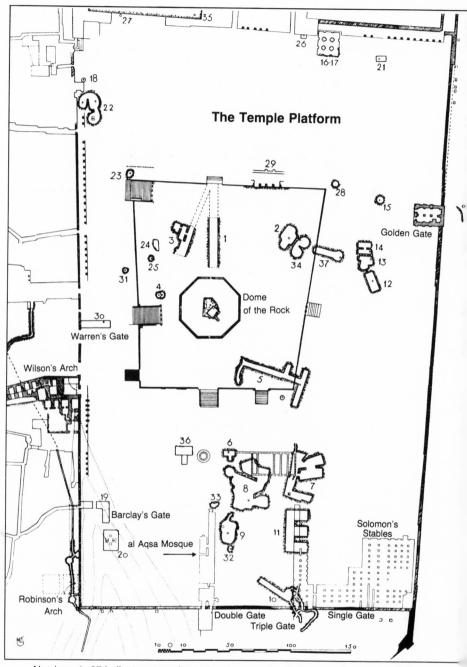

The Temple Platform

Dome
of the Rock

Golden Gate

Warren's Gate

Wilson's Arch

Barclay's Gate

al Aqsa Mosque

Solomon's
Stables

Robinson's
Arch

Double Gate
Triple Gate

Single Gate

Numbers 1–37 indicate reservoirs and underground halls beneath the temple platform.

The Golden Gate.

constructed of heavy Herodian stone blocks, cuts its way in toward the north under the Single Gate, about 112 feet west of the southeast corner of the platform. The underground passage ends at a doorway which then leads into a hall under part of the vaulted substructures mentioned above. The temple platform surface is 40 feet above the floor of this subterranean area. These so-called "Solomon Stables" extend 260 feet west and 200 feet north from the southeast corner of the platform. Finegan comments that the lower part of some of the piers there show Herodian masonry while the upper parts display Crusader rebuild. The vaults[45] were probably used as storerooms for the temple. Josephus says that in his day when the Romans were laying siege to Jerusalem the Zealots "took refuge in the temple vaults" (*War* 5.102), and later when the city had been taken, the conquerors found in these caverns "upwards of two thousand dead" (*War* 6.429).

On the east of the northeast corner of the temple platform part of a Herodian tower is to be seen; it was part of Herod's platform wall north of the temple.[46]

45. Finegan, *Archaeology of the New Testament*, pp. 125-26.
46. Mazar, *The Mountain of the Lord*, p. 151

Although Josephus mentions the east (Solomon's) colonnade, he does not mention a gate on the eastern wall of the temple platform. However, the present Golden Gate is located 1,023 feet north of the southeast corner of the platform. It is disputed as to whether this site is the location of the eastern gate of Herod's time, and it is to be noted that the walled-up Golden Gate seen today is from Byzantine or Umayyad times.[47] In 1971 and 1972 preliminary investigations were made by J. W. Fleming, R. Hayden, and G. Giacumakis of a tomb area about 7 to 8 feet below the present Golden Gate. The investigation showed evidence of an arch equally as large as the two arches of the Golden Gate above.[48] This evidence suggests that there were earlier gates at a lower level at this location; it is possible, therefore, that this is the proper location of the eastern gate, possibly the Beautiful Gate of Acts 3:2, 10. It is not possible to date this lower gate precisely; yet based on the type of the two or three lowest courses of the wall adjacent to the lower gate, which show affinity to the masonry to the right (north) of the straight joint of the east wall masonry (i.e., the section of wall to the right of a perpendicular straight joint which divides the earlier masonry to the right from the later Herodian masonry to the left) which some date as early as the Solomonic, Persian, or Hellenistic periods, it is possible to date the lower gate to a time considerably earlier than the present Golden Gate—that is, to a time prior to the Herodian period. This suggests that this gate area was used over a long period of time, including the time of Jesus and the apostles, who may well have used this very gate.[49]

Just to the west of the Golden Gate is an inner vestibule dating to the fourth–fifth centuries A.D. (Byzantine period), a vestibule which has support columns from the debris of the Herodian temple courts. Also to be seen at the eastern wall of the platform near the southeastern corner and in a position opposite Robinson's Arch, is the remnant of an arch, which also suppported a stairway that came up from the road below the eastern wall. "The top of the stairway opened onto a gate which led to the vaulted halls known as the 'Solomon Stables.' "[50]

47. Ibid., p. 148.

48. G. Giacumakis, "The Gate Below the Golden Gate," *Bulletin of the Near East Archaeological Society*, ns. 4 (1974): 23–26.

49. James Fleming, "The Uncovered Gate Beneath Jerusalem's Golden Gate," *Biblical Archaeology Review*, 9.1 (1983): 24–37.

50. Mazar, *The Mountain of the Lord*, pp. 150–51.

Turner

Southeast corner of temple platform,
the probable site where Satan tempted Jesus.

Structures South of the Temple Platform

To the south of the temple mount, in the area called the Ophel, Mazar found remains of two large structures connected with the Herodian period. One of these structures, located 64 feet south of the Double Gate, contained a series of huge cisterns and a plastered pool. It was originally built in Hellenistic times, as evidenced by the finds, especially the pottery, including Rhodian (Hellenistic) jar handles with Hebrew inscriptions stamped on them and an Aramaic ostracon. The second structure is located about 295 feet south of the Triple Gate on the southeast edge of Ophel at the top of the Kidron Valley. The building, projected to have been there in the Judean monarchy period, was superseded by a massive tower (discovered earlier by Charles Warren) which was part of a fortification system built at the edge of the scarp overlooking the Kidron Valley. This building was built on the rock terraces of the upper slopes of Ophel, terraces leveled out with fill containing Bronze Age and Iron Age sherds.

These building remains, the excavator feels, might well be ascribed to the Beth Millo mentioned in 2 Kings 12:20, razed at the time of Nebuchadnezzar's destruction and reutilized in the Herodian period as the base of a large two-story building, the upper story of which is attested by a small piece of mosaic. Mazar hypothesizes that this building was one of the palaces built by the royal family of Adiabene, who were converts to Judaism. According to Josephus (*War* 4.567; 5.252-53; VI. 355), this palace stood in the Lower City.[51]

In summary, Mazar notes that the physical modifications in the topography of the area south of the temple mount are due to Herod's projects. Most of the pre-Herodian buildings were razed to make room for his massive construction, while pools and cisterns, some channels, and even early tombs were reutilized and made a part of his constructions.

Interesting objects and other artifacts have been uncovered outside the temple platform, including Herodian lamps, stone sundial, and coins.

The Antonia

In *War* 1.401 Josephus describes the Antonia fortress, which Herod had named in honor of Mark Antony. He states that Herod rebuilt the Antonia on the site of an older castle, called Baris, which had been constructed by John Hyrcanus (*Ant.* 18.91; cf. 15.403; *War* 1.75). Herod must have built the Antonia by 31 B.C. when Antony was defeated by Octavian, for it would have been folly for Herod to have named the fortress after Antony subsequent to transferring his allegiance to Octavian. The Antonia must have served Herod as his palace for a good number of years, since he did not build his elaborate palace on the west side of the city until about 24–23 B.C.[52] Josephus indicates that the Tower of Antonia (he says that the whole gave the appearance of a tower) was erected at the northwest corner of the temple platform, on a hill about 75 feet high, on the rock

51. Mazar, "Herodian Jerusalem in the Light of the Excavations South and South-West of the Temple Mount," *Israel Exploration Journal*, 28 (1978), pp. 236–37.
52. See Finegan, *Archaeology of the New Testament*, pp. 156–57.

surface of which Herod laid smooth flagstones. Behind a wall about 4½ feet high he erected the fortress itself to a height of about 60 feet. Three of the towers were about 75 feet high, but the tower at the southeast corner was about 105 feet high. Josephus says that the Antonia included apartments, cloisters, baths, and large courtyards for troops. On the south side, next to the two temple colonnades, there was a stairway that led down to both colonnades; the guards of the Roman cohort permanently stationed there could use this stairway to watch for any outbreak of trouble among the people. Paul stood on this stairway when he addressed the Jewish people (Acts 21:40). Josephus likens the magnificent Antonia with all its facilities and luxury to a town and a palace, and comments that the Roman cohort there guarded not only the temple but also the whole city.

The street that led west from St. Stephen's Gate (also called the Lion Gate or St. Mary's Gate or, in Arabic, *Tariq Bab Sitty Mariam*) proceeds parallel to the north side of the temple area in the neighborhood where the Antonia was located. On the north side of this street the following sites are located from the east to west, starting from St. Stephen's Gate: Bethesda, with its two pools and five covered colonnades (John 5:2); the Franciscan Convent of the Flagellation situated farther up the hill; the Convent of Our Lady of Sion (also called the Ecce Homo Orphanage); and the Greek Orthodox Convent. It is to be remembered that Jerusalem has been inhabited for the last two thousand years, and the accumulated debris has raised the level of the present street several feet. Therefore, explorations for ancient sites has had to take place under these buildings. From 1931 to 1937 M. Godeleine and L. H. Vincent excavated under the Convent of Our Lady of Sion, and in 1955 the Franciscans did likewise under the Convent of the Flagellation, located across the street from the present-day minaret which is evidently at the site of the northwest corner of the temple complex. Underground in these areas, for instance, in the basement of the Convent of our Lady of Sion is an extensive water system including cisterns and basins. One large cistern adjoins the large section of paved courtyard exposed in the basement of the convent. The dimensions of the cisterns are: 170 feet long, 45 feet wide, and up to 33 feet deep.[53] This ancient water system no doubt served the Antonia well in time of siege and may well have been part of the water installation which Josephus called Struthion and against the middle of which Titus's Fifth Legion built up an embankment in the siege against Jerusalem (*War* 5.467).

Extensive portions of the very large courtyard of the ancient An-

53. Ibid., pp. 159–60.

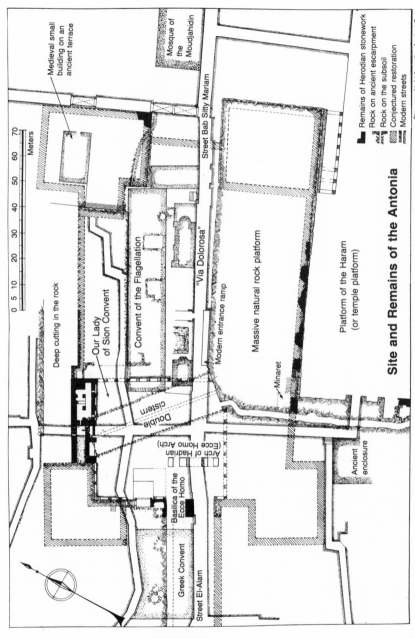

Meters
0 5 10 20 30 40 50 60 70

Medieval small
building on an
ancient terrace

Mosque of
the
Moudjahidin

Street Bab Sitty Mariam

Deep cutting in the rock

Our Lady
of Sion Convent

Convent of the Flagellation

"Via Dolorosa"

Double
cistern

Modern entrance ramp

Massive natural rock platform

Minaret

Platform of the Haram
(or temple platform)

Arch of Hadrian
(Ecce Homo Arch)

Basilica of the
Ecce Homo

Ancient
enclosure

Greek Convent

Street El-Alam

Remains of Herodian stonework
Rock on ancient escarpment
Rock on the subsoil
Conjectured restoration
Modern streets

Site and Remains of the Antonia

Finegan, *Light from the Ancient Past*

The Sheep Gate, also known as St. Stephen's Gate, Lion's Gate,
and St. Mary's Gate.

tonia are to be seen in and under the Convent of the Flagellation,
and also under the Convent of Our Lady of Sion and the Greek
Orthodox Convent. This pavement extended west to east about 104
feet and north to south about 156 feet, covering an area of well over
16,000 square feet. "Architectural remains around the area show
that this was an impressive courtyard surrounded by galleries. The
paving stones are slabs of limestone, some square and some rectangular, as much as a meter on a side, sometimes as much as two
meters or more. Some channels are cut out into the stones for the
drainage of rain water."[54]

On the south side of the courtyard a transverse section of stones
with grooves cut into the stone runs east to west. This section of the
paved courtyard, frequently visited by pilgrims today, is part of a
roadway which was striated to keep the horses from slipping. As the
roadway extends west, one can position the location of the west
entrance to the Antonia. This roadway and the entrances can be
seen on the model displayed in the Convent of Our Lady of Sion. On
some of the courtyard stones were cut patterns, one of which suggests a game board (*lusoria tabula*), used by the Roman troops.

54. Ibid., p. 160.

Plan of the Lithostrotos Section of Antonia Fortress

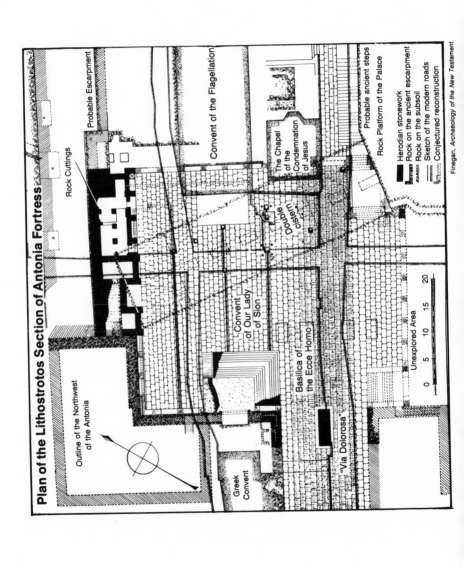

Outline of the Northwest of the Antonia

Rock Cuttings

Probable Escarpment

Convent of the Flagellation

The Chapel of the Condemnation of Jesus

Double cistern

Convent of Our Lady of Sion

Basilica of the Ecce Homo

"Via Dolorosa"

Greek Convent

Probable ancient steps

Rock Platform of the Palace

Herodian stonework
Rock on the ancient escarpment
Rock on the subsoil
Sketch of the modern roads
Conjectured reconstruction

Unexplored Area

0   5   10   15   20

Finegan, *Archaeology of the New Testament*

General view of the Lithostroton.

Ecce Homo Orphanage

Some scholars have questioned the exact location of the Antonia and have posited that the structure is to be located to the south of the street running west from St. Stephen's Gate. But it would seem that Josephus is correct (*War* 5.238) that the fortress was built on the hill to the west of St. Stephen's Gate.

Some of the remains of columns, capitals, etc., in the area of the Antonia come from Herod's time and some from the time of Hadrian (A.D. 117–138). I have seen these items in the arches in the walls of the altar of the Basilica of Ecce Homo in the Convent of Our Lady of Sion. These items show marked similarity to the architectural segments in Hadrian Arch at Gerasa (modern Jerash). Such intermingling of Herodian and Hadrian architectural features argues for the use of the arches in the period from the first century B.C. to the second century A.D.[55]

Bethesda

The Pool of Bethesda was located to the east of the hill on which the Antonia was built, on the north side of the street running west from St. Stephen's Gate. It was near the Sheep Gate, as is indicated in John 5:2. Nehemiah 12:39 also mentions the Sheep Gate, and from Nehemiah's description that it was located in the north in the vicinity of the Tower of Hananel (which may be the site where the Antonia was later built) and the Tower of the Hundred, we may gather that the Sheep Gate was at the northeast corner of the walled city. The Tower of the Hundred would then be to the west and the Tower of Hananel to the northwest.[56] It is here that we find the Bethesda pools today, at the northeast corner of the walled city of Jerusalem, not far west of St. Stephen's Gate.

Josephus (*War* 5.149–151) speaks of a hill north of the temple which he calls Bezetha; it lay opposite the Antonia and was separated from it by a deep valley purposely dug, a district which had been recently built and which carried the Greek name of New Town. Finegan argues that this name *Bezetha*, or *Bethzatha* (the Greek transcription of the Aramaic for the word) is a variant spelling of the Hebrew word *Bethesda*, meaning House of the Twin Pools. The pool is identified by all three names, Bezetha, Bethzatha and Bethesda as attested by the variant Greek manuscript evidence in John 5:2. Finegan further notes that the Hebrew text of the Copper Scroll from Qumran, dated between A.D. 25 and 68, uses the word *Bethesda*

55. Ibid., pp. 162-63.
56. Ibid., p. 143.

Excavations at Bethesda.

with a Hebrew dual ending which suggests that site contained two pools.[57] The Bordeaux pilgrim also talks about the two pools and the five porches, and Cyril of Jerusalem (A.D. 348–386) speaks of the Sheep Pool with five porches, one of which extended across the center.

Finegan further notes that modern excavations at Bethesda by the White Fathers have confirmed the existence of two pools of rectangular shape; they were separated by a wall of stone about 20 feet wide. Jeremias reports that there were drainage channels connected with the cross wall separating the two pools. One of these channels, an old conduit located 26 feet above the floor of the north pool, conducted water from the north pool to the south pool. This hydrological engineering technique might help explain the meaning of the invalid's statement in John 5:7, "when the water is stirred." Passage of water from time to time from the north pool into the south pool could have produced what seemed to be a "stirring" effect to the

57. Ibid., pp. 143–44.

viewer.[58] The two pools, somewhat rectangular in shape, averaged about 185 feet east-west and about 290 feet in length north-south, for a combined total of about 53,650 square feet, or an area in excess of one acre. The vaulted cistern in the southeast corner of the northern pool measures about 52 feet east-west and 20 feet north-south. Although the cistern was cut out of rock on three sides, a wall was built up on its north side, the lower part being of Roman construction. This wall suggests an attempt to keep part of the northern pool suitable for drinking water. Being in a valley these pools would naturally serve in the collection of rain water.

In the Bethesda excavations many fragments of columns, capitals, and bases were found, many of which can be seen by visitors today. Investigation of these remains has led to the conclusion that the columns were about 25 feet high, the colonnades about 26 feet high, and the colonnade between the two pools 20 feet wide. All this fits the general description of Bethesda in John 5:2—that it included a pool of water surrounded by five covered colonnades. In 1932 a graffito in Hebrew was found on the south wall of the southern pool. Hadrian excluded the Jews from living in Jerusalem, so it would seem that such Hebrew writing would have been scribbled there before that emperor's time. Together with the elegant work done on the colonnades as evidenced by the fragments, reminding one of Herod's type of construction, this suggests that the work at the pools was done under Herod's direction.[59] Actually, the original construction of the reservoir or pool(s) seems to date to the Hellenistic period when in the days of Simon the Just it is said that a great reservoir named Beth Hasda (House of Mercy) "was dug, a deep pool as extensive as the sea" (Ecclus. 40:1–3).[60]

The House of Caiaphas and St. Peter in Gallicantu

Josephus (*War* 2.426) tells us that the revolutionaries went into the Upper City (the southwestern ridge or hill) and burned the palaces of Agrippa II and Bernice and the house of Ananias, the high priest. A plausible assumption is that this was also the house of the earlier high priests, and if so, it could have been the house of Caiaphas and Annas (John 18:13–15). But just where on the southwest-

58. Joachim Jeremias, *The Rediscovery of Bethesda* (Louisville, Ky.: Southern Baptist Theological Seminary) pp. 17, 37, 38.

59. Finegan, pp. 146-47.

60. Mazar, *The Mountain of the Lord*, p. 202. M. Avi-Yonah suggests that Jesus' miracles were not performed at these pools but at a cave to the east, but he gives no evidence for this theory.

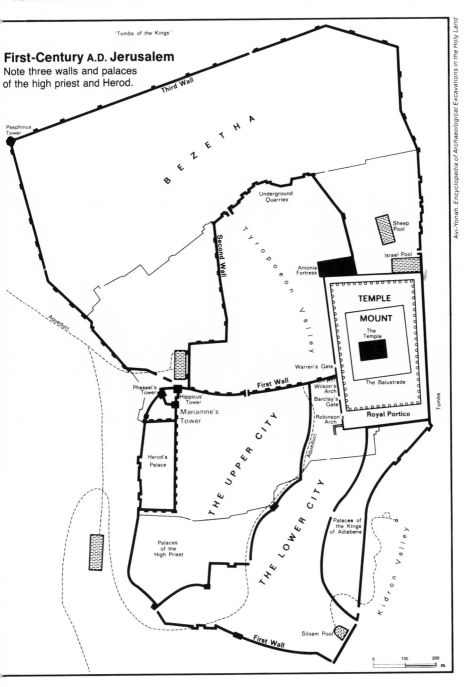

First-Century A.D. Jerusalem
Note three walls and palaces
of the high priest and Herod.

"Tombs of the Kings"

Third Wall

Psephinus
Tower

B E Z E T H A

Underground
Quarries

Second Wall

Sheep
Pool

Israel Pool

Antonia
Fortress

TEMPLE

MOUNT

The
Temple

The Balustrade

Warren's Gate

First Wall

Phasael's
Tower

Hippicus
Tower

Wilson's
Arch

Barclay's
Gate

Mariamne's
Tower

Robinson's
Arch

Royal Portico

THE UPPER CITY

Herod's
Palace

Palaces of
the Kings
of Adiabene

Palaces
of the
High Priest

THE LOWER CITY

Kidron Valley

Siloam Pool

First Wall

0   100   200
                m

Avi-Yonah, Encyclopedia of Archaeological Excavations in the Holy Land

ern ridge was the house of Caiaphas located? According to early Christian tradition it was located on Mount Zion. The Bordeaux Pilgrim (A.D. 333) says he saw the place on Mount Zion where the house of Caiaphas was located. Theodosius (A.D. 530) suggests that Caiaphas's house was about 50 paces (Latin *passus*, a length of about five Roman feet) from the Cenacle, the traditional place of the Last Supper (this traditional place is located on the top of the southwestern ridge), but he does not indicate in which direction. The present Armenian Chapel, located about 165 feet north of the Cenacle, is thought by some experts to be the site of Caiaphas's house. Although the chapel is from the fifteenth century, excavations show that a Byzantine church was built there in the sixth century. A threshold and Byzantine mosaic pavement 3 to 16 feet long and 8 feet wide have been found at this site. These ruins point to the presence of a church estimated to have been about 100 feet long. This may have been the Church of St. Peter, the place of the house of Caiaphas. Theodosius so identifies it.

But a Crusader tradition located the Church of St. Peter on the declivity to the south and east of Mount Zion; this tradition held that this place was called Gallicantu (i.e., "of the cock-crowing"), the place where Peter wept bitterly after his denial of the Lord. This corresponds to the location of the present Church of St. Peter in Gallicantu, built in 1931, where excavations uncovered ruins of an ancient church. Coins found there from the time of Theodosius II (408–450) to Leo I (457–474) help date the original construction of the church to the fifth century. Rock-hewn chambers below the church have been argued to be the place below Caiaphas's house where prisoners were incarcerated and where Jesus was imprisoned. The upper chamber of the underground structures is thought to have been the room for the guards; it contains rings in the stone walls where, it is argued, prisoners were tied for flagellation. The lower chamber, a deep pit, in these subterranean rooms, thought to have been the place where the prisoners were kept, has in its walls and roof fourteen Byzantine crosses. In the lower chamber one can see holes cut in the support columns at which prisoners could have been tied and whipped. In favor of accepting the tradition that Caiaphas's house is to be located at the site of St. Peter in Gallicantu is the fact that this site places Caiaphas's house farther away from the traditional place of the Last Supper on the southwestern ridge. It could be argued that the disciples would have chosen a place some distance away from Caiaphas's house, a situation which would not have been possible had Caiaphas's house and the Cenacle both been located near the Armenian Chapel on the top of the ridge.

Kent

First-century steps near house of Caiaphas.

However, the earlier, and probably more reliable, Christian tradition places the house of Caiaphas near the Cenacle (site of the Lord's Supper) on Mount Sion. Theodosius says that the house of Caiaphas (which in his day was the Church of St. Peter) was only fifty paces from the Church of Holy Zion. If this interpretation is correct, then the Church of St. Peter in Gallicantu is not to be identified with the site of the house of Caiaphas, but is simply the traditional site for commemorating the place where Peter wept.[61]

Whichever interpretation is accepted, one is impressed with the ancient stone stairs that run from the vicinity of the Cenacle down past the Church of St. Peter in Gallicantu to the Pool of Siloam, stairs that are thought to be from the Jewish period. It could be that these were the very stairs used by Jesus as he went down from the Last Supper to the Kidron Valley and on to Gethsemane (John 18:1).

The Palace of Herod

Comparable to his great work on the temple and the Antonia were Herod's endeavors in building his palace on the western ridge in the

61. Finegan, *Archaeology of the New Testament*, pp. 152–54.

vicinity of the present Citadel near the Jaffa Gate. Josephus (*War* 5.173–75) describes the area as containing a lofty hill and a higher crest on which Herod built his three towers. These towers were constructed of immense white marble blocks, 30 feet long, 15 feet wide, and 7 to 8 feet thick; they were perfectly joined together. The tower Hippicus, named after a friend of Herod and probably to be identified as the northwest tower of today's Citadel, was about 32 feet square and rose to a height of 45 feet. Josephus says this tower had built in it above this mass of masonry a reservoir 30 feet deep, over which was a double-roofed 32-foot high chamber, and above that, turrets; the structure was 120 feet high.

The tower Phasael located to the northeast, was named for Herod's brother. It was 60 feet square. Josephus tells us (*War* 5.166–169) that its 60-foot-high solid base was the foundation for a cloister 15 feet high "protected by parapets and bulwarks;" above the center of the cloister arose another 135-foot tower containing apartments and baths, embellished with bulwarks and turrets. Josephus likens it to the Pharos lighthouse at Alexandria.

The Mariamne tower, named for Herod's Hasmonean wife, was apparently located east of the Phasael tower. It had a solid base 30 feet high, and the structure was 30 feet square. The total height of the upper structure was 80 feet and included luxuriously decorated apartments (*War* 5.170–171).

As ornate and luxurious as the towers were, they did not compare with Herod's palace located just to the south. Josephus describes it in *War* 5.176–182. The palace was enclosed by a wall 45 feet high, with ornamental towers at frequent intervals. It contained large banquet halls, bedrooms for 100 guests, circular cloisters, each of whose columns was different, and a wide variety of rare stone and decorated ceiling beams. The apartments enclosed were ornately designed and furnished, and included numerous gold and silver objects. This palace also contained spacious gardens, with long walks, deep canals, and ponds bordered with bronze figures. The magnificence of this second palace-fortress in Jerusalem was breathtaking.

When Titus destroyed Jerusalem, he left the Hippicus, Phasael, and Mariamne towers standing as testimony to the grandeur of Jerusalem's magnificent structures which Rome had devastated. He also left a portion of the western city wall (Josephus, *War* 7.1).

In subsequent years others used the site of Herod's palace. These included the early Arabs, the Crusaders, the Mamluks, and the Turkish governors, who in turn brought about further destruction and change to the region. The site now called the Citadel contains a castle that comes mainly from the Mamluk period, based on a plan

The Citadel.

of a Crusader castle from the twelfth century. Of the several towers of this castle the northeastern one, called from Crusader times David's Tower, is the most prominent and is probably the site of the Phasael Tower. C. N. Johns excavated in the Citadel area close to the Jaffa Gate from 1934 to 1948 and uncovered the lower Hasmonean and Herodian levels of this Tower. Johns's excavations showed that the tower had been built into an earlier Hasmonean wall. Four different building phases have been identified here.[62] The first phase of the wall was Hasmonean, with Hellenistic pottery and arrowheads, and potsherds from the monarchy period; the second phase of the wall (from the Phasael tower south to the Mariamne tower) was also Hasmonean, shown by the coins found there from the time of Alexander Jannaeus. The third phase, evidenced in the section of the wall east of the Phasael tower, was Herodian; and the fourth phase was attributed to the time of the First Jewish Revolt against the Romans.

The more recent excavations in the Citadel conducted by R. Amiran and A. Eitan uncovered along the interior of the Hasmonean wall the remains of a massive tower preserved to a height of about

62. Finegan, *Archaeology of the New Testament*, p. 134; Mazar, *The Mountain of the Lord*, p. 30.

10 feet. This wall has also been traced by M. Broshi in his new excavations in the Armenian Garden.[63] This wall, remains of which were uncovered by Bliss and Dickie in 1894, continued south to enclose the western hill (Mount Zion) in an angle running east, south of the Pool of Siloam.[64]

Houses of the Herodian Period

Excavations conducted since 1967 in the Upper City on the eastern slope of the western ridge, in an area to the west of the temple platform called the Jewish Quarter, have revealed a considerable number of houses that belonged to upper-class Jews. These houses come from the Hasmonean period and particularly from the Herodian period. One such house, which may have been built in the Hasmonean period, was quite extensive, covering over 2,000 square feet and containing a number of rooms arranged around a central courtyard, in typical Roman pattern. Among the houses excavated was one called the Mansion, which had a frescoed wall preserved to a height of 8 feet. In another structure called the Burnt House a stone weight was found with the Aramaic inscription "[of]Bar Kathros," indicating that this house belonged to the family of Kathros. Most of these houses were burned in the Roman destruction of A.D. 70.

In the ruins of these houses were found numerous mosaics, clay vessels such as lamps of the Hellenistic and Herodian types, stone tables, kitchen utensils, storage vessels, and dishes. The coins found here dated from the Ptolemaic, Seleucid, and Hasmonean periods (third to first century B.C.) into the times of Herod the Great, Archelaus, and the Roman procurators of Judea (A.D. 6–59). In one outstanding discovery there was found incised on the wall of a house an 8-inch-high representation of the seven-branched candlestick of the temple, the earliest depiction of its kind. In the area of the Armenian cemetery on Mount Zion, Magan Broshi excavated a house of the same Herodian period which contained some fine frescoes.[65] In another excavation, one which went down some 60 feet under the Siebenberg residence in the Jewish Quarter of the Old City, evidence representing the Second Temple Herodian period was uncovered,

63. *Encyclopedia of Archaeological Excavations in the Holy Land*, 2:599–600.

64. Mazar, *The Mountain of the Lord*, p. 30. Kenyon, *Digging Up Jerusalem* (p. 246), suggests that it was Herod Agrippa "who completed the enclosure of the western ridge by joining the tips of the two ridges across the mouth of the Tyropoeon" (p. 246).

65. N. Avigad, "How the Wealthy Lived in Herodian Jerusalem," *Biblical Archaeology Review*, 2.4 (1976): 23–35.

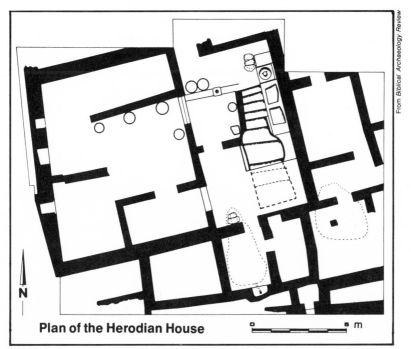

Plan of the Herodian House

From Biblical Archaeology Review

The rooms are arranged around a central courtyard. The four circles in the same area are four ovens sunk into the ground. There are three niches in the left wall which were used as cupboards for dishes, many of which were found just as they had been left. Steps leading down to a large reservoir are in the upper middle of the plan. At the head of the stairs is a small footbath for use before descending into the pool.

including a bronze bell, a rhyton (drinking vessel), arrowheads, a ritual bath, and a half-burned gold pen and inkwell, evidence of the Roman conflagration.[66]

We have already mentioned the paved street that ran down the eastern side of the central Tyropoeon Valley. Bliss and Dickie were the first to discover this in 1894–97, and Kenyon obtained further information of this from her excavations in the area.[67] R. Weill in 1914 found meager remains on the southern Ophel of a synagogue and an asylum built by Theodotus, son of Vettanius.[68]

66. Leroy Aarons and Goldie Feinsilver, "Jerusalem Couple Excavates Under Newly Built Home in Search of Their Roots," *Biblical Archaeology Review* 8.2 (1982): pp. 44–49. Also in this excavation were found evidence of a Byzantine cistern and, down at the burial chambers at bedrock, much earlier evidence probably representing the eighth century B.C.

67. Kenyon, *Jerusalem* (New York: McGraw-Hill, 1967), p. 164.

68. *Encyclopedia of Archaeological Excavations in the Holy Land*, 2:610.

Akeldama

Akeldama (Acts 1:19), or the Field of Blood, where Judas went and hanged himself (Matt. 27:3–10), cannot be located because the archaeological evidence is insufficient. However, early Christian tradition has it that it was located in the Valley of Hinnom, probably not far from En-rogel, the spring at the junction of the Kidron and Hinnom Valleys. The Hinnom Valley was the high place of Topheth where the people of Judah burned their sons and daughters in the fire (Jer. 7:31), and later refuse was continually burned there; hence Jesus' graphic expression, Gehenna, used to indicate hell, that place of final and eternal torment (Matt. 5:22; cf. Rev. 20:15).

The Problem of the Three Walls

M. Avi-Yonah has stated:

With all due deference to the excavators who have toiled to solve the problem of the three walls of Jerusalem, their course still remains far from being clear. We may hope that with the now changed conditions in the city, large scale excavations will be possible along the Old City wall, and that the remains of the Third Wall will be cleared and studied once again. Perhaps this century old problem will then finally be laid to rest.[69]

Although Avi-Yonah indicates he has problems with the three walls, he does grant that "Dr. Kenyon's soundings near the German School in the Old City (her Site C) have shown—for all their exiguity—that this area was outside the city wall in Roman times."[70]

In the light of the research by Kenyon and others that has shed light on this problem, we can review the literary and archaeological evidence for the three walls in the time of the first and second centuries A.D. From this evidence conclusions can be drawn as to the location of Calvary and the tomb of Jesus. We can also draw some conclusions about the site where Jesus was tried by Pilate and the general route taken by Jesus on his way to the place of crucifixion.

Since the route of the second wall mentioned by Josephus (*War* 5.146) is more difficult to determine, it is best to examine first the courses of the first and third walls and then relate the problems concerning the second wall to the conclusions drawn about these two.

69. Avi-Yonah, "The Third and Second Walls of Jerusalem," *Israel Exploration Journal* 18 (1968): 125.
70. Ibid., p. 123.

The First Wall

The first, or innermost, wall was called by Josephus (*War* 5.142) the most ancient wall. Josephus thought that this wall goes back, in part at least, to the time of David and Solomon and their successors. Kenyon, however, thinks that its northern extremity was of Maccabean origin.[71]

There is general acceptance, though without any solid evidence, that this first wall extended from the Herodian Citadel on the west across the Tyropoeon Valley to the temple platform on the east. Josephus (*War* 5.143–45) says that this wall began on the north at the Hippicus tower and extended east to the Xystos, a building which was connected to the temple by a bridge. Then it joined the council chamber—a hall in or adjoining the southern part of the temple area, a place in which the Sanhedrin usually met—and terminated at the temple's western porches. He describes the southern direction, beginning at the Hippicus tower:

> Beginning at the same point in the other direction, westward, it descended past the place called Bethso [unidentified] to the gate of the Essenes [unidentified], then turned southward above the fountain of Siloam, thence it again inclined to the east towards Solomon's pool, and after passing a spot which they call Ophlas [Ophel], finally joined the eastern porch of the temple.

In his excavations in the 1970s in the Kidron Valley along the modern asphalt road east and south of the City of David, David Adan uncovered what he calls a first-century A.D. pool, containing first-century pottery in its plastered floor. He argues that the overflow of the Gihon water coming from the Pool of Siloam ran through a canal (Weill's Canal IV) into this pool. Adan claims that this is the pool which Josephus calls Solomon's Pool and may, therefore, attest to the existence there of an earlier pool. Adan notes that Solomon was anointed at Gihon (2 Kings 1:33–34), apparently identified later by Josephus as the Pool of Siloam. Thus the name Solomon's Pool would have been particularly appropriate if the Pool of Siloam overflowed through Canal IV into this valley pool. According to Josephus, this pool is located in the right place between the Pool of Siloam and Ophel. The consistent overflow of the Pool of Siloam would explain Josephus's term "fountain of Siloam." Based on the fact that there is no pottery evident at the valley pool after the first century, Adan concludes that this pool

71. Kenyon, *Jerusalem*, p. 147.

fell into disuse after A.D. 70.[72] It would seem from Josephus' description that the southern section of the first wall crossed east above the Pool of Siloam.

Finegan analyzes the wall described by Nehemiah and concludes that the northern section of Nehemiah's wall must have run along virtually the same line as Josephus's first wall. In working through Nehemiah's survey Finegan thinks that Nehemiah's Tower of the Hundred and the Tower of Hananel must have corresponded to a degree with the later Antonia. Then in comparing Nehemiah 3:6–11; 12:38–39 with 2 Kings 14:13; 2 Chronicles 25:23 and 26:9, he comes to the conclusion that the Corner Gate (2 Kings 14:13; 2 Chron. 25:23) could have been the site of the Tower of the Furnaces (Neh. 3:11), which in turn was the site of one of the towers of Herod the Great, possibly Hippicus.[73]

However, the line of the north course of this first wall does not exclude either the Church of the Holy Sepulchre or the area of Gordon's Calvary and the Garden Tomb from being the place of Calvary and the tomb of Jesus, since both were obviously outside this wall (Heb. 13:12).

The Third Wall

Excavations in 1961 show that the third wall encircled the southern end of the western ridge of the Jerusalem area, but not before the first century A.D., according to Kenyon.[74] Her map of this time shows not only a trace of a postexilic wall running south beyond Siloam, but also a part of a wall and gate of Agrippa's time located below Siloam at a point near the joining of the Hinnom and Kidron valleys.[75] Further evidence of this third wall being no earlier than the first century, she says, was obtained from investigation of the time of occupation of the western ridge. Conclusions regarding this date were determined through excavations conducted at several places, some of which were done in the grounds of St. Peter in Gallicantu. She concludes:

It would therefore appear that there was no appreciable occupation of the southern portion of the western ridge, at least down to the 700 metre contour prior to the 1st. century A.D. In that century there was a

72. David Adan (Bayewitz), "The 'Fountain of Siloam' and 'Solomon's Pool' in First Century C.E. Jerusalem," *Israel Exploration Journal* 29 (1979): 92–100.

73. Finegan, *Archaeology of the New Testament*, p. 136.

74. Kenyon, "Excavations in Jerusalem, 1965," *Palestine Exploration Quarterly*, 98 (1966): 87.

75. Kenyon, *Jerusalem*, p. 157.

sufficient growth to warrant the construction of the southern wall by Herod Agrippa. The stratigraphical evidence does not suggest that the wall had a long life, and this would agree with a destruction by the Romans c. A.D. 70, after the First Revolt.[76]

Avigad, however, in excavations in the Jewish Quarter in 1970 and 1971 found evidence of a new wall on the eastern edge of the western ridge which goes back to the eighth century B.C. He believes that this may well argue for a wall connecting the eastern and western ridges on the south in Old Testament times.[77] If such a southern wall was rebuilt by Herod Agrippa, it was no doubt destroyed by the Romans in A.D. 70, as is indicated by the stratigraphic evidence pointed out by Kenyon.

On the north, the third wall has been argued to have been in line approximately with the present north wall of the Old City.[78] However, it has also been argued that the third wall ran farther north, a theory which connects that wall with the remains of the wall located within the vicinity of the American Consulate and area of the old Mandelbaum Gate, and of the Albright Institute of Archaeological Research. Remains of this outer third wall were excavated by Sukenik and Mayer in 1925–27.

Avi-Yonah has espoused this view that the wall excavated in 1925–27 is the third wall planned by Herod Agrippa I and completed after the outbreak of the Jewish War in 66/67. He argues that if this wall be counted as the Roman siege wall, then it would be behind Titus's Roman camp, which the Roman general had moved inside the third wall (the so-called Camp of the Assyrians; Josephus, *War* 5.303), leaving the Roman camp between the circumvallation wall and the enemy.[79] Sarah ben-Aryeh in 1972 excavated again along this same wall and uncovered substructures of the wall with sherds of the Herodian period and remains of a tower which projected northward some 30 feet for a length of 148 feet between the Nablus Road and the Road of the Engineering Corps. The wall was 14 feet wide. She and Mazar also think that this wall was Josephus's third wall.[80]

Based on the excavations at the Damascus Gate in 1964–66, J. B.

76. Kenyon, "Excavations in Jerusalem, 1961," *Palestine Exploration Quarterly* 94 (1962): 85.

77. Avigad, "Excavations in the Jewish Quarter of the Old City of Jerusalem, 1970, 1971," *Israel Exploration Journal* 20 (1970): 134-35; 22 (1972): 193–95.

78. Kenyon, "Excavations in Jerusalem, 1963," *Palestine Exploration Quarterly* 96 (1964): 16.

79. Avi-Yonah, "The Third and Second Walls of Jerusalem," pp. 113-14.

80. Mazar, *The Mountain of the Lord*, pp. 82–84.

Pedestrian gate section of Damascus Gate.

Hennessey says that the Roman ruins there show no occupation surfaces within the lowest levels. He states that this archaeological evidence, together with several internments (two cist graves and one early first-century A.D. jar burial similar to jar burials uncovered at Abila of the Decapolis and other sites) found at a level 25 feet beneath the present Damascus Gate, points to the area of the Damascus Gate being outside the city, unoccupied, and used as a cemetery in at least part of the first century A.D. He further reports that shortly after this period there is evidence of intensive occupation. Starting with the reign of Herod Agrippa I a number of well-made plastered and paved roads appear; one produced within its surface a coin dating to A.D. 42–43. In commenting on the entranceway at the Damascus Gate, Hennessey states:

> There seems little reason to doubt that Agrippa's wall here included a triple-arched entrance to the city, with its line, flanked on either side by towers, practically identical with that of the present day. Certainly the lower courses of the small eastern pedestrian entrance, the engaged columns and the massive lower courses of the central gateway are in their original positions.[81]

81. J. B. Hennessey, "Preliminary Report on Excavations at the Damascus Gate, Jerusalem, 1964–6," *Levant* 2 (1970): 22–24.

Damascus Gate, exterior view.

Hennessey concludes that there can be little doubt that this is a part of the commonly argued third wall of Jerusalem, started by Herod Agrippa I, but probably never finished by him. The gate complex seems to have been reconstructed and incorporated into Hadrian's Aelia Capitolina.

In holding that Josephus's third wall is approximately on a line with the north wall of the present Old City, Kenyon concludes that the "outer" third wall excavated in 1925–27 is to be taken as part of the circumvallations Titus built around besieged Jerusalem, not a part of the headquarters of the Tenth Legion Fretensis. A number of tiles bearing the stamp LEG.X.FR. found in the general neighborhood of Herod's towers argue for that area as the location of the legion's fortress.[82] Kenyon states that Sukenik and Mayer were wrong in claiming that the wall excavated in 1925–27 was Agrippa's third wall, because the visible portions of that wall seem to face south, not north which would fit the circumstances of Titus's siege wall as he (the attacker) faced the Agrippa third wall to the south.[83] In 1965 and 1966 Kenyon conducted a number of excavations along the wall and found that it was cut into a fill with a foundation trench; in the fill were a number of coins, two of which were of the Roman procurators to be dated to A.D. 54 and 59. She argues that "the wall was therefore built after that date, and cannot possibly be the work of Herod Agrippa. . . . The identification of this wall as part of Titus's circumvallation wall seems to be convincing.[84]

In his survey of the northern course which the third wall took, Josephus (*War* 5.147–51) states that this wall began at the tower Hippicus and went north to the tower Psephinus. The tower Psephinus, located at the northwest angle of the third wall, was 70 cubits high and octagonal in form. Finegan indicates that some pilasters built of blocks of drafted stone, similar to the masonry observed at the southwest angle of the temple area and now found in the basement of the Collège des Frères buildings, could be part of the tower of Psephinus of Herod Agrippa's time.[85]

Josephus' third wall then descended east from the Psephinus Tower, continued opposite the Helena (Queen of Adiabene) monuments, and went past the royal caverns. As Finegan notes, the statement that the wall was opposite the Helena monuments could indicate that there was a considerable distance between these monuments and the wall. (Cf. *Ant.* 20.95, where it is said that the tomb of Helena was 3 stadia, about 1800 feet, from the city; Josephus must have been speaking rather generally, for the distance is greater.) Next, Josephus says, the third wall went through the royal caverns, as does the present north wall, breaking through the roof of Solomon's quarry in the process.[86] After the royal caverns, Josephus's third wall "bent" around the Corner Tower over against the so-called Fuller's Tomb and joined the ancient rampart at the wall's termination at the Kidron Valley. All of Josephus's description corresponds rather closely with the course of the present north wall.

The north course of this third wall, whether identified with the line of the present north wall or the outer wall excavated in 1925–27, does not affect the location of Calvary and the burial place of Jesus. In either case the evidence supports the view that this third wall was built subsequent to the time of Jesus' death.

The Second Wall

All that Josephus says about the second wall is that it started from the gate in the first wall, which the ancients called Gennath, meaning Garden Gate. It enclosed only the northern district of the town, extending up as far as Antonia (*War* 5.146). In one other reference (*War* 5.158) Josephus states that this second wall (he now calls it the middle wall) had fourteen towers. From these remarks we gather that

84. Kenyon, *Digging Up Jerusalem*, p. 254.
85. Finegan, *Archaeology of the New Testament*, p. 139.
86. Ibid., p. 140.

North wall of the Old City.

these towers were placed at intervals of about 300 feet. The conclusion is that Josephus's second wall ran a relatively short distance.

The location of the Gennath Gate, mentioned by Josephus only in *War* 5.146 and otherwise unknown, has raised a good deal of discussion. That this gate was at the location of Herod's towers seems very unlikely, since Josephus doesn't mention these towers in connection with the beginning of the second wall; in describing the courses of the first and third walls he begins at the tower Hippicus. The natural conclusion is that since the second wall branched off from the Gennath Gate in the first wall at a point other than at the towers, the Gennath Gate must have been located at a distance east of the Herodian towers.

Kenyon's excavation location called Site C is located directly south of the Church of the Holy Sepulchre and north of the old first wall, which presumably ran approximately along the line of the present David Street. Kenyon showed from her excavations at Site C that this area was outside the city wall until the second century A.D.[87] At bedrock she found evidence of quarrying. This quarrying

87. Kenyon, *Jerusalem*, p. 153.

was sealed by a seventh-century B.C. level and a tipped fill that had been placed there through a massive leveling operation. The fill contained seventh-century B.C. and first-century A.D. pottery and enough second-century A.D. pottery to suggest that the leveling operation occurred at the time of Hadrian's building of Aelia Capitolina in 135.[88] Also, a drain halfway down in the fill, which ran down to join the great main Roman drain in the central valley, suggests that both drain and fill must have been part of the second-century town-planning operation in laying out Aelia Capitolina. Kenyon comments, "A filling in of a hollow in one area with material derived from cutting down in other areas fits well into the picture of a plan to obliterate Jewish Jerusalem."[89] She says further, "It can therefore be said confidently that the area was a quarry outside the town walls in the 7th century B.C., and remained outside them until the 2nd century A.D."[90] The excavations under the Lutheran Church of the Redeemer just to the south and east of the Church of the Holy Sepulchre also showed a fill of material from the seventh century B.C. to the second century A.D. deposited by Hadrian's building.

On this kind of evidence Bruce Schein argues that the area south of the Church of the Holy Sepulchre was a stone quarry which was later a moat located just outside the second wall; the second wall, then, would be just east of the Church of the Redeemer excavations and Kenyon's excavations at Site C. It is further argued that the second wall, running north, turned toward the Antonia at the northeast corner of the stone quarry.[91]

In conclusion, Kenyon observes that though the precise location of the Gennath Gate is unknown, the evidence from the Site C excavations is clear: the only logical location for this gate is in the center of the first north wall, which ran east from Hippicus. The line of the second wall, going north from the Gennath Gate, would have run just to the east of Site C and the Church of the Holy Sepulchre.[92] The quarry area then would have been west, "without the gate" (Heb. 13:12). Kenyon's projected location of the second wall may well fit in with the findings of Avigad in his excavations on a newly exposed wall in the nearby vicinity of the Jewish Quarter. This wall, which goes back to the eighth century B.C.,[93] may have continued in exis-

88. Kenyon, "Excavations in Jerusalem, 1963," p. 14.
89. Ibid.
90. Ibid.
91. Bruce E. Schein, "The Second Wall of Jerusalem," *Biblical Archaeologist* 44.1 (1981): 21–26.
92. Kenyon, "Excavations in Jerusalem, 1963," p. 16.
93. Avigad, "Excavations in the Jewish Quarter, 1970, 1971," pp. 134-35, 193–95.

tence to A.D. 70 and have been a part of Kenyon's second wall. Amiran argues this way,[94] but Avi-Yonah doubts it.[95]

Using arguments similar to those of Schein, cited above, Kenyon projected that the second wall turned more immediately east to the Antonia after it had gone north past the quarry and Church of the Holy Sepulchre.[96] This seems to agree with Josephus's statement that the second wall, starting from the Gennath Gate and encircling only the northern district of the town, went up as far as Antonia. Avi-Yonah disagrees. He argues that such a projection does not fit Josephus's description of the second wall as running from the "rock cutting" still farther north to the Damascus Gate and then around east and south to Antonia.[97] Neither of these views, however, affects the conclusion based on the Site C and Lutheran Church of the Redeemer excavations that the Church of the Holy Sepulchre and Gordon's Calvary were both outside the Jerusalem walls in Jesus' time. Thus far the evidence shows that either one could have been the site of Calvary and Jesus' tomb.

The Location of Calvary and the Tomb of Jesus

Three possible views may be held regarding the location of Calvary and the tomb of Jesus. The first holds that though these places are to be located somewhere in Jerusalem, we do not know exactly where they are. This solution is not satisfactory since it does not take into consideration concrete evidence available.

The second view posits Gordon's Calvary and the Garden Tomb as the site of these important events of Christianity. Gordon's Calvary and the Garden Tomb are located a short distance north of the present Damascus Gate and just east of Nablus Road. We have already seen that this fits the requirements of being outside the gate. The general area includes the Grotto of Jeremiah, a quarry across the road and north of Solomon's Quarry. These two quarries were probably at one time part of one ledge of rock but were separated when the rock was cut away. The quarries no doubt produced material used in building projects undertaken since New Testament times. In 1842 Otto Thenius proposed that the rocky hill above the Grotto of Jeremiah, the face of which looks like the face of a skull

94. R. Amiran, "The First and Second Walls of Jerusalem Reconsidered in the Light of the New Wall," *Israel Exploration Journal* 21 (1971): 166–67.

95. Avi-Yonah, "The Newly Found Wall of Jerusalem and Its Topographical Significance," *Israel Exploration Journal* 21 (1971): 168–69.

96. See Kenyon's map in *Jerusalem*, p. 157.

97. Avi-Yonah, "The Third and Second Walls of Jerusalem," pp. 123–25.

(with eyes and a nose), was the biblical Golgotha. A rock-hewn tomb was found in 1867 in the northwestern face of this hill. The British general Charles G. Gordon in 1883 espoused Thenius's view, and the hill and tomb became known as Gordon's Calvary and Gordon's Tomb. The latter is now called the Garden Tomb.

Gordon's Calvary looks like the face of a skull. But the likeness may have occurred as a result of quarrying. Scripture says that Calvary was named Golgotha, the place of a skull (Matt. 27:33; Mark 15:22; Luke 23:33; John 19:17), but this does not necessarily mean that the place looked like a skull. It could as easily mean that it was a place where the skulls of criminals crucified there were scattered. So whether the place of Calvary did or did not look like the face of a skull is not essential in our understanding the Scripture text.

In addition, the nearby rock-hewn Garden Tomb, though aesthetically satisfying, does not meet the requirements of a first-century tomb of Christ's time. Of the three ledges for burial, the one the visitor today sees on the north side is best preserved, but shows a trough burial place, a type most characteristic of the Byzantine period. When the tomb was first discovered, two Byzantine crosses were found painted in red on the east wall of the chamber. Finegan has well observed, "The fact that there are other Byzantine tombs in the neighborhood also tends to point to a Byzantine date for this tomb."[98]

The Church of the Holy Sepulchre

The third view posits the Church of the Holy Sepulchre as the site of Calvary and the tomb, a view that is almost certainly correct. It has already been established that this site, along with Kenyon's Site C nearby, was outside the city wall in the time of Christ. It was included within the walled city when Herod Agrippa I built his third wall. This establishes the fact that the church can be the authentic site of Golgotha and the tomb of Jesus.

There is another piece of archaeological evidence which helps establish the fact that the Church of the Holy Sepulchre was outside the walls and was the place of Calvary: ancient Jewish tombs have been found and may be seen today inside the area of the church itself. Certainly such a cemetery would not have been located within the city walls. Further, in addition to the tombs the Church of the Holy Sepulchre has within it a large rock which could have been seen from afar (Matt. 27:55); thus it meets the requirements of a site capable of housing both tomb and place of crucifixion. The biblical

---

98. Finegan, *Archaeology of the New Testament*, p. 173.

The Church of the Holy Sepulchre.

narrative summarizes the situation: "At the place where Jesus was crucified there was a garden and in the garden a new tomb" (John 19:41).

Parrot has shown in a diagram of the rotunda of the church the location of ancient Jewish tombs off the southeast of the rotunda.[99] This is in the area where there have been found some sections of ancient masonry which are part of a curving wall. Finegan argues that here we probably have part of the structure Constantine built around the tomb in the rotunda, and Finegan notes that opposite a part of this ancient masonry are "two ancient *kokim* graves[100] known as the family tomb of Nicodemus."[101]

In 1976 excavations conducted by Christos Katsimbinis in the

99. André Parrot, *Golgotha and the Church of the Holy Sepulchre,* (London: SCM Press, 1957), pp. 42–43. See also P. B. Bagatti, *L'Église de la gentilité en Palestine* (Jerusalem: Franciscan Press, 1968), pp. 140–53.

100. In the kokim-type grave a horizontal shaft was cut straight back into the rock face. In the arcosolium type a ledge with a vaulted top was cut into the side of the rock.

101. Finegan, *Archaeology of the New Testament,* p. 166. It is also popularly called the Tomb of Joseph of Arimathea.

Church of the Holy Sepulchre uncovered a 35-foot-high mound of gray rock containing two small caves, which gave it a skull-like appearance. This hill, which is claimed as the genuine Calvary, would have been located just outside the north wall of Jerusalem in Christ's time, standing in a corner where the wall formed an angle.

The testimony of the early Christian tradition that the Church of the Holy Sepulchre is the site of Calvary and the tomb of Jesus is fully analyzed by Finegan. He includes the witness of Jerome (Letter 58 to Paulinus, A.D. 395), who states that in Jerusalem from the time of Hadrian to Constantine the place of the resurrection was occupied by a statue of Jupiter and the rock where Christ was crucified had on it a marble statue of Venus.[102] Finegan also presents the record of Eusebius (*Life of Constantine* 3.26, A.D. 337), who tells that Hadrian covered the area containing the traditional sepulcher of Christ with earth, laid down a stone pavement, and then erected a Venus shrine. Eusebius goes on to say that Constantine ordered the Venus structure removed, and in doing so, came upon the tomb of Christ. Then Constantine had a basilica built there (this is the first occurrence in known literature of the word *basilica* being used for a Christian church).[103] Other ancient witnesses Finegan cites include the Bordeaux Pilgrim (A.D. 333), Cyril of Jerusalem (Catechetical Lectures), and Aetheria (A.D. 385).[104] All point to the Church of the Holy Sepulchre as the place of Calvary and the tomb of Jesus.

In further argument pointing to the church as the proper site, it can be stressed that accurate knowledge concerning the location of the crucifixion and the tomb was likely to have been handed down from the very times the events occurred. Early Jewish Christians who fled to Pella just before the Jewish War and who were only 50 miles from the place of the events no doubt had vivid memories of the details of the crucifixion and resurrection. Subsequent to the time in the second century when the Jews were deprived of the privilege of entering Jerusalem, Gentile Christians were there; they by their very presence helped keep the tradition alive.

It was evidently this strong tradition that persuaded Queen Helena and Constantine to build the Church of the Holy Sepulchre in the early fourth century on this very site. This site, in seeming contrast to Hebrews 13:12 that Christ suffered without the gate, was not officially within the walls of the Roman city. Helena would not have known that this was not the case in the time of Christ. Interesting too is the testimony of Cyril of Jerusalem, who in his Catechetical

102. Ibid., pp. 22-23.
103. Ibid., pp. 137–38, 164.
104. Ibid., pp. 166–68.

Lectures to his catechumens, given at the church site, points out in the church the sites of Golgotha and the tomb.

All of this archaeological and literary evidence strongly points to the Church of the Holy Sepulchre as the authentic site of Calvary and of the tomb of Jesus.

The Pavement

The praetorium (Matt. 27:27; Mark 15:16; John 18:28, 33; 19:9) and the pavement, the *lithostroton* (John 19:13), where Jesus was judged before Pilate, can be located in one of two sites: either at the tower of Herod's palace on the west side of the walled city, or at the Antonia on the northwest corner of the temple area. Based on his excavation at the area of Herod's palace in 1971, Broshi believes the square in front of the palace was the place of the praetorium.[105] However, Finegan argues effectively that the fortress-palace of Antonia was the site where Pilate had his residence and judgment hall. Finegan bases this assertion on Josephus's statements (*War* 2.224–27; 5.244; *Ant.* 20.106–12) that a Roman cohort was permanently stationed there and that military precautions were taken in that area at festival times. As an additional argument, he notes that a large paved courtyard of striated stones has been excavated in the area of the Antonia, an area which corresponds to the pavement reference in John 19:13.[106] In addition, it may be argued that in time of potential political trouble it would be more logical for Pilate to have had his headquarters in the Antonia near the temple area. Here Pilate would have been near to monitor the troublesome and milling crowds. Also he would be near the council chamber at the temple area where the Sanhedrin usually met.

At any rate, whether the pavement and praetorium are to be located at the Antonia or at Herod's palace, the distance for Christ to have carried his cross, with the help of Simon of Cyrene, to Calvary at the Church of the Holy Sepulchre would not have been great.

The Via Dolorosa

The modern Via Dolorosa, "The Way of Sorrows," lays out quite definitely the route that Christ supposedly took from the place where he was judged by Pilate to Calvary. But any such route is hard to determine with any accuracy, both because of the very brief and general scriptural statements (Matt. 27:31–33; Mark 15:20–22;

---

105. Dan Bahat and Magan Broshi, "Jerusalem, Old City, the Armenian Garden," *Israel Exploration Journal* 22 (1972): pp. 171–72.
106. Finegan, *Archaeology of the New Testament*, pp. 156–57.

Luke 23:26–33; John 19:16–17) and because of the lack of opportunity to do any extensive excavating in the area between the two points. The whole area is now thickly inhabited. All Scripture says is that Jesus was led off to be crucified, and that along the way Simon of Cyrene was recruited to carry the cross. Further, Scripture indicates that many people followed him and women mourned for him, an act which he encouraged them not to do. Two criminals were led out with him to be crucified at a place called Golgotha, the place of the skull. Nothing is said of the route they took.

However, based on the conclusions that the Church of the Holy Sepulchre is the place of Calvary and the tomb of Jesus, and that the Antonia is the place where Christ was judged, we can argue that the general route Jesus took to the cross was west and south. At a certain point this route ran along the westward and southern course of the second wall, but again, the specifics are not known. Thus we cannot count on the traditional route with its fourteen stations of the cross to give us exact information as to the course Jesus took to the cross.

Conclusions

Examination of the evidence for the Jerusalem walls spoken of by Josephus and examined by archaeology has shown that in the time of Christ the first and second walls were in existence and that these two walls in their northern and eastern courses ran in such a direction as to leave the area of both the Church of the Holy Sepulchre and Gordon's Calvary outside the city wall. From additional evidence we have seen that only the Church of the Holy Sepulchre meets the requirements as the site of Calvary and the tomb of Jesus.

If we are correct in locating Pilate's judgment hall at the Antonia at the eastern end of the second wall, then the route that Christ took to Calvary might well have been along the route of the second wall as it went west and then turned south. We have argued that the second wall would have passed just east of the area where the Church of the Holy Sepulchre was built, a place that in the first century A.D. was a quarry. At this point Jesus was probably led west out of a gate in this north-south section of the second wall. This projection agrees with the scriptural statement, "Jesus suffered without the gate."

The Jewish Revolt and the Roman Conquest

In A.D. 70, not long after the death of Herod Agrippa I, the wall he built and many other structures in Jerusalem suffered massive destruction. Josephus describes these events in vivid detail in *The Jewish War*. The Jewish revolt against the Romans broke out in 66. By degrees the Romans overcame the opposition, crushing the uprising in the outlying regions, such as Galilee and Judea. In the spring of 70 the Roman general Titus started his final assault against Jerusalem. By September of the same year he had gained complete mastery of the city. To accomplish his task Titus had with him four legions, the Fifth, Tenth, Twelfth, and Fifteenth. He planned his attack on the city from the north, the weakest and least defensible side, since it did not have the protection of valleys such as the Kidron and the Hinnom. He set up his headquarters on Mount Scopus, a region to the north and east of the city, with three of the legions at hand and the Tenth Legion camped on the Mount of Olives.

In the course of his campaign Titus had to penetrate the three walls of Jerusalem described earlier. Titus and his troops first overcame the outer wall built by Herod Agrippa I. Then came his conquest of the second wall, which was connected with the fortress of Antonia. His capture of these two walls was accomplished quickly and with relative ease. At this point the Roman general encouraged the Jews to surrender. When they refused to do so, Titus renewed his attack using battering rams and other siege instruments. Also he hoped that famine and the fierce struggles of rival factions in the city would help bring Jerusalem to its knees. To hasten the surrender Titus built an enclosure wall around the whole city of Jerusalem. We cannot locate all the sites that the wall encompassed, as listed by Josephus (*War* 5.499). We know that the wall took in the Mount of Olives on the east, Siloam on the south, and the area north of the temple called New Town. In circumference the enclosure wall was 39 stadia, or about 4½ miles long. As a military backup Titus established thirteen forts attached to the outer side of this enclosure wall. We have seen that the north part of this enclosure wall is that outer wall found north of Herod Agrippa's third wall, parts of which are exposed near the Albright Institute of Archaeological Research.

The end of the siege and the final collapse of Jerusalem came in September of 70 after the capture of the Antonia. It was accompanied by the burning and destruction of the temple. The destruction of this sacred sanctuary was contrary to Titus's wishes. Josephus tells us the carnage and stench of the dead witnessed prior to the final destruction was unbelievable (*War* 5.512–19; 567–72; 6.193–213).

What then is left archaeologically from all of this destruction? There are the remains of the enclosure wall that we have already

Section of the Arch of Titus in Rome depicting the temple furniture being carried away.

noted. There are the remains of a number of Jewish houses recently excavated in the Jewish Quarter of the Old City, which have been described above. Further, there are the remains of the Herodian tower at the Citadel. Nearby to the south, in the area of the Armenian Patriarchate, Kenyon's site L, a good number of tiles inscribed with the stamp of the Tenth Legion—LEG.X.FR.—were found, suggesting that this famed legion was camped in the vicinity.

In contrast, as a testimony to the massive destruction of Jerusalem by the Romans, Kenyon's later excavations at the City of David on the eastern ridge showed no remains of structures from the first century A.D. to the Byzantine period. These excavations give stark testimony to the total devastation. In the accumulated wash layers down the slope of the eastern ridge, the pottery and coins found show that the area was abandoned in the latter part of the first century. The later evidence from Yigal Shiloh's excavations from the City of David produces the same conclusion: following the A.D. 70 destruction the ridge of the City of David was abandoned. Shiloh summarizes it thus:

> The structures of the "Lower City" on its ridge, and the supporting walls on its slopes, collapsed and tumbled down. The eastern slope for its entire length became covered with a layer of debris several meters thick. This debris included many finds from Stratum 6 [37 B.C.–A.D. 70], carried down from the buildings at the top of the slope. They have

been defined by us as a separate stratum, Stratum 5 [first century A.D.], which also contains almost nothing later than A.D. 70.[107]

There is more archaeological evidence pointing to the disaster. On the west slope of the eastern ridge, along the Tyropoeon Valley side, Kenyon found ruins of houses, with a Roman-type drain and pottery to be dated to the mid-first century A.D. The walls were razed and the pavement torn up; the drains were clogged with, among other things, human skulls and bones that had been washed down after the destruction of the city farther north. North of this Kenyon found further evidence of the Roman destruction: a collapsed stairway leading east from the main north-south street up to another street; a number of the slabs of the street had fallen to the bottom of the stairs. Kenyon also uncovered the ruins of buildings made of fine ashlar Herodian masonry; at the base of this debris lay a hoard of coins corresponding to the date of the destruction of Jerusalem. Human bones were found in these ruins, including three skulls. All this was indicative of the horrendous destruction described by Josephus.

Shiloh, in his Area H in the region of the Central Valley side of the City of David and adjacent to the Pool of Siloam, uncovered remains of three buildings with a street in between which showed evidence of the massive Roman destruction and conflagration following the burning of the Herodian temple as described by Josephus (*War* 6.434).[108]

The Tyropoeon Valley gives graphic evidence of the monstrous destruction wrought by the Roman army.

Burial Sites

There are early Jewish tombs of the first century A.D. west of the temple platform. In the Church of the Holy Sepulchre there are two ancient kokim-type graves, known as the family tomb of Nicodemus. Near the King David Hotel is a burial complex called the Herodian family tomb. This tomb may be the memorial mentioned by Josephus, which was located near the Serpent's Pool (*War* 5.108). The tomb does not contain kokim or arcosolia burial niches. Rather, burial in sarcophagi seems to have been the method used. Although Herod himself was not buried here (he was buried at the Herodian;

---

107. Yigal Shiloh, *Excavations at the City of David, I, 1978–92, Qedem,* 19 (Jerusalem: The Hebrew University, 1984), p. 30.
108. Ibid. p. 30.

War 1.673), it is possible that some members of his family were.[109] The stone that closed off the entrance to this tomb, a type of closure one sees also at the tomb of Queen Helena of Adiabene and mentioned in the Gospels, is a type used by the Jews only in the Roman period up to A.D. 70.[110] Two similar rolling stone tombs were excavated at Heshbon, Jordan, one (Tomb F1) in 1971 and the other (Tomb G 10) in 1974. Items found in Tomb G 10 included a bronze fibula, a Nabataean coin and three Herodian lamps pointing to its use in the early Roman period.[111]

The tomb of Queen Helena of Adiabene, misnamed the Tombs of the Kings and located just north of St. George's Cathedral at the junction of Nablus and Saladin Roads, also exhibits characteristics of the Herodian period. Helena, ruler over Adiabene in northern Mesopotamia, had become a convert to Judaism. In the time of the great famine prophesied by Agabus (Acts 11:28), when Tiberius Alexander was procurator and Claudius was emperor, she supplied grain for the starving people of Jerusalem (Josephus, *Ant.* 20.51–52; 101). Her tomb on the north of the city was a familiar landmark at Jerusalem. Josephus speaks of it as Helena's monuments (*War* 5.55, 119), and describes the third wall of Jerusalem on the north as "descending opposite the monuments of Helena" (*War* 5.147). The remains of this tomb complex include stone steps, water channels, cisterns, a large courtyard in front of the tomb, a part of an entablature over the tomb entrance, kokim- and arcosolium-type burial places cut into a number of different chambers, and a rolling stone in a stone track similar to the one at the Herodian family tomb. The inner chambers were closed with hinged stone doors. One of the lower chambers contained a sarcophagus with the dust of the deceased still in it.[112] One of the sarcophagi had the bilingual inscription: *Zadan Malkata'* (in Aramaic) and *Zada Malkatah* (in Syriac), meaning Queen Zadda. This is probably a reference to Queen Helena of Adiabene.[113]

However, the more usual places for Jewish burials in the first century B.C. and first century A.D. were the Kidron Valley and lower western slopes of the Mount of Olives.

In the Kidron Valley tombs have been found on both sides of the ravine. On the side opposite the east wall of the temple platform is the so-called Tomb of James. It had a Doric-style columned en-

109. Finegan, *Archaeology of the New Testament*, pp. 198, 202.
110. Ibid.
111. "Hesbon, 1974," Andrews University Studies, 14.1 (Spring, 1976), pp. 103–06
112. Finegan, *Archaeology of the New Testament*, pp. 199–202.
113. Mazar, *The Mountain of the Lord*, p. 230.

An example of the rolling-stone-type entrance to an ancient tomb.

trance. As we observed earlier, this was the family tomb of Hezir
and is to be dated to the second half of the second century B.C., the
Hellenistic-Hasmonean-Maccabean period. Just to the south of the
Tomb of James is the so-called Tomb of Zechariah, a monolith with
a pyramid top cut out of the rock, about 30 feet high and 17 feet
wide. It is to be dated to the second half of the first century B.C. Not
having an entrance, the Tomb of Zechariah may well have been a
burial monument (nephesh) rather than a tomb. Farthest to the
north in this necropolis complex is the 52-feet high Tomb of Absalom, also a monolith cut out of the cliff. It has a cylindrical superstructure and is equipped with corner pilasters, Ionic columns,
upper entablature with architrave, Greek Doric-type frieze and cornice. There is an opening for a stairway above the cornice on the
tomb's south side; this leads below to a small burial chamber containing two arcosolia. This type of burial chamber is reminiscent of
Hellenistic and Roman sepulchers and is to be dated to the first part
of the first century A.D. Because of its resemblance to a pillar, the

The facade of the tomb of Queen Helena of Adiabene.

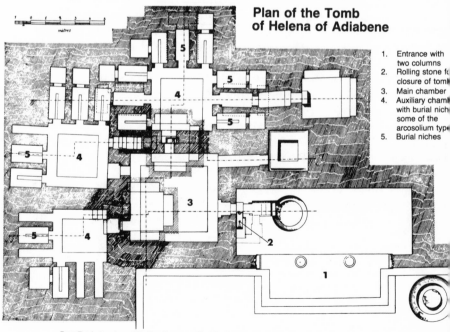

Plan of the Tomb of Helena of Adiabene

1. Entrance with two columns
2. Rolling stone fo closure of toml
3. Main chamber
4. Auxiliary chaml with burial nich some of the arcosolium typ
5. Burial niches

The Kidron Valley tombs.

name of Absalom became attached to this tomb on the assumption that it was the pillar which 2 Samuel 18:18 says Absalom set up in the King's Valley (i.e., the Kidron) as a monument to himself. The Tomb of Jehoshaphat, located behind the Tomb of Absalom, is reached by a flight of stairs which enter into a large oblong chamber with side chambers containing both kokim and arcosolia burial places.[114] This type of structure resembles others built at the beginning of the first century A.D.

On the basis of the architectural features described above we can safely state that all four of these tombs were in existence in the time of Jesus, and were seen by him and his disciples as they traveled across the Kidron Valley.[115]

Part way down the west slope of the Mount of Olives, opposite the temple platform, is the Franciscan chapel of Dominus Flevit. At this place the Lord's weeping over Jerusalem (Luke 19:41) is commemorated. No doubt many pilgrims in the Middle Ages came to this place for a time of remembrance. Of extreme interest in the area of this chapel is a large cemetery with burials of both the kokim and arcosolium types.

Besides seven sarcophagi, many ossuary (bone) boxes were excavated at the Dominus Flevit cemetery. The ossuary boxes, made of stone or wood and averaging 25 inches long, 15 inches wide, and 13

114. Finegan, *Archaeology of the New Testament*, pp. 194–96.
115. Finegan, *Archaeology of the New Testament*, p. 196.
116. Finegan (*Archaeology of the New Testament*, p. 101) suggests that there were two burial periods represented here; 1) 135 B.C.–A.D. 70, when kokim burials were characteristically used; and 2) the third and fourth centuries, when arcosolia were featured.

Ossuary boxes from Dominus Flevit cemetery.

inches high, were decorated with inscribed designs on the sides and tops and often had names inscribed on them as well. Examples of these boxes can be seen in site in the excavation area at the Dominus Flevit and at the Israel Museum, Jerusalem. These boxes were used to contain the bones of the dead in secondary burials after the disintegration of the flesh. They were evidently used in Jerusalem until A.D. 70 or possibly until 135.[117] Biblical names such as Martha, Mary, Salome, Sapphira, Simeon, Jonah, John, Joseph, and Zechariah are inscribed on some of the ossuaries at Dominus Flevit.

Besides this cemetery of the New Testament period at Dominus Flevit there are Herodian family tombs on Mount Scopus, just to the north of the Mount of Olives. An inscription on one of the ossuaries there identifies the bones as belonging to someone from the family of Nicanor, the Alexandrian who donated the copper gates of the inner court of the temple. The Aramaic inscription of another tomb bears testimony to a certain Simon, who is honored as "builder of the temple." One of the most intriguing burials excavated here uncovered the skeleton of a Jew in his twenties who had been crucified in the earlier part of the first century A.D. The remains show heel

117. Finegan, *Archaeology of the New Testament*, pp. 101, 218. Rahmani states that the ossilegium practices (the secondary burial of entire skeletons in ossuary boxes) were abandoned in the early third century A.D. (L. Y. Rahmani, "Ancient Jerusalem's Funerary Customs and Tombs, Part One," *Biblical Archaeologist* 44.3 [1981]: 176).

Based on a drawing in Mazar, *The Mountain of the Lord.*

A Roman crucifixion victim.

bones pierced with a nail still fixed to a wooden piece. The man's knees had been doubled up and laid sideways and his shins had been broken. This evidence gives vivid illustration of some of the aspects of Roman crucifixion which Jesus experienced.[118]

Bethany and Bethphage

Before leaving Herodian Jerusalem, we should note two places on the Mount of Olives: Bethany and Bethphage. Bethany, located on the east slopes of the Mount of Olives almost two miles from Jerusalem, was the home of Lazarus and Mary and Martha (John 11:1, 18; 12:1). It was also the home of Simon the leper (Matt. 26:6; Mark 14:3) and was the place where Jesus often stayed (Matt. 21:17; Mark 11:11). Luke 24:50–51 tells us that it was near the place of his ascension. In 1914 near the village of Bethany (present-day el-

118. Mazar, *The Mountain of the Lord,* pp. 226–28. Besides these tombs discussed above, Rahmani lists other tombs in the area, including the Sanhedria Tombs, the tombs of Umm el 'Amad, the Frieze Tomb, the Giv'at Shahin Tomb, the Ruppin Road Tomb, the Nazarite's Tomb, and the Abba Cave Tomb (Rahmani, "Ancient Jerusalem's Funerary Customs and Tombs, Part Three," *Biblical Archaeologist* 43.1 [1982]: 43–53).

-'Azariyeh) shaft tombs from the Canaanite period were found. Other finds from the area indicate occupation from 1500 B.C. to A.D. 100. Excavations in 1951–53 uncovered pits, caves, cisterns, tombs, and grave objects which pointed to site occupation from the sixth century B.C. to the fourteenth century A.D. Clay lamps, other vessels, and coins of the first century A.D. were found, artifacts that are to be dated to the time when Jesus frequented Bethany. In the coin evidence, the times of Herod the Great and Pontus Pilate were represented.[119] The churches built to commemorate the traditional tomb of Lazarus are, of course, later, but the tradition about the location of this Bethany tomb is very early. In the fourth century A.D. Eusebius says, "The place of Lazarus is still pointed out even until now."[120]

Bethphage, a village near Bethany mentioned in the Gospels, is to be located on the southeast slope of the Mount of Olives on the way west from Bethany across the Mount of Olives to Jerusalem. It is the place where Jesus told his disciples to get the colt for him (Matt. 21:1; Mark 11:1; Luke 19:29). The church there today commemorates the story of the colt. Archaeological finds in the vicinity of Bethphage include caves, coins, cisterns, pools, a wine press, and various types of tombs which point to occupation at the site from the second century B.C. to about the eighth century A.D. One trough-like tomb (No. 21) featured a rolling stone and graffiti in Greek and archaic Semitic letters. It also contained representations of crosses, trees, palms, harps, and squares.[121]

119. Finegan, *Archaeology of the New Testament*, pp. 91–92.
120. Ibid., p. 93; S. J. Saller, *Excavations at Bethany*, (Jerusalem: Franciscan Press, 1957), p. 30.
121. S. J. Saller and E. Testa, *The Archaeological Setting of the Shrine at Bethphage* (Jerusalem: Franciscan Press, 1961), pp. 9–30, 72–74, 83–120; Finegan, *Archaeology of the New Testament*, pp. 90–91.

The Roman Period

A.D. *70–324*

The City After Titus's Conquest

Titus with his Roman legions laid siege to Jerusalem in the spring of A.D. 70 and by September of the same year had completely conquered it. The city lay in ruins. This, however, did not eliminate Jewish resistance, either at Jerusalem or at various places where the Jews were dispersed. The Roman emperors Trajan (98–117) and Hadrian (117–138) had to deal with these rebellions. Statements from the Talmud indicate that following A.D. 70, Jews continued to come to the temple area and had hopes of rebuilding the temple. Since there was no longer a temple, the Jews who lived in the city could worship only in the synagogues.

Throughout the Diaspora messianic expectations had helped stir up Jews. In particular, in about 115 uprisings occurred in Egypt, Cyrene, Cyprus, and Mesopotamia. These events no doubt influenced Hadrian's attitude toward the people when he came to the area in 130–132. The emperor finally decided to deal with the center of the rebellion, the city of Jerusalem. He obliterated the city and

201

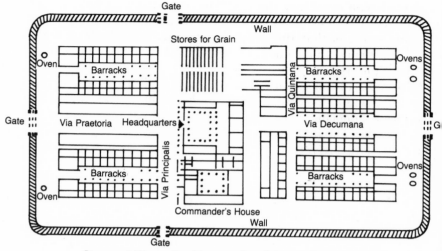

General Plan of a Roman Legionary Camp (Fort)

established on its ruins a pagan Roman city which he called Aelia Capitolina, named after himself (Publius Aelius Hadrianus). One of the severe actions in the destruction occurred when the legate Tinus plowed the confines of the city (the Latin term is *pomoerium*), an act which is depicted on Roman coins. Mazar comments that to Jews this was a sign forecasting the city's destruction prophesied by Micah 3:12: "Zion will be plowed as a field. (NIV)"[1]

Because of the thoroughness of Hadrian's demolition of what was left of old Jerusalem and the establishment of this new Roman city, not much archaeological evidence from 70 to 135 has survived. However, there is some evidence during this period of the presence of the famous Roman Tenth Legion (Fretensis) which Titus left to keep watch over what was left of the ruined city. This legion continued on there until the last part of the third century A.D. We have already seen that Titus had left the three Herodian towers standing in the Citadel area and also spared part of the western wall. These formed the defenses of the Tenth Legion's headquarters. Kenyon found some evidence of buildings at her Site L, some distance south of the three Herodian towers. Her finds there, however, did not seem to fit the plan of a legionary headquarters. Still, she found one bit of valuable evidence. Although numerous fragments of tiles and bricks stamped with the Tenth Legion's signature, LEG. X. Fr., and some

1. Benjamin Mazar, *The Mountain of the Lord* (Garden City, N.Y.: Doubleday, 1975), p. 235. See also Talmud, Makkoth 24b.

with the legion's emblem, the wild boar, were found in various parts of the city, a greater concentration of them were discovered at Site L.[2] This suggests that the headquarters was not far off, probably located to the north of Site L, along the west wall in the direction of the three towers.

In the excavation south of the southern wall of the temple platform there was found a section of a broken column carrying a Latin inscription honoring Vespasian, Titus, and the commander of the Tenth Legion. The inscription is fairly well preserved, except for the right side and the fifth line. The inscription as restored reads as follows:[3]

The expanded inscription[4] reads:

IMPERATOR CAESAR
VESPASIAN[US]
AUGUSTUS IMPERATOR T[ITUS CAE]
SAR VESP(ASIANUS) AUG(USTUS) [f(ilius)]
L[UCIUS FLAVIUS SILVA]
AUG(USTI) PR PR (PRO-PRAETOR)
LEG[IO] X FR[ATENSIS]

The translation then is:

Emperor Caesar Vespasian Augustus,
Emperor Titus Caesar Vespasian
Augustus, his son; Lucius Flavius
Silva, Propraetor[5] of Augustus,
the Tenth Legion Fretensis.

2. Kathleen Kenyon, *Digging Up Jerusalem* (London: Ernest Benn, 1974), p. 256; Mazar, *The Mountain of the Lord*, p. 232.

3. Restored portions are shown by dotted lines.

4. Letters in parentheses or brackets fill out the forms that are known Latin abbreviations.

5. A Latin term indicating a Roman military governor.

"Judaea Capta" coin.   Coin of Vespasian.

This inscription is to be dated 70–80, since it commemorates Vespasian, who ruled from 69 to 79, and his son Titus, who ruled from 79 to 81. It also honors the commander of the Tenth Legion, who, judging from the letter L seems to have been Lucius Flavius Silva. This Roman commander is the one who finally captured Masada in 73 (Josephus, *War* 7.252) and was the governor of the new Roman province of Judea from 73 to 80. The inscription alludes to the conquered status and military occupation of Jerusalem following the fall of the city in 70.[6]

Further evidence of the captive status of Jerusalem and Judea is seen in the numerous Roman coins excavated which depict the conquest of the area. The coins struck by the Flavian emperors—Vespasian, Titus, and Domitian—are particularly revealing. Some are bronze coins with the emperor's head on the obverse and the Greek *Iudaias Ealokias* (Captive Judea) on the reverse side. A series of gold, silver, and bronze coins bear on the obverse the emperor's image and on the reverse the figure of a Jewish woman, with her hands tied and seated under a palm tree. The legend on the reverse reads *Judaea Devicta* (Defeated Judea) or *Judaea Capta* (Captive Judea). These latter coins were struck by all three Flavian emperors, a fact which shows how important the subjugation of Jerusalem and Judea was to them.[7] The presence of these coins in the late-first-century ruins of Jerusalem suggests that such coins were the ordinary means of exchange for the Tenth Legion, the military occupants of the decimated city. Many of the coins just mentioned were found on the western ridge. This evidence, together with that from Kenyon's excavations at

6. Mazar, *The Mountain of the Lord*, pp. 232–33.
7. Ibid., pp. 233–34; Ya'akov Meshorer, *Jewish Coins of the Second Temple Period* (Tel-Aviv: Am Hassefer and Massada, 1967), pp. 107–8, plate XXXI.

Site L, indicates that the Tenth Legion was garrisoned somewhere inside the west wall of the ruined city.

Aelia Capitolina

This period began with the disastrous Second Revolt of the Jews (132–135). What events sparked this rebellion so soon after the devastating Roman destruction in 70? The suggestion has been made that the revolt was ignited because of suspicion that the Romans were going to pass a law against circumcision, or because the Jews suspected that Hadrian was going to establish a Roman city on the site of Jerusalem and build a temple to Jupiter Capitolinus on the temple platform. Eusebius (*Ecclesiastical History*, 4, 6), seems to indicate the rebellion was increasing in intensity and then Hadrian sent an auxiliary force to Rufus, governor of Judea, to put down the rebellion and their leader Bar Kochba.

Evidence given by Dio Cassius indicates that in his various travels throughout the provinces, Hadrian altered, removed, and built cities and their garrisons and forts (*Roman History*, LXIX, 9, 1). At "Jerusalem he founded a city in place of one which had been razed to the ground, naming it Aelia Capitolina, and on the site of the temple of the god he raised a new temple to Jupiter" (*Roman History*, LXIX, 12, 1). By the words "at Jerusalem he founded a city" (ἐς δὲ ἱεροσυλυμα) it is not clear whether Hadrian was actually at Jerusalem when it was refounded. However, Dio Cassius tells us that the emperor at this period was at least close by in Egypt and again in Syria (LXLX, 12, 2). He may well have been in Jerash (see Hadrian's arch at the site).[8] Whether Hadrian's decision to superimpose the Roman city on Jerusalem was the cause or the result of the revolt under Bar Kochba, the new Roman city, Aelia Capitolina, was established when the revolt was put down.

The Second Revolt erupted in 132 under the leadership of Simon Bar Kochba, who at that time captured Jerusalem. How long Bar Kochba and his followers were able to control Jerusalem is not easy to determine. Nor can we be certain whether or not he was able to begin reconstruction of the temple or of the city walls. He was able to reestablish sacrifices at the altar and to reinstitute other religious ceremonies. Coins found inscribed with Year 1 and Year 2 of the revolt establish the fact that the Jewish victory continued for some time. Coins struck in 132 and 133 indicate that the Jews had estab-

---

8. Jack Finegan, *The Archaeology of the New Testament: The Life of Jesus and the Beginning of the Early Church* (Princeton: Princeton University Press, 1969), p. 62.

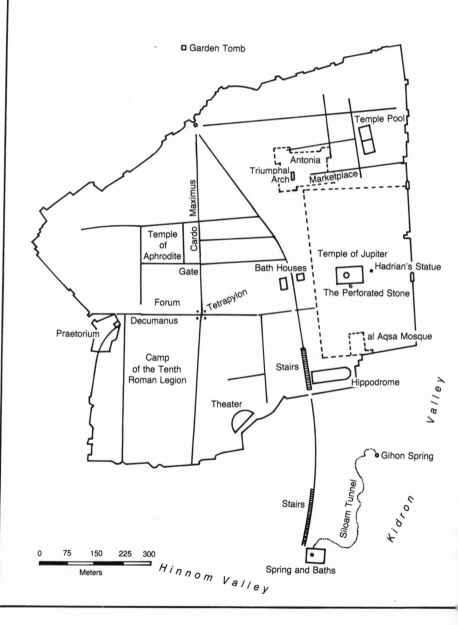

General Plan of Roman Jerusalem

Garden Tomb

Temple Pool

Antonia

Triumphal Arch

Marketplace

Cardo Maximus

Temple of Aphrodite

Gate

Temple of Jupiter

Bath Houses

Hadrian's Statue

The Perforated Stone

Forum

Tetrapylon

Decumanus

Praetorium

al Aqsa Mosque

Camp of the Tenth Roman Legion

Stairs

Hippodrome

Theater

Valley

Gihon Spring

Stairs

Siloam Tunnel

Kidron

0   75   150   225   300

Meters

Hinnom Valley

Spring and Baths

lished a dual leadership for the community—civil and religious. The coins bear the inscriptions "Simon *nasi* of Israel" and "Eleazer the Priest"; these refer to Bar Kochba as the civil leader and Eleazer as the religious leader. Other coins identified with Bar Kochba's leadership point to the Jewish character of the city at this time with the inscription "To the Liberation of Jerusalem." Since only two of the latter coins were found in Mazar's excavations here, and since the excavations south of the temple platform produced no other certain evidence of extended Jewish occupation, in all likelihood Bar Kochba's control of the city was short-lived, probably lasting only for the years 132–133.[9] By 135 the Romans had suppressed the revolt and reconquered Jerusalem. At this point Hadrian set in progress his plan to level Jerusalem and rebuild it as Aelia Capitolina.

Archaeological evidence of Hadrian's direction and leadership in the establishment of the new city is seen in an inscription cut into the base of a Roman statue, assumed to be that of Hadrian. The base was found as a part of rebuild material used in the Double Huldah Gate. The inscription reads:[10]

> TITO   AEL   HADRIANO
> ANTONINO   AUG   PIO
> PP   PONTIF   AUGUR
> DD

The translation is:

> To Titus Aelius Hadrianus
> Antoninus Augustus Pius
> Of the Fatherland, Pontifex Augur
> By decree of the Decurions.[11]

There is only a little literary evidence regarding the building of Aelia Capitolina. Part of this comes from a late Byzantine source, the anonymous Christian writing called *The Chronicon Paschale*. This document is based on earlier records which dealt with details

---

9. Kenyon, *Digging Up Jerusalem*, p. 257; Mazar, *The Mountain of the Lord*, pp. 235–36.

10. Mazar, *The Mountain of the Lord*, p. 235.

11. An augur was a diviner or seer at Rome, a member of a particular group of priests who were counted on to make known the future. The decurions were military commanders of a *decuria* (division) of cavalry; when Roman dominion was expanded, the members of the senate of the municipia (i.e., free towns, especially in Italy, with the right of Roman citizenship and often voting) and the colonies were called *decuriones*.

about Aelia Capitolina. According to Mazar the *Chronicon Paschale* states that Hadrian

> pulled down the temple (*naos*) of the Jews at Jerusalem and built the two *demosia* (public baths), the theatre, the *Trikameron* (the Temple of Jupiter, divided into three parts with statues of Jupiter, Juno, and Minerva), the *Tetranymphon* (one of the public baths), the *Dodekapylon* (the colonnade) . . . formerly known as the *Anabathmoi* (the "steps") and the *Kodra* (the square podium of the Temple Mount); and he divided the city into seven quarters (unidentified to date).[12]

The reference to Hadrian's pulling down the temple may refer to the partial rebuilding of the temple by Bar Kochba.

There is some archaeological evidence to add to this meager literary testimony as to the building of the new city. In addition to the literary evidence indicating the continued presence of the Roman Tenth Legion in the city, numerous bricks, tiles found as far south as the present-day south wall of the city point to the same fact. These bricks, tiles, and pottery dated to the second and third centuries A.D., reveal the expansion of the new city in this period. In addition to those bricks and tiles inscribed with LXF (identification of the Tenth Legion), some carry the inscription Ael(ia) C(olonia) C(apitolina). A baking oven lined with bricks carrying the Tenth Legion's insignia was found in a building just to the south of the major pier at the bottom of Robinson's Arch. Baths found to the northwest of Robinson's Arch were probably also used by the legion, since a number of their stamped bricks were found in the area.[13] Quantities of Roman glass, pottery, and coins found in the area also indicate a developing city. Most of the coins found were those of Roman cities, including those struck in Aelia Capitolina itself. Evidence of such coinage points again to the presence of the Roman Tenth Legion in the area from the time of the First Revolt to the time of Diocletian (284–305). Recovery of second- and third-century coins, dice, and bronze figurines in an area south and southwest of the temple platform reveals aspects of the Tenth Legion's daily life.[14] The Tenth Legion was probably moved to Eilat (Aqaba) in 285. South of the temple platform fragments of statues belonging to the Aelia Capitolina period were found. No doubt these had belonged to the temple of Jupiter which had been erected on the platform above. Among these fragments are a statue of a youth, with head missing, and the statue of a woman

12. Mazar, *The Mountain of the Lord*, p. 236.
13. Ibid., pp. 242–43.
14. Ibid.

dressed in the costume of the second–third century A.D.; the Latin inscription on this statue's pedestal reads: "Valeria Emiliana dedicated [it] by her vow." To the south and west of the temple platform were found fragments of marble statues, gems, seals, and bronze figurines. One figurine was of a barbarian horseman. One fragment of a Latin inscription gave the names and titles of Emperor Septimius Severus and his son Caracalla. The inscription was in commemoration of the completion of a building project in the city.[15]

Hadrian had established a ban prohibiting the Jews from living in the city, a proscription which continued for many years.[16] However, by the middle of the second century, during the reign of Antoninus Pius, local authorities relaxed the restrictions. Thus at this time a small Jewish community called "the holy community of Jerusalem" was living there. Talmudic references going back to the second–third centuries testify to this. This liberalization policy which took place during the reign of the Severan emperors allowed the Jews to have their own community life throughout Palestine. One of the church fathers of the fourth century, Epiphanius, seems to be referring to this period when he mentions that there were synagogues on Mount Zion, one of which existed up to the time of Constantine.[17] The Bordeaux Pilgrim (333) also indicates that there had been seven synagogues there but only one remained in his day.

The Romans decided to use the north and west parts of Herod Agrippa's city. Thus the walled part of their city encompassed basically the same area included in the walled Old City today. The temple platform, which survived the A.D. 70 destruction, was located on the east side of the new city. This situation forced an alteration in the typical Roman plan, which provided for a symmetrical north-south, east-west layout. In Jerusalem the north-south axis now ran slightly west of south from the Damascus Gate to intersect with the east-west street extending east from Herod's towers. This main north-south street, called cardo maximus, runs south through the souk (market) just to the east of the Church of the Holy Sepulchre. It

15. Ibid., p. 237.
16. Hadrian brought foreign races into Jerusalem as well as keeping Jews out. Eusebius (*Ecclesiastical History* 4.6–3), in citing evidence from the Jewish Christian Ariston of Pella, states that Hadrian decreed that the whole Jewish nation "should be absolutely prevented from entering thenceforth even the district around Jerusalem, so that not even from a distance could it see its fatherland (πατρῷον)." Justin Martyr (*Apology* 1.47) says that this was enforced by the death penalty, and Tertullian indicates (*An Answer to the Jews* 13) that the order included Bethlehem. Eusebius (*Theophany* 4.20) seems to indicate that the rule was in force in his time.
17. Mazar, *The Mountain of the Lord*, pp. 237–39.

Excavated portion of the cardo maximus.

is the colonnaded roadway depicted on the historic Madaba map.[18] The street running east from the Jaffa Gate (the present David Street) intersected the north-south street at the tetrapylon (like the town square) represented on the Madaba map almost due east of the Jaffa Gate and then the street continued east to the temple platform; because of the platform, the rest of the street had to skirt the platform on its north, running along the present-day "Via Dolorosa" there on east to St. Stephen's Gate.[19]

That the city was laid out in Hadrian's time as nearly as possible on the typical Roman north-south axis is supported by the discovery of bases of some of the columns that lined the street in the vicinity

18. A mosaic map, dated about 575, to be seen on the floor of a Greek Orthodox church in Madaba, Jordan (see Chapter 9 below). In the Jewish Quarter Avigad found part of the *cardo*—a beautifully paved road, 60 feet wide, with a central line of vertical pavement stones, flanked on either side by a many-columned colonnade—a street which looked like the *cardo* on the Madaba map. Avigad argues that his find is Byzantine in date, but Y. Tsafrir and others argue that it is Roman. "Is the Jerusalem Cardo Roman After All?" *Biblical Archaeology Review*, 3.4 (Dec.) 1977: 10–12.

19. Kenyon, *Digging Up Jerusalem*, p. 258.

of the Church of the Holy Sepulchre. These bases were found in the vicinity just east of the Russian Alexander Hospice and the German Evangelical Lutheran Church. Additional bases were found near the Damascus Gate where the street begins to run south. A number of columns of the colonnade found in the shops of the souk on the west side of the street also witness to the fact that this was a typical Roman street.[20] An example of this colonnaded street plan can be seen in the ruins of Jerash in Jordan. The Madaba map, referred to above, clearly shows the colonnaded north-south street (cardo maximus) and also another colonnaded street which diverges off to the east and then extends south. The main point from which these streets in the map project is the column seen in the semicircular plaza located just inside the Damascus Gate. The region of the Damascus Gate was important not only in the time of the Madaba map (ca. A.D. 575) but also in Hadrian's time, when the north gate of the city was at the site of the present-day Damascus Gate. This is shown by an inscription in the stone rebuild at the Damascus Gate above the eastern pedestrian entrance to the Herod Agrippa gateway.[21] In a stone above the keystone the inscription, though mutilated and incomplete, can be restored to read:

C O L [onia] A E L [ia] C A P [itolina] D [ecurionum] D [ecreto],

meaning, "Colonia Aelia Capitolina by order of the Decurions."[22] The north wall of the city then seems to have followed the same general line as the north wall of the present-day city. Portions of the wall on both sides of the Damascus Gate may be dated to the fourth century A.D.[23]

On the east, the main gate of the Hadrianic city was no doubt St. Stephen's Gate. The projection of a street in a line directly west from St. Stephen's Gate is supported by evidence in the area of the Convent of Our Lady of Sion of a triple triumphal arch spanning the street. Due to centuries of accumulated debris the ancient street level is a number of feet below the present level of the street. Today the central archway spans the Via Dolorosa. The arch is 17 feet wide and 20.5 feet high. The northern segment of the arch is to be seen over the altar in the present basement church of the Convent of Our

20. Ibid., p. 260.
21. The lower part of the arch associated with the wall east of the Damascus Gate is probably the work of Herod Agrippa. The upper part of the arch is of different masonry. See Finegan, *Archaeology of the New Testament*, p. 140.
22. Kenyon, *Digging Up Jerusalem*, p. 243.
23. Mazar, *The Mountain of the Lord*, p. 239.

Lady of Sion.[24] The arch adjoins the striated pavement which we
have previously indicated was the likely place of the stone pavement
(John 19:13). This pavement, preserved in the basement of the convent and in other nearby buildings, covers a cistern with a vaulted
roof. P. Benoit has argued, without too much evidence, that the
pavement is to be taken as belonging to the Hadrianic triumphal
arch; he also posits that the pavement represents the area of a small
forum through which this east-west road coursed.[25]

At any rate, the main forum of Aelia Capitolina seems to have
been located in the area some 500 feet south and east of the Church
of the Holy Sepulchre where there are preserved in the Russian
Alexander Hospice portions of two walls of plain large stone blocks
which meet at right angles. At a point where the east-west portion of
these walls continues toward the east, two well-worn stones with
depressions in them appear. These suggest a position for a gate
through which many persons traveled. On the line of the north-
south portion of these walls, a little to the south of the gate area,
there is to be seen a portion of an arch with a Corinthian capital
built into it. This suggests the remains of a Roman-type structure.[26]
Vincent posits that this is part of a side arch of a triple-arched
Roman gateway.[27] Eusebius (*Life of Constantine* 3.26) tells us that
Hadrian covered up the traditional tomb of Christ. Then it is said
that he laid a stone pavement over the whole area and erected a
shrine of Venus. At this site Hadrian built the forum for Aelia Capitolina, an area which may have been Nehemiah's square by the
Gate of Ephraim (Neh. 8:16), possibly the area of the garden leading
to the tomb of Jesus (John 19:41). From this evidence, the arch in
the Russian Alexander Hospice may well have been part of the eastern threefold arched entrance leading into the Roman forum of Aelia Capitolina.[28]

Hadrian's purpose in the area south of the German Evangelical
Lutheran Church and south and east of the Church of the Holy

24. Kenyon, *Digging Up Jerusalem*, p. 260; Mazar, *The Mountain of the Lord*,
p. 241.

25. P. Benoit, "L' Antonia d' Herode le Grand et le Forum Oriental d' Aelia
Capitolina," *Harvard Theological Review* 64 (1971), pp. 135–167; Kenyon, *Digging Up
Jerusalem*, pp. 223, 260–61.

26. Finegan, *Archaeology of the New Testament*, p. 137.

27. L. H. Vincent, *Jérusalem recherches de topographie, d'archeologie et d'histoire.*
Vol. II, L. H. Vincent and F. M. Abel, *Jérusalem Nouvelle* (Paris: Libraire Lecoffre, J.
Gabalda et Cie, 1954–56), p. 75, figure 42.

28. Finegan, *Archaeology of the New Testament*, pp. 137–38.

Sepulchre was to fill in the depressions, making the foundation for Aelia as level as possible and to fit it into a rectangular schema. The evidence at Kenyon's Site C and the site of Lux's excavations of the Lutheran Church shows an extensive fill laid over quarried bedrock. The fill did not contain any stone or architectural fragments, showing that this was not destruction debris. About 8 feet down from the top of the fill was found a drain that Hadrian's workmen had put in; it ran down to join the main drain beneath the main north-south street that ran down the central valley. Part of the main drain, as well as portions of the paving of the main street, have been found in several places. This drain has served Jerusalem down to the modern period.[29]

The walls encompassing Aelia Capitolina are fairly well established. The east wall of the city, of course, ran east of the temple platform. The north wall, east of the Damascus Gate, ran along the same line as it does today. But from the Damascus Gate there is uncertainty about how far west and northwest the north wall ran. On the west side of the city the line of the wall is uncertain. We do know that the south wall of the city at this period went no farther south than the south wall of the present Old City; as evidence, a section of this south wall of Hadrian's time is exposed in the lower courses east of the Dung Gate; here the wall runs east 695 feet and then turns north to join the temple platform. The large blocks of stone in the wall in this region display well-defined margins and protruding irregular central bosses; the stones are well set and, in the northern part of this section, they are built right on the vertical edge of a quarry of Herodian date. The type of construction suggests that this segment of wall was erected in the time of Hadrian's building of Aelia Capitolina.[30]

Kenyon's Site S, south of the temple platform, and Site R, at the Kidron Valley side of the eastern ridge, give evidence of Hadrianic quarrying. East, below Site S, the noticeable bulge with erosion channels cut into the loose soil may indicate that this material is first-century A.D. debris that Hadrian pushed over into the Kidron Valley to make room for his quarrying farther to the west. The loose soil here produced numbers of coins of the period of the First Jewish Revolt. Very dramatic evidence of Hadrianic quarrying is to be seen toward the southern end of the eastern ridge at the City of David, at the place where R. Weill excavated in 1913–14. In nearby Site V, Kenyon was able to date the quarrying to the second century A.D.[31]

29. Kenyon, *Digging Up Jerusalem*, pp. 261–62.
30. Ibid., pp. 262–63.

Salient wall of the Roman Aelia Capitolina. Note the large blocks of stone with
irregular central bosses.

The only evidence Shiloh found at the City of David representing
this period was a few late Roman sherds in area H.[32]

Thus we see that Hadrian covered up much of Herodian Jerusalem on the north, and south of the temple he quarried extensively
for stone to build Aelia Capitolina. We have seen that he built a
temple of Jupiter Capitolinus on the site where the Herodian temple
stood. According to Jerome (Commentary on Matthew 24:15) there
was also at this site a statue of Hadrian on horseback, which, he
says, was erected on the site of the Holy of Holies. David Jacobson
argues that the present rock in the Dome of the Rock is not the
summit of the temple platform that existed prior to the destruction
of the temple in A.D. 70.[33] He suggests that Hadrian's workmen
lowered the rock summit in preparation for the building of the
temple of Jupiter, and for statues and any other structures Hadrian
wanted to place there.

In this period Hadrian's triumph was complete in rebuilding Je-

31. Ibid., pp. 263–64.

32. Shiloh, *Excavations at the City of David, I, 1978–82*, pp. 6, 30.

33. David M. Jacobson, "Ideas Concerning the Plan of Herod's Temple," *Palestine
Exploration Quarterly*, January–June, 1980, p. 39.

rusalem as a Roman city, and the Roman Tenth Legion was dominant in the city, overshadowing all its activities. We have no specific archaeological evidence as to developments on the Mount of Olives in this period. Possibly some of the artisans and laborers who worked in the city lived there.

The Byzantine Period
313–638

A dramatic change took place in the course of the history of Jerusalem when the Roman emperor Constantine espoused Christianity for himself and for the empire. In 313 he declared Christianity the official religion of the Roman Empire and moved the empire's capital to Byzantium, which he named Constantinople. Changes ensued on every level, and, of course, the Holy Land was affected. The great amount of church building activity that occurred in the Byzantine period in Jerusalem and its environs reflected the strong influence of Christianity. Numbers of pilgrims flocked to Jerusalem, and it was befitting that a great church commemorating the death, burial, and resurrection of Christ should be erected. In about 325 this great monument, the Church of the Holy Sepulchre, was built under the direction of Queen Helena, the mother of Constantine.

In the centuries that followed Christian emperors, empresses, and other leaders were interested in building edifices to commemorate persons and events related to the history of Christianity. Empress Eudocia was probably the most influential in the erection of Chris-

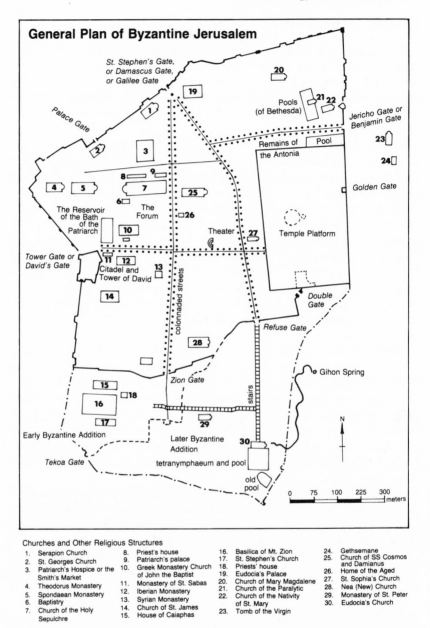

General Plan of Byzantine Jerusalem

Churches and Other Religious Structures

1. Serapion Church
2. St. Georges Church
3. Patriarch's Hospice or the Smith's Market
4. Theodorus Monastery
5. Spondaean Monastery
6. Baptistry
7. Church of the Holy Sepulchre
8. Priest's house
9. Patriarch's palace
10. Greek Monastery Church of John the Baptist
11. Monastery of St. Sabas
12. Iberian Monastery
13. Syrian Monastery
14. Church of St. James
15. House of Caiaphas
16. Basilica of Mt. Zion
17. St. Stephen's Church
18. Priests' house
19. Eudocia's Palace
20. Church of Mary Magdalene
21. Church of the Paralytic
22. Church of the Nativity of St. Mary
23. Tomb of the Virgin
24. Gethsemane
25. Church of SS Cosmos and Damianus
26. Home of the Aged
27. St. Sophia's Church
28. Nea (New) Church
29. Monastery of St. Peter
30. Eudocia's Church

tian monuments in Jerusalem. The wife of the emperor Theodosius, she lived in Jerusalem from 450 to 460. The emperor Justinian was also active and influential in building in the Holy Land.

Literary Sources for Byzantine Jerusalem

Fortunately, a number of literary sources from the early Christian centuries exist to help us understand what structures were built and where they were located in Jerusalem. These records can help us examine the archaeological evidence at Jerusalem for the Byzantine period. The most important of these sources, with their dates, follows.

Justin Martyr, born about 110 in Neapolis, Samaria, is one of the early church apologists who mentions the cave in Bethlehem where Christ was born (*Dialogue with Trypho,* 78) and also the Mount of Olives, "situated opposite the temple in Jerusalem, where Jesus prayed before he was seized by his enemies" (*Trypho,* 99, 101). Since Justin lived before the Byzantine Holy Land building activity, he could not be alluding to nearby Christian church structures. Justin Martyr at first studied philosophy. Later at Ephesus he became a Christian and eventually served in Rome as a Christian teacher. He was martyred in 165 under the reign of Marcus Aurelius. Besides the *Dialogue with Trypho,* Justin Martyr wrote two *Apologies* in defense of the persecuted Christians and other assorted discourses and exhortations.

Melito, Bishop of Sardis, the capital of Lydia, is the first pilgrim to Palestine we are told about (160). Among his many works is one called *Extracts* which no longer exists. Eusebius (*Church History* 4, 26, 13) quotes the *Extracts* where Melito says that in order to have more knowledge of the events regarding the Christian faith, he "went East and came to the place where these things were preached and done." In other words, about the middle of the second century he and others were being shown places where the events of Christianity took place.

Alexander, a friend of Origen, became a bishop in Cappadocia (212). Subsequently he went to Jerusalem where he established a library later used by Eusebius. In telling of Alexander's trip to Jerusalem, Eusebius says that he went there "for prayer (or to fulfill a vow) and for gaining information about the [Holy Land] places" (*Church History* 6.11.2), evidently the sacred places connected with Christ's life, death, and resurrection.

Origen, a Church Father, was born about 185 at Alexandria and died and was buried about 253 at Tyre. He visited the Holy Land (215) and lectured in Caesarea (Eusebius, *Church History* 6.19.16; Schaff, *History of the Christian Church,* 3, pp. 786–7).[1] He also bore

---

1. Philip Schaff, *History of the Christian Church,* 3 (Grand Rapids: Eerdmans, 1956), pp. 786–87.

witness to the early Christian tradition that Jesus was born in a cave in Bethlehem. He states that beyond the prophecy of Micah and the history recorded in the Gospels, additional evidence pointing to the birth of Jesus is the cave shown "at Bethlehem where he was born and the manger in the cave where he was wrapped in swaddling clothes" (Origen, *Against Celsus*, 1.51).

Eusebius was born in 263 at Caesarea, educated at Syrian Antioch as well as Caesarea, and died in 339 or 340. He was elected Bishop of Caesarea in 313 and continued in that position until his death. He participated in the Council of Nicaea in 325 and also participated in the dedication of the Church of the Holy Sepulchre in 335; that same year he lectured in Constantinople. His *Church History* records events from the time of Christ to 324. His *Life of Constantine* tells of the church buildings erected by the emperor and of Queen Helena's journey to Palestine, while his *Onomasticon* gives an alphabetical listing of place names in the Bible, with annotations on their history and location (cf. Schaff, *History of the Christian Church*, 3, 871–879).

The **Bordeaux Pilgrim** was an anonymous Christian who made a pilgrimage from Bordeaux to Jerusalem and other parts of Palestine and then back to Milan by way of Rome in 333. His treatise on his pilgrimage is titled, *The Journey from Bordeaux to Jerusalem and from Heraclea through Aulona, through Rome to Milan.*

Cyril of Jerusalem was probably born in Jerusalem about 315, and died in 386. He became Bishop of Jerusalem in 347 and in that year gave a series of twenty-four catechetical lectures at Easter time in the Church of the Holy Sepulchre. A member of the congregation took shorthand notes of these lectures which were later published. It is said that Cyril wrote a letter to the Emperor Constantius in which he describes the miraculous appearance of a luminous cross covering the distance from the site of Golgotha to the Mount of Olives (cf. Schaff, *History of the Christian Church*, 3, pp. 923–25).

Epiphanius was born about 315 near Gaza, Palestine, and died about 403. He founded a monastery in Eleutheropolis of which he was the leader for many years. In 367 he became Bishop of Salamis. He wrote a number of treatises, including *On Weights and Measures* (392); this was a Bible dictionary dealing, among other things, with the geography of Palestine.

Aetheria, also known from the manuscript evidences as Eihera or Echeria or Egeria, a nun from northern Spain or Southern France in 385–388, made a pilgrimage to the Holy Lands and left a record of it, a part of which has been preserved. Her document is called *The Journey of the Holy Silvia to the Holy Places* or, in short, *The Journey of Aetheria or Egeria.*

Jerome was born at Stridon on the borders of Dalmatia about 345. He lived in a cave at the Church of the Nativity in Bethlehem from 386 to his death in 420. He was a prolific writer. In *Letter* 46 written in 386 in Bethlehem he invites his friend Marcella to leave Rome, come to Palestine to see first hand where the events of Christ's life took place, "the cave of the Savior, and weep together in the sepulchre of the Lord with his sister and his mother and touch with our lips the wood of the cross." He talks about rising in prayer and resolve on the Mount of Olives with "the ascending Lord," and the privilege of seeing "Lazarus come forth bound with grave clothes" at Bethany. He must have seen these commemorated places often and absorbed some of the inspiration they gave.

Paula, an aristocratic Roman lady, became a pupil of Jerome, studying Hebrew, Greek, and Latin under him in Bethlehem. In his Letter 108 to Eustochium, comforting her over the recent death of her mother, Jerome describes Paula's journey to Egypt, to other places in the East, and particularly to the Holy Land and Jerusalem which included a visit to the tomb of Queen Helena of Adiabene, to the place of the cross, and the tomb of Jesus.

Sozomen was born at Bethelia in the vicinity of Gaza and raised in a Christian family; he was influenced by the monastic life practiced in the area. He studied civil law at Beirut, Phoenicia, and practiced law in Constantinople, as he relates in Book 2, chapter 3, of his *Church History.* In this history which covers the period from 324 to 425 he talks about Constantine building the Church [of the Holy Sepulchre] "near the place called Calvary," including the "Great Martyrium" sanctuary; he also talks about Helena, mother of the emperor, finding the wood of the cross and the nails, and erecting two "temples," one at Bethlehem and the other on the crest of the Mount of Olives where Jesus ascended to heaven [the Inbomon Church].

Socrates, born about 380 in Constantinople, was raised and educated in that city. He, too, was trained in law, and practiced in the city and gained the title Scholasticus. He wrote an *Ecclesiastical History* which was to continue the history of Eusebius to the year 439; he had time to revise part of the work so he must have lived several years beyond that date. He describes the events leading to the Emperor Constantine's conversion to Christianity in 312 (Book 1, 2). He tells how (Book 1, 17) Helena, Constantine's mother later went to Jerusalem and found the tomb of Christ which had been desecrated by a temple and statue of Venus imposed on it, a sacrilege she immediately destroyed. In doing so she is said to have found three crosses in Christ's tomb, the one of Jesus, and two of the thieves. He relates how Helena built the Church of the Holy Sepulchre which she called the New Jerusalem Church, and also the Church of the Nativity and the Ascension Church [Inbomon]. At the end this work (Book 7, 147) he tells how Eudocia wife of Emperor Theodosius II went to Jerusalem and adorned all the churches with expensive gifts.

Peter the Iberian, son of a prince in Georgia (southern Russia), came to Jerusalem in 451 and became a priest. Later he became the Bishop of Majuma, near Gaza, where he died in 485.

The Jerusalem Breviary (sixth century) by an unknown author gives a brief enumeration and description of the sanctuaries in Jerusalem. It lists, among others, the Church of the Holy Sepulchre (including Calvary, the three crosses, and the tomb); the place of the Lord's Supper; the basilica at the temple mount; the Great Basilica of Holy Sion [the Mother of All Churches] with its column where Jesus was beaten; the Great Church of St. Peter at the House of Caiaphas; the Great Basilica of St. Sophia at the house of Pilate; the Basilica of St. Mary; and the basilica at the pinnacle of the temple which was laid out in the form of a cross.

Theodosius, otherwise unknown, left for us his pilgrimage itinerary to places in the East and particularly in the Holy Land, giving precise notations on the holy places as they existed in the early sixth century. In the Jerusalem area he depicts Bethany and the tomb of Lazarus; the place of Christ's ascension; the Holy Sepulchre, Calvary and Golgotha where the cross of Christ was found; Saint Sion, the Mother of All Churches; the Church of St. Peter at the house of Caiaphas; the Church of St. Sophia at the praetorium of Pilate; St. Stephen's Church, beyond the Galilean (northern) Gate built by Eudocia, wife of the Emperor Theodosius; the sheep pool (Bethesda) where Christ healed the paralytic, and the nearby Church of Queen Mary; the Church of Mary in the Valley of Jehoshaphat (Kidron Valley); and the churches of Ancona (the arms of Christ) and St. Thecla at Bethphage, where the Lord started his ride on the foal of a donkey to go through the Gate of Benjamin into Jerusalem.

The Anonymous of Piacenza, or *The Itinerary Under Antoninus of Placentina* is a document by an unknown author describing his Holy Land pilgrimage about 570 under the protection of the Blessed Antoninus Martyr, who was the patron saint of Placentina, i.e., Piacenza, in Italy. It describes the holy sanctuaries and the stories connected with them at the zenith of the Byzantine period.

Sophronius, born in Damascus, later served as a learned and revered monk at Jerusalem where he became a patriarch in 633–34;

he journeyed to Egypt, Rome, and Constantinople. He died as patriarch of Jerusalem in 638, the year the city was overthrown by Caliph 'Umar and the Muslims. His poems, called the *Anacreontica*, describe the holy places in Jerusalem and Bethlehem.

Peter the Deacon, although he is from the twelfth century, as librarian at the monastery at Cassino, Italy, he used pilgrim itinerary materials as early as those from the journey of Aetheria (385) to describe Jerusalem and its environs. Thus his description of the Holy City is in part Byzantine. The name of his work was *The Book of Peter the Deacon on the Holy Places.*

Concerning archaeological evidence for this period Kenyon says, "Within the area enclosed by the Byzantine walls, the sites of thirty-five churches identified in pilgrims' records can be located, and certainly there were many more originally."[2]

The Madaba Mosaic Map[3]

The Madaba mosaic map, a good portion of which is preserved as part of the floor of a Greek Orthodox church in Madaba, Jordan, is to be dated to about 560–575. It is very important and instructive archaeologically, depicting what the designer of the mosaic understood were the important structures in sixth-century Jerusalem. The name for the Holy City of Jerusalem (HÁΓIA ΠΟΛIC I(POUCA[ΛHM]) appears just outside the upper left of the walled city.

The schematic drawing accompanying the photo identifies several buildings and places pictures on the map.

Part of the name Gethsemane (ΓHΘI-[IMANH] appears outside the east wall of the city. For some reason the Basilica of St. Stephen, built by Eudocia in 461 in the area where Stephen was buried, does not appear on the map. Neither do the Church of the Ascension and the Church of Eleona on the Mount of Olives. Perhaps they were represented on a part of the map that has been destroyed.

Another source for evidence regarding Jerusalem in the Byzantine period is to be seen in the considerable archaeological remains uncovered in the city itself. Much additional evidence waits to be revealed.

2. Kathleen Kenyon, *Digging Up Jerusalem* (London: Ernest Benn, 1974), p. 274. See also E. A. Moore, *The Ancient Churches of Old Jerusalem: The Evidence of the Pilgrims* (Beirut, Lebanon, 1961).

3. Michael Avi-Yonah, *The Madaba Mosaic Map* (Jerusalem: Israel Exploration Society, 1964) gives a full description of the map.

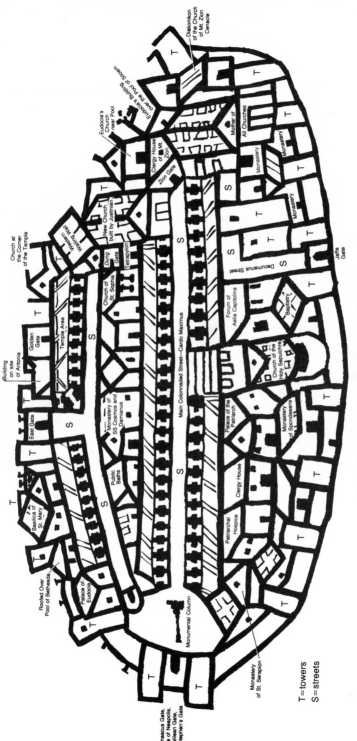

Sketch of the Madaba Mosaic Map

T = towers
S = streets

Diakonikon
of the Church
of Mt. Zion
Canacle

Eudocia's Building
over the Pool of Siloam

Eudocia's
Church near Pool

Mother of
All Churches

Clergy House
of Mt. Zion

Zion Gate

New Church
built by Justinian

Monastery

Monastery

Tetrapylon

Monastery

Church at
the Corner
of the Temple

Western
Wailing Wall

Dung
Gate

S

Decumanus Street

Jaffa
Gate

Building
on site
of Antonia

Golden
Gate

Temple Area

Church of
St. Sophia

S

Forum of
Aelia Capitolina

S

S

East Gate

S

Monastery of
SS. Cosmos and
Damianus

Main Colonnaded Street—Cardo Maximus

Church of the
Holy Sepulchre

Baptistry

S

Public
Baths

S

Palace of
the Patriarch

Monastery
of
Spondeans

Basilica of
St. Mary

Roofed Over
Pool of Bethesda

Palace of
Eudocia

Clergy House

Patriarchal
Hospice

T

Monumental
Column

Monastery
of St. Serapion

T = towers
S = streets

Damascus Gate,
Gate of Neapolis,
Galilean Gate,
St. Stephen's Gate

The Church of the Holy Sepulchre

The most famous Jerusalem church, of course, is the Church of the Holy Sepulchre. The emperor Constantine instructed Bishop Macarius to build the structure "as a house of prayer worthy of the worship of God" in about 327. In the account of Eusebius (*Life of Constantine* 3.31) it is actually called a basilica, the first time in literature that this word is used for a Christian church. Information about the place of Calvary and the tomb of Christ was alive in the memories of the early Christians who lived in the vicinity. These living memories were a prime source of information for Hadrian, who ordered these sacred Christian sites covered over and pagan statues erected. Two centuries later Constantine ordered Hadrian's Venus shrine removed. He unexpectedly came upon a tomb here which he understood to be the tomb of Christ. The emperor ordered the church to be built on the site. The church was dedicated in 335, eight years after the order to build it.

Archaeologically, the present structure is not anywhere near like the representation on the Madaba map. The reason for this is that the church has been damaged and rebuilt more than once over the centuries. The Persians destroyed the original structure in 614. What we see today is in large part the Crusader church, which includes some foundations belonging to the Constantinian structure, and a few remains of other rebuilding periods. Such early Christians as the Bordeaux Pilgrim give us valuable information regarding Golgotha, the burial crypt, and the church built by Constantine. Eusebius (*Life of Constantine* 3.33–40) gives us a description of the church. His account informs us that the entrance, located on the east of the structure, extended off the colonnaded north-south street, the *cardo maximus*. Entrance was gained through monumental gates, the remains of which are to be seen north of the Russian Alexander Hospice; these remains seemingly are a part of the entrance arch belonging to the forum of Aelia Capitolina. Eusebius continues: "After these, in the midst of the open market-place, the general entrance gates which were of exquisite workmanship . . . could not fail to inspire astonishment."

From the archaeological evidence it has been determined that the entranceway to the Holy Sepulchre Church was about 33 by 164 feet. Several steps led up through three doors into the first atrium (or open court), which was surrounded by columns. Eusebius calls them porticos.

The main basilica, the Martyrion,[4] lay farther to the west and was

4. Latin or Greek meaning witness or testimony to the death of Christ.

Entrance to the Church of the Holy Sepulchre.

approached by three doors. The Martyrion was a rectangle measuring approximately 98 by 130 feet;[5] it contained four rows of columns, had a floor composed of colored marble slabs, walls lined

5. Based on the archaeological evidence available, Jack Finegan (*The Archaeology of the New Testament: The Life of Jesus and the Beginning of the Early Church* [Princeton: Princeton University Press, 1969), p. 165] estimates the dimensions were 128 feet square, while Dan Bahat (*Carta's Historical Atlas of Jerusalem: An Illustrated Survey* [Jerusalem: Carta, 1983], p. 45) figures them to be 85 by 148 feet. If Charles Coüasnon's calculations are true, that parts of the north wall of the Martyrion show evidence of being from Hadrian's time, then "the Basilica of Constantine would be a transformation of the civic basilica of Hadrian, whose central nave could have measured [62 by 130 feet]" (*The Church of the Holy Sepulchre in Jerusalem* [London: Oxford University Press, 1974], pp. 41–42). Coüasnon's suggested measurements for Hadrian's civic basilica on which the Martyrion of the Church of the Holy Sepulchre could have been built are closer to the measurements of Bahat than those of Finegan. For examples of church basilicas built on earlier Roman structures, see the basilica in Area A, Heshbon, Jordan, and possibly the basilica on the north tell at Abila of the Decapolis ("Heshbon, 1976," *Andrews University Seminary Series*, 16:1 [Spring, 1978], p. 24; "1984 Abila of the Decapolis Excavation," *Near East Archaeological Society Bulletin*, No. 24 [Winter, 1985], pp. 32–33).

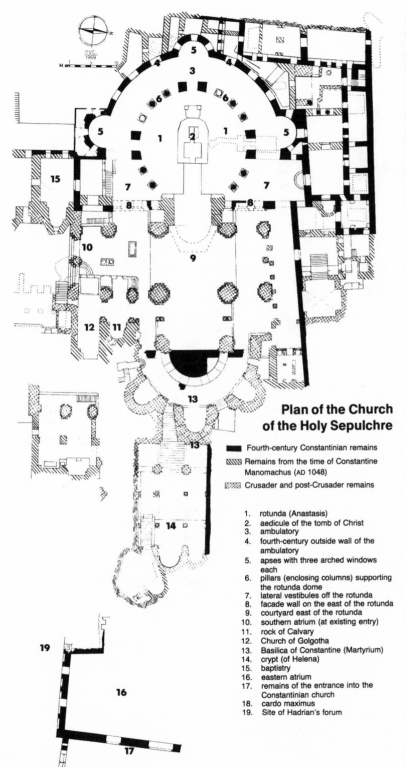

Plan of the Church of the Holy Sepulchre

■ Fourth-century Constantinian remains

▨ Remains from the time of Constantine Manomachus (AD 1048)

▨ Crusader and post-Crusader remains

1. rotunda (Anastasis)
2. aedicule of the tomb of Christ
3. ambulatory
4. fourth-century outside wall of the ambulatory
5. apses with three arched windows each
6. pillars (enclosing columns) supporting the rotunda dome
7. lateral vestibules off the rotunda
8. facade wall on the east of the rotunda
9. courtyard east of the rotunda
10. southern atrium (at existing entry)
11. rock of Calvary
12. Church of Golgotha
13. Basilica of Constantine (Martyrium)
14. crypt (of Helena)
15. baptistry
16. eastern atrium
17. remains of the entrance into the Constantinian church
18. cardo maximus
19. Site of Hadrian's forum

with polished stones, and a lead roof. The interior paneled ceiling was overlaid with gold. The porticos also had roofs that were ornamented with gold. A flight of stairs descended from the center of the Martyrion down to the Helena Chapel and, below that, to a room called the Place of the Finding of the Cross. An apse crowned with a half dome was located on the west side of the Martyrion. This was enclosed with twelve columns whose capitals were crowned with large silver bowls, a gift from the emperor. Another colonnaded courtyard, paved with polished stone, extended to the west of the Martyrion. The rock of Calvary (or Golgotha), some 15 feet high and cut away at the sides, was located at the south-east corner of this court (a fact Eusebius does not mention). The holy tomb itself was to be found a little farther west. Eusebius comments regarding the tomb that it was "beautified with rare columns, and profusely enriched with the most splended decorations of every kind." The baptistry was located to the south of the tomb. The Bordeaux Pilgrim mentions the baptistry, but Eusebius does not.[6]

The church's impressive arrangements can be gathered from the remarks of Cyril, Bishop of Jerusalem, who only a dozen years after it was completed gave his famous catechetical lectures in the church. His catechumens, or initiates, were apparently assembled in the inner colonnaded courtyard near the rock of Calvary. Cyril refers to "this blessed Golgotha, in which we are now assembled" (Lecture 4.10); it is "the holy hill standing above us here" (10.19) where Jesus was crucified "on Golgotha here" (4.14), "in this most holy Golgotha" (13.22). Following Easter, when the newly initiated were assembled at the tomb, Cyril instructed them to come "into the holy place of the resurrection" (*Mystagogical Lectures* 19.23). Finegan comments: "This must assuredly mean that there was a building around and over the tomb, and a building of proportions sufficient for such a meeting as Cyril was announcing."[7] The building was named Anastasis.

Epiphanius, Bishop of Salamis, on his visit to Jerusalem in 394 gave a lecture to the clergy and people who were meeting in front of the Lord's tomb. That such a group was assembled here also suggests that there was some kind of structure built around the tomb. About a century after Constantine's original construction Egeria (also known as Aetheria) is reported to have seen the tomb within a large building.[8]

    6. See Bahat, *Carta's Historical Atlas*, p. 24; R. W. Hamilton, "Jerusalem: Patterns of Holiness," *Archaeology in the Levant*, ed. Moorey and Parr, (Warminster, Wilts, Great Britain: Aris and Phillips, Ltd., 1978), p. 198. Finegan, *Archaeology of the New Testament*, pp. 164–165.
    7. Finegan, *Archaeology of the New Testament*, p. 167.
    8. Benjamin Mazar, *The Mountain of the Lord* (Garden City, N.Y.: Doubleday, 1975), p. 245.

Whether there was actually a building around the tomb at the time the church was built is debatable. Coüasnon argues that the basilica for the congregation was built first, and that later in the fourth century the Anastasis[9] (rotunda) was built over the tomb of Christ. The chapel of the Calvary rock was built as a separate unit.[10] However, at this time the tomb and Golgotha could be seen by Cyril and his congregation regardless of whether or not they were enclosed within buildings. When the church was built, or before, the tomb and its environs may have looked different. Cyril tells us that at a previous time there was a cave before the door of the sepulchre and that this outer cave was cut away for the tomb's embellishment (Lecture 14.9). This work may have been done to provide space for the erection of Constantine's "rare columns" and "splendid decorations" placed as embellishments around the tomb (Eusebius, *Life of Constantine* 3.34). Cyril continues his description by saying that a stone which closed the tomb was rolled away and was still "lying by the tomb to this day" (13.39). This description fits one of the types of tomb used by Jews in the first century A.D., which consisted of a *dromos* (passageway) cut into the rock, possibly with steps, leading to a rectangular or circular entrance into an inner chamber, closed at the entrance by a rolling stone or stone door (i.e., Heshbon, Abila of the Decapolis). The inner chamber or chambers contained the burial places which were kokim (or loculus) or arcosolium type. When Cyril says the outer cave of the tomb was cut away, he may be referring to the work Constantine's laborers did in cutting away the *dromos*, or antechamber, of the tomb. An example of this simple type of early Jewish tomb may be seen today within the church just to the West of the Anastasis behind the Coptic Shrine. Here there are a number of rock-cut horizontal loculi (or niches) and pits to hold ossuary boxes; this tomb is popularly known as the sepulchre of Joseph of Arimathea.[11] Part of the ancient wall of the church can be seen in front of these ancient tombs, and underneath the Anastasis can also be seen part of the ancient curved wall that was built around the tomb either by Constantine or by someone later.

The Greek architect Oekonomopolis in restoring parts of the church has reported that he found the edge of the apse of the Con-

---

9. Latin, *anastase;* Greek, *anastasis;* meaning resurrection, a commemoration of the place where our Lord Jesus Christ arose from the dead. Aetheria expresses it vividly: "Those days are called the days of dedication on which the holy church in Golgotha called the Martyrium, and the holy church at the Anastasis, where the Lord rose again after his passion, were on that day consecrated to God."

10. Coüasnon, *Church of the Holy Sepulchre in Jerusalem*, pp. 21, 38, 50–52.

11. Mazar, *The Mountain of the Lord*, p. 255.

stantinian basilica and part of the eastern stylobate, which was the foundation for a row of columns in the court that surrounded the rock of Calvary.[12] Charles Coüasnon, the architect representing the Latin community, has also done considerable restoration work in the Holy Sepulchre Church. Based on Coüasnon's work and that of others Kenyon believes that the plan of the original Constantinian church can be established. She states: "The archaeological contribution concerning the church comes from the identification of the foundation trenches and the isolation of the pottery from them, which is, on my assessment, fourth century A.D."[13] A vivid early picture of what the tomb area in the Constantinian church may have looked like comes from an unusual artifact found in a sixth-century Byzantine building south of the temple platform. The artifact is a gold ring with a design representing the domed Anastasis building, including a row of columns and piers around the tomb of Jesus. This visual representation corresponds to the written record depicting what the ancients saw. Mazar comments: "The ring is contemporaneous with the church erected by Emperor Constantine in the fourth century, a circular and domed small building that stood over the traditional tomb of Jesus before its renovation and inclusion under the Crusader-built Church of the Holy Sepulchre."[14]

One further bit of archaeological evidence from the Constantinian church was uncovered by Magan Broshi in recent excavations at the Church of the Holy Sepulchre. On a wall beneath the church in the eastern extremity of the Armenian Orthodox Patriarchate east of St. Helena's Chapel, a place known to the Armenians as St. Gregory's Chapel, Broshi found a red-and-black graffiti of a small Roman sailing vessel. Beneath the drawing were the Latin words *Domine ivimus*—"Lord we went." These could be interpreted as the words beginning Psalm 122, the psalm of pilgrimage. Or the words could be the statement of a pilgrim, "We went to the tomb of the Lord." The ship represents a type depicted elsewhere in the first centuries A.D. The Christian inscription, however, would not likely have been painted on a public wall before 313.

Broshi also discovered the eastern wall of the Crusader's St. Helena Chapel, and at a level 40 feet down at the site he found that in the seventh century B.C. the area was a rock quarry.[15] The excava-

12. Ibid., p. 245; Coüasnon, *Church of the Holy Sepulchre in Jerusalem*, pp. 37, 41.
13. Kenyon, *Digging Up Jerusalem*, pp. 266–67.
14. Mazar, *The Mountain of the Lord*, pp. 244–45.
15. Cf. Kenyon's find at Site C, south of the German Lutheran Evangelical Church, showing that the area was "without the gate" when Jesus was led to the cross.

tions showed that the area was covered with a seventh-century B.C. beaten-earth floor into which were dug foundations of a Roman structure, no doubt part of the Roman forum built by Hadrian. At Broshi's site some pagan substructures were found untouched by Constantine's workers. Broshi also uncovered foundations of the north stylobate (or platform) of the nave of the Constantinian basilica (a find agreeing with Coüasnon's calculations) as well as the foundations that supported the rock ledge on which the façade of the church was built.[16]

Gordon's Calvary and the Garden Tomb

In connection with Byzantine Jerusalem, Gordon's Calvary and the Garden Tomb call for further discussion. Charles G. Gordon, an Englishman, is largely responsible for the view that this was the area where the crucifixion and burial of Jesus took place. There are geographical and structural difficulties with this view. First, although the face of the rocky hill of Gordon's Calvary presents the rough outline of human eyes and nose (the so-called "face of a skull"), the geographical historical evidence argues that this face of the hill was not there in the first century A.D. but was part of the rock ledge, a section of which one sees under the north wall of Jerusalem. Second, as Finegan points out, the trough-like ledge in the Garden Tomb is characteristic of the Byzantine period. Finegan also notes that when the tomb was discovered in 1867, two Byzantine crosses were found on the east wall of the tomb chamber. Third, other Byzantine tombs found in the area give additional support for a Byzantine date for this Garden Tomb.[17] Fourth, the narrowness of the stone-cut trough that runs in front of the Garden Tomb argues against its being used for a rolling stone; an alternative conclusion is that this trough was used to carry rainwater from the cliff. Thus, we can conclude that the site of Gordon's Calvary and the Garden Tomb served as part of a Byzan-

16. Magan Broshi, "Evidence of Earliest Christian Pilgrimage to the Holy Land Comes to Light in Holy Sepulchre Church," *Biblical Archaeology Review*, 3.4 (1977): 42–44; cf. Coüasnon, *The Church of the Holy Sepulchre*, pp. 41–42.

17. In the grounds of the Basilica of St. Stephen, 320 meters north of the Damascus Gate and near the Garden Tomb, were found a number of rock-hewn tombs, one of which, from the Herodian period, appears to have been converted into a Byzantine burial type of the fifth century A.D. In the north gallery of the basilica was found another Byzantine tomb covered by a large stone with an inscription: "The private tomb of the deacon Nonnus Onesimus of the holy Anastasis of Christ and of this monastery." These tombs suggest that the graves in the Garden Tomb nearby may have been another group of Byzantine date (Finegan, *Archaeology of the New Testament*, p. 176).

Gordon's Calvary.

Garden tomb.

tine cemetery. There is no commanding evidence that it was the place of the crucifixion and burial of Jesus.

The Church on Mount Zion

Mark 14:15 says that Jesus and his disciples were to gather in Jerusalem in an upstairs room (Greek *anagaion*) for the passover.

Acts 1:13 states that, following the ascension of the Lord, the disciples gathered in an upstairs room (Greek *huperōion*) where a number of days later they were filled with the Holy Spirit. In his Latin translation Jerome renders the two Greek words by the one Latin word *cenaculum*, dining room—no doubt because he thought that as the disciples in Mark 14:15 met in a dining room on the upper floor, so they must have met in the same kind of room, a dining room, as recorded in Acts 1:13. Possibly this was the same room in both instances, and may have been in the house of Mary, the mother of John Mark (Acts 2:12). Tradition has it that this house was located on Jerusalem's highest southwestern hill, a hill that came to be called Zion, or Sion, or Mount Zion. We remember that when Titus destroyed Jerusalem in A.D. 70, he spared the Herodian towers at the Citadel and part of the western wall. This meant that the area near Mount Zion was not as completely destroyed as other parts of the city. Subsequent to A.D. 70, building must have begun again in the area. Epiphanius (*On Weights and Measures* 14 [54c]) says that when Hadrian came into the area in 130 he found on Mount Zion "the Church of God which was small where the disciples, when they had returned after the Savior had ascended from the Mount of Olives, went to the upper room." Epiphanius also says that the emperor found "the seven synagogues which alone remained standing in Zion, like solitary huts, one of which remained until the time of Maximona the bishop and Constantine the king, 'like a booth in a vineyard,' as it is written [Isa. 1:8]."

When the Bordeaux Pilgrim came to Jerusalem in 333, he went up on Zion and found only one of the seven synagogues remaining; the rest he states had been "plowed over and sown upon" as Isaiah the prophet said [cf. Micah 3:12, "Zion will be plowed like a field"]. However, the Bordeaux Pilgrim does not refer to a church on Mount Zion—unless he considered the synagogue to be a Jewish-Christian church (cf. James 2:2, *synagogē*, synagogue; James 5:14, *ecclesia*, church). But in the fourth century such a view of a synagogue would be unlikely. Cyril in his catechetical lectures gives further evidence concerning the sacred character of this Mount Zion site. He speaks of the Holy Spirit "in the Upper Church," which must be a reference to the Church on Mount Zion, a church that, no doubt, was now much larger than the small church Hadrian saw. Theodosius calls this church "the mother of all churches." He says that this church was on the site of the house of St. Mark the Evangelist, and locates it 200 (i.e., ca. 970 feet)[18] paces from Golgotha. In 940 Eutychius

18. Based on 1,000 paces to a Roman mile, or 4,854 feet.

of Alexandria gives further evidence when, depending on earlier sources, he states that "the Church of the Holy Mount Zion bears witness that Christ ate the passover of the law in the upper room there on the day of the passover of the Jews." Arculf, a Frankish bishop who visited Jerusalem in 670, also bears witness to the church structure when he speaks of it as a "great basilica." He gives a drawing of it with legends indicating that there were two other traditions connected with the site—that here was the column where Jesus was scourged and that Mary, the mother of Jesus, died in this place.

Thus the cumulative early church tradition pointed to the fact that the Church on Mount Zion commemorated the place of the upper room of the Last Supper and the place where the disciples gathered at Pentecost, and that this is the site where the house of Mary, the mother of John Mark, was located.

This site on Mount Zion today is outside the walled city of Old Jerusalem. It contains a number of buildings: the Dormition Church (commemorating the death of Mary) and Monastery of the Benedictines; the building containing the traditional Tomb of David (which had been used at an earlier time as the Mosque of the Prophet David); and the so-called room of the Last Supper (of fourteenth-century date) located on the second floor of the Tomb of David. The Church on Mount Zion was no doubt destroyed by the Persians in 614, but it was then rebuilt, only to fall into ruins again. Later the Crusaders rebuilt it into what they called the Church of Zion, or the Church of St. Mary.[19] Mazar reports that "part of its original wall was uncovered when the foundations of the Basilica of the Dormition were laid in 1898–99."[20] This excavation, conducted by Heinrich Renard, uncovered the remains of the Byzantine church of the fourth century, a structure that was about 197 feet long, 131 feet wide, and had three or possibly five aisles. One of the ancient columns of this church is visible in the garden of the Dormition Church.[21]

The So-called Tomb of David

The so-called Tomb of David includes two rooms. The north one contains a large stone cenotaph (memorial) in front of an apse. Behind the plaster on the apse J. Pinkerfeld in 1951 found a wall of

---

19. Finegan, *Archaeology of the New Testament*, pp. 147–48, 151.
20. Mazar, *The Mountain of the Lord*, p. 246.
21. Finegan, *Archaeology of the New Testament*, pp. 150–51.

squared stones he dated to the Late Roman period. The same kind o masonry was found on the east wall and also on the eastern part o both the north and south walls. The apse faces north and eas toward the temple platform. Pinkerfeld believed that he had found an ancient Jewish synagogue, since it was characteristic of the an cient synagogue to have the torah niche or apse on the side of the building facing in the direction of the temple. Examples of relevant ancient synagogues are the Galilee-type synagogues with facades and three doors facing Jerusalem (i.e., the structures at Capernaum and Chorazin), or the broad-house-type with the torah niche facing the Holy City (Dura Europos and Eshtemoa, south of Hebron).[22]

The question is, could this be one of the seven synagogues on Zior which Hadrian saw when he came to Jerusalem in 130? And could it have still existed there when the Bordeaux Pilgrim came in 333?

The Nea (New) Church

Justinian dedicated the Nea, or New, Church, which he had built in 542. It is located at the southern wall of the present Old City somewhat west of the Dung Gate. Here, in the Jerusalem Archaeological Park, a portion of the Nea Church's foundation can be seen protruding just outside the southern wall. The site is in the old Jewish Quarter. Recently Avigad excavated a section of the church's wall and found it consisted of massive late Byzantine masonry blocks, about 40 feet long and over 20 feet wide. This wall was laid on bedrock; large square and rectangular stone blocks were placed on the exterior of the wall and smaller ones on the interior. Avigad compared his findings with the representation of the church on the Madaba map and with Procopius's description of the church and concluded that what he had excavated was the eastern wall of the Nea Church. The apse of the church was located on the east, as was the normal orientation in the Byzantine period. Using the plans of other Byzantine churches as examples, he concluded that the Nea Church had three external apses, in contrast to inscribed apses built within the external east wall of a church. He also found two additional walls to the west of the wall containing the apse, one parallel to the massive wall and one perpendicular to that wall.

Additional remains of the Nea Church have also been found. Out-

22. Ibid., p. 150; W. Harold Mare, "Archaeological and Literary Evidence Regarding Building Remains and Worship in the Early Church," *Near East Archaeological Society Bulletin*, New Series No. 1 (1971), pp. 13–16.

side the south wall of the city west of the present Dung Gate Ben-Dov found the southeast corner of the Nea Church protruding from the base of that wall. He also found the south apse, which helped confirm Avigad's conclusion. The Nea masonry is much larger than that of the southern city wall.[23] A number of these large stone blocks can be seen protruding from the wall. Some have margins with rough center bosses, while others have smooth surfaces. The rectangular blocks measure from about 5 feet to 6½ feet long by about 2⅔ feet wide; others are about 2⅔ feet square.

The Nea Church was a basilica consisting of a central nave and matching side aisles. Its facade had three entrances, the middle one being larger than the other two. The southern wall of the Nea was a retaining wall for several buildings, and the foundations of these have been uncovered.[24] Close to the southeast corner of the Nea one can see today remains of a building protruding from the southern city wall. This was probably a hospice, or hospital, one of a series of public buildings Justinian in the sixth century built adjacent to the Nea Church. Ben-Dov says that the walls of the church no doubt supported the two hospices that Procopius tells us Justinian built next to the church. Procopius said that "one of these is destined for the shelter of visiting strangers, while the other is an infirmary for poor persons suffering from disease."

Additional work at the Nea Church was done in 1976. In that year Avigad excavated inside the southern city wall and uncovered a subterranean structure of vaulted halls connected with the Nea Church. Warren had discovered these halls in the nineteenth century. In the midst of the subterranean vaulting Avigad found a beautifully preserved Greek inscription containing the name of Justinian.

In 614 the Persians destroyed the Nea, as they did a good many other churches in the Holy Land. After the Christians retook Jerusalem in 628, there was little time for repairs to be made on the Nea before the Muslims conquered the city in 638. In the Islamic Umayyad period (A.D. 638–750) the remains of the Nea and other damaged churches were used as ready-made quarries from which to obtain materials for building Islamic structures.

In the old Jewish Quarter, not far from the Nea Church, remains of ancient Jewish synagogues, from the Byzantine and later periods, have been found. These include the Ramban synagogue, built somewhere between the fourth and twelfth centuries, according to the

23. M. Ben-Dov, "Found after 1400 years—The Magnificent Nea," *Biblical Archaeology Review*, 3.4 (1977), pp. 33–34.
    24. Ibid., p. 34.

Remains of the Nea Church.

evidence of columns found there; two of the columns are Roman and two Byzantine.[25]

The Church of St. Anne and Bethesda

The pools of Bethesda were discussed in the context of first-century Jerusalem (see pp. 166–68). In succeeding centuries Christians associated with Jerusalem gave a consistent description of this place just northwest of St. Stephen's Gate where Jesus healed the lame man. Eusebius (*Onomasticon*) speaks of the place as Bezatha and describes it as

> a pool in Jerusalem, which is the Sheep Pool . . . , which formerly had five porticoes [i.e., colonnaded courts]. And now it is shown in the twin pools which are there, each of which is filled by the yearly rains, but one of which paradoxically exhibits water colored purple-red . . . , a trace, it is said, of the sacrificial animals formerly washed in it. That is also why it is called Sheep Pool . . . on account of the sacrifices.

25. Sylvester J. Saller, *Second Revised Catalogue of the Ancient Synagogues of the Holy Land* (Jerusalem: Franciscan Press, 1972), p. 47.

Cyril of Jerusalem also speaks of the Sheep Pool and its five colonnaded porches. When Peter the Iberian came to Jerusalem in 451, he spoke of going into the Church of the Lame Man. Eutychius of Alexandria in 940 speaks of "the church which is called the Place of the Sheep in Jerusalem."

The site of the pool is also associated with the birth of Mary, the mother of Jesus. Theodosius speaks of the Church of St. Mary there, and *The Anonymous of Piacenza,* in commenting about the five colonnaded porches, states that "one has the basilica of St. Mary." This statement suggests that the Byzantine church was built into one of the colonnaded porches; it was probably the same church, or its replacement as the Church of the Lame Man. Eutychius of Alexandria further remarks that the church here bore witness to the birth of Mary, whose parents were Joachim, of the tribe of Judah, and Anne, of the tribe of Aaron; they supposedly placed Mary under the charge of Zacharias in the temple. The fuller account of all this is in the Protevangelium of James. There Joachim is pictured as a shepherd; this would give reason for him to be connected with the Sheep Pool.

In the Persian destruction of 614 the church at the pool was destroyed; after this a small chapel was built on the site. Later the Crusaders built the new Church of St. Anne, which must have been to the east of the Pool of Bethesda, where the Church of St. Anne stands today. As testimony to this, the *Deeds of the Franconians Conquering Jerusalem* (1108) states that the Crusader Church had in front of it the remains of the old pool and the five porches.

In excavations in the vaults of the Church of St. Anne in 1866 an inscription was found on a broken marble foot which reads, "Pompeia Lucilia dedicated (this as a votive gift)." On paleographical grounds the script may be dated to the second century A.D. The marble foot may have commemorated a healing, and, if so, a pagan healing cult may have existed at the site in that day. Compare such votive offerings found in the excavations in Corinth.[26] Paintings in Pompeian red found in an underground vaulted gallery in 1962 may have been part of this cult. Excavations by the White Fathers have uncovered remains of a Byzantine church, probably of the fifth century. The west side of the church, including its main entrance was constructed on the rock dike between the two pools. The north side of the church rested on the Roman built cistern and the south side

26. W. Harold Mare, I Corinthians, *Expositor's Bible Commentary* Vol. 10, (Grand Rapids: Zondervan, 1976) p. 241; Oscar Broneer, "Corinth," *Biblical Archaeologist,* Vol. 14, No. 4 (Dec. 1951) pp. 80–83.

rested on a series of arches, which Jeremias calls "mighty arched substructures."[27] As customary, the apse area of the church (in this case there were three apses) was found on the east end. An underground Roman sanctuary east of the pools had been destroyed and filled in. The church narthex evidently had a mosaic floor; other areas of the church had been paved with marble. This church was also destroyed by the Persians in 614. Subsequently a small chapel was built above the north aisle of the basilica. It eventually fell into ruin. On these ruins and the ruins of the Byzantine church over the pool the Crusaders erected a chapel which they called the Moustier (the Monastery); it was built over the Roman cistern in the southeast corner of the north pool. Under a Byzantine vault a stairway was constructed to lead down into the cistern, the stairway that leads to the cistern today.[28]

The Basilica of St. Stephen

Peter the Iberian, arriving in Jerusalem in 451, indicates that he approached the city from the north and that he saw first the Basilica of St. Stephen, called the Martyrion of Stephen. This indication that the Basilica of St. Stephen was on the north of Jerusalem is confirmed by the statement of Theodosius. He testifies that the church which commemorated the stoning of Stephen was built by Eudocia outside the north gate of Jerusalem (Theodosius calls the north gate the Galilean Gate). Further testimony comes from *The Anonymous of Piacenza*, which says that Eudocia, in addition to extending the walls of the city south to enclose the pool of Siloam, built the basilica and tomb of Stephen and put her tomb beside Stephen's.

The site of the Basilica of St. Stephen is 1,050 feet (one-fifth of a mile) north of the Damascus Gate on the Nablus Road, about 490 feet northwest of the Garden Tomb. The French Dominicans began excavating here in 1885. They found on the site a fifth-century basilica, probably the remains of the one built by Eudocia. A cistern was found under the courtyard of the church. In plan the basilica had a nave, two side aisles, and an apse oriented toward the east, as was the general pattern for Byzantine churches. In the fifth-century debris were found fragments of columns and capitals and portions of a mosaic pavement.[29] No doubt this basilica also was destroyed by the Persians, and a new chapel was built there at the end of the seventh

27. Joachim Jeremias, *The Rediscovery of Bethesda* (Louisville, Ky.: Southern Baptist Seminary, 1949), pp. 28–32.

28. Finegan, *Archaeology of the New Testament*, p. 147.

29. *The Quarterly of the Department of Antiquities of Palestine* 2 (1932), pp. 176–177.

century. Later the Crusaders restored the structure. The present church of St. Stephen was built in 1900 on the foundation of the Byzantine basilica built by Eudocia; the courtyard of the modern church is built over the ancient one, and in it one can see part of a column of the Byzantine church. The Dominican Abbey and the Ecole Biblique et Archéologique Française are located on the grounds of the modern church.[30]

The Church at the Pool of Siloam

The Bordeaux Pilgrim states that there was a four-sided portico above the Pool of Siloam, but does not mention any church there. However, at a later time Antoninus Martyr (560–570) gives a full description of the church and the pool. Also the Madaba map knows of the church there. We are told that the roofed structure over the Pool of Siloam and the church near it, both pictured on the map, were built by Eudocia.

The church that Bliss and Dickie discovered at the Pool of Siloam no doubt is the one built by Eudocia. It was difficult for these excavators to reach much of the remains of the church because a minaret which can be seen today had been built on top of it. It was only through a tunneling procedure that they were able to piece together the basic plan of the church. The church was built over the northern side of the arcade, or colonnaded porches, that surrounded the pool. Hampered by ownership problems of the land at the Pool of Siloam and limited basically to tunneling at the site, Bliss and Dickie were still able to outline, describe, and draw the architectural features of the church at the Pool of Siloam. They determined that the inside measurements of the church itself were: 84 feet long, and 51½ feet wide; the nave was 25 feet, 10 inches wide; the two aisles 10.51 feet wide each, and the atrium 62 feet long and 17⅔ feet wide. From their plan we gather the overall dimensions of the church were about 115-125 feet long by 100 feet wide, including the narthex and atrium located on the north side of the church.[31]

Mazar estimates the church's dimensions as 116 by 53 feet. The difference between these two sets of figures no doubt is to be attributed to the lack of availability of the entire site for close examination. Mazar says that a large vault on four piers covered the church itself.[32]

30. Finegan, *Archaeology of the New Testament*, pp. 174–75.

31. F. J. Bliss and A. C. Dickie, *Excavations at Jerusalem*, 1894–1897 (London: The Committee of the Palestine Exploration Fund, 1898), pp. 179, 180; Plate XVIII.

32. Mazar, *The Mountain of the Lord*, p. 249.

Evidently all the Bordeaux Pilgrim saw in his day was what he
calls "the fourfold colonnade," that is, the arcade, 64 feet long, on
the northern part of which the church was built; Bliss and Dickie
also found parts of this structure and from their investigation determined that the arcade surrounded the four sides of the Pool of
Siloam.[33] *The Anonymous of Piacenza* not only saw the colonnaded
pool divided to accommodate men and women bathers, but also the
vaulted basilica, the latter of which he at least implies Eudocia had
built when she enclosed the Pool of Siloam area within the city
wall.[34] Further evidence, beyond the testimony of the Bordeaux Pilgrim, that the colonnaded porches were built at an earlier time than
the church of Eudocia is seen through the archaeological discovery
that the original flight of steps leading to the porches had been
altered ("enlarged and extended," Bliss and Dickie call it) at a time
prior to the building of the church; these steps may be of Roman
date. The church had a simple geometric mosaic pattern on the
floor.[35]

Kenyon reports on the scanty remains of a Byzantine church she
uncovered at her Site L along the west wall below the Citadel, in the
Armenian Quarter. This church is not mentioned in any written
record. She found the east apse of this church and enough of the
foundation of the walls to suggest that there were two smaller side
apses; this evidence suggested that the structure was a basilica with
a nave and side aisles. Also found was a portion of a fine mosaic
with a damaged inscription which indicates that the church was
associated with a noble lady, Bassa, a friend of Eudocia.[36]

Shiloh found a small amount of Byzantine remains in the form of
some pottery deposits in areas A1 and G. In area A2 he found some
thick support walls of the Byzantine period and what he thinks may
be part of the fortifications àt the City of David which ran above the
Pool of Siloam. Shiloh's excavation in area H uncovered the corner
of a large structure with massive walls, with evidence of poorer
buildings abutting this large building. Shiloh argues that the City of
David's First Wall fortifications of Strata 7–6 (second century B.C. to
A.D. 70) may well have served as a base for Eudocia's fifth-century
city wall which included the Pool of Siloam.[37]

33. Bliss and Dickie, *Excavations at Jerusalem*, pp. 157, 184–85; plate XVIII.
34. Bliss and Dickie, *Excavations at Jerusalem*, pp. 192–93; 196–99.
35. Kenyon, *Digging Up Jerusalem*, pp. 28, 273; Bliss and Dickie, *Excavations at
Jerusalem*, pp. 151–55, 179–208, 329.
36. Kenyon, *Digging Up Jerusalem*, pp. 273–74; plates 113, 114.
37. Shiloh, *Excavations at the City of David, I, 1978–82*, pp. 30, 31.

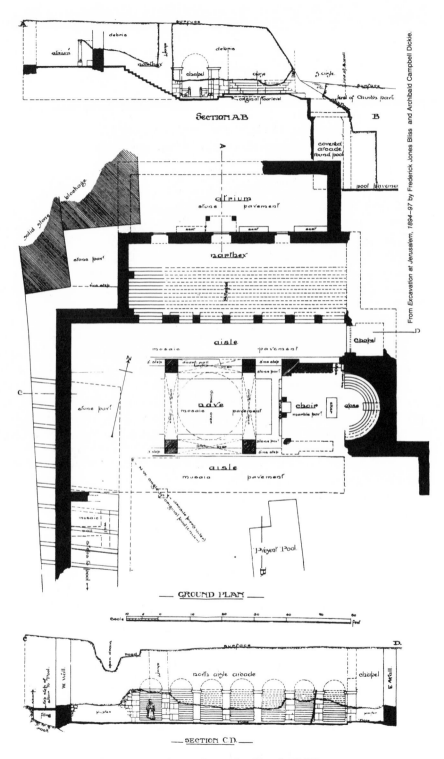

SECTION AB

atrium

debris

debris

narthex

chapel

apse

s. aisle

level of Church pav't.

original floor level

surface

surface

line of s. wall

A

B

covered arcade round pool

pool pavement

solid stone

blockage

atrium

stone pavement

stone pav't

seat

seat

seat

one step

narthex

aisle pavement

mosaic

D

Chapel

one step

dwarf wall open

one step

stone pav't

N

stone pav't

nave

mosaic

choir

marble pav't

apse

chancel step

marble pav't

one step

stone pav't

one step

stone pav't

aisle mosaic pavement

mosaic wall

pool

Present Pool

A

C

B

_ **GROUND PLAN** _

Scale .... feet

10 5 0 10 20 30 40 50 60

SECTION CD

C

D

surface

road

open drain

north aisle arcade

chapel

W. wall

pilaster

pilaster

W. wall

E. wall

top step down to Pool

filling

pool

Plan of the Church at the Pool of Siloam

The dome building behind the wall
is the Church of St. Peter in Gallicantu.

The Church of St. Peter in Gallicantu

In an earlier chapter we examined the archaeological evidence regarding the house of Caiaphas and the Church of Peter, which seem to have been located on Mount Zion at the site of the present Armenian Chapel, across a narrow street from the Dormition. At the site of the Armenian Chapel which is a fifteenth-century building, a Byzantine mosaic pavement 13 to 16 feet long and 8 feet wide was found and a threshold was discovered to the west, suggesting that the sixth-century church there was about 100 to 115 feet long. Finegan suggests that these might be the remains of the Church of Peter, or really the church of the Denial of Peter.[38] The *Jerusalem Breviary* speaks of the Great Basilica of St. Peter at the house of Caiaphus where St. Peter made his denial.

But what of the Church of St. Peter in Gallicantu? The monk Epiphanius (780–800) places the location of the Last Supper and the assemblage of disciples on Mount Zion and indicates that the house of Caiaphas, the place where Peter denied the Lord, was close by. But he places the location where Peter wept bitterly and the church erected to commemorate it elsewhere. Specifically he states, "To the right outside the city and near the wall there is a church where Peter, when he went out, wept bitterly; and to the right from the church, approximately three bowshots distant, is the Pool of Siloah." The location of the Church of St. Peter in Gallicantu which

38. Finegan, *Archaeology of the New Testament*, p. 153.

one sees today satisfies the requirements of this description. The monk Bernard (870) also indicates that there was a church to the east of the Mount Zion church where Peter denied the Lord. Saewulf (1102) also agrees with this assessment. He indicates that below "on the declivity of Mount Zion is the Church of St. Peter which is called Gallicantus, where he hid himself in a very deep cave, which may still be seen, after his denial of our Lord, and there wept over his crime most bitterly." Our conclusion then is that the Church of Peter on Mount Zion preserved the location and commemorated Peter's denial of the Lord, and that the Church of St. Peter in Gallicantu was built some distance away to commemorate Peter's bitter weeping.

On the eastern slope of Mount Zion, 820 feet east of the Cenacle, there is a church which is owned by the Assumptionist Fathers. Excavations in 1888 and 1911 revealed remains of an ancient church there. Coins from Theodosius II (408–450) to Leo I (457–474) found in the ruins suggest that the original construction of the church is to be dated to the end of the fifth century. The coins of Phocas (602–610) and Heraclius I (610–642) found at the site suggest that the church was in existence before and at the time of the Persian invasion in 614, when the structure was probably destroyed, and that after the destruction there was a smaller edifice there. This early church, in a location corresponding to the citations above, is surely to be identified as the Church of St. Peter in Gallicantu. The present church is a modern building erected by the Assumptionist Fathers in 1931. Beneath this church are several rock-hewn rooms. Connected with one room are recesses radiating off a central court; rings are attached high up on the walls of the room. Over to one side of the room one looks down into a deep pit on the sides of which Byzantine crosses are painted or incised in the rock. This deep pit may have served in ancient times as a cistern.[39]

Byzantine Buildings in the Temple Area

After the destruction in A.D. 70 the temple area lay in ruins, and it remained in this state until the Muslims came in 638. Eusebius comments on how sad it was in his day to see the stones of the temple being taken away for use in other buildings.

However, in the Byzantine period considerable building was carried on southwest of the temple platform. A partial Hebrew inscription from Isaiah 66:14 found on part of the western Wailing

39. Ibid., pp. 153–54.

Wall bears testimony to the raised hopes of the Jews during the fourth century when Julian the Apostate (362–363) gave the Jews a short-lived reprieve and allowed them to resettle Jerusalem and to work on rebuilding the temple. Of particular interest are two buildings which Mazar excavated. These buildings had been originally constructed in Roman time and had been renovated in the fourth century. The latest coins found there date from the end of the reign of Julian the Apostate. One building was well-preserved including arches and well constructed doorways and windows. A heavy layer of ash in some of the rooms indicates that the building was destroyed by fire.[40] Byzantine structures were built all along the southern wall of the temple platform, including a cloister south of the triple and single gates near the southeastern corner of the temple platform. This is the cloister or monastery of the fifth century which Theodosius (530) describes as being below the pinnacle of the temple (cf. Matthew 4:5). He says that the monastery was for nuns who entered, never to leave again. Water for the monastery was provided by cisterns. Other needed provisions were brought to and placed on the walls for the nuns to take inside. Mazar says the structure was built to take care of six hundred nuns. In the sixth century the monastery was a three-storied structure with one gate on the west wall. Mazar's excavations revealed two cisterns and several tombs in the basement; he speculates that in the fifth-century phase it was Eudocia's palace, later it was turned into a monastery.[41]

In the nineteenth century R. A. S. Macalister and S. W. Crowfoot excavated other Byzantine structures, mainly late Byzantine dwellings on the southeastern ridge. Other buildings of the late Byzantine era were found by Mazar south and southeast of the temple area. Some of the brick and tiles of these structures had Greek markings and insignia and Greek inscriptions. All of this points to a considerable Late Byzantine population in the area.[42]

M. Avi-Yonah excavated another public building at Giv'at-Ram near the Hebrew University on Mount Scopus. The evidence showed that this building was a home for the aged (Gerokomion). It had a chapel dedicated to St. George which was laid out as a basilica with prayer cubicles in the aisles; in the mosaic pavement was the inscription, "Lord, God of Saint Georgios, remember the donor."[43]

40. Mazar, The Mountain of the Lord, p. 247.
41. Ibid., p. 254.
42. Ibid., pp. 256–57.
43. Ibid., p. 254.

The Byzantine Walled City

From the buildings described above we can see that in the Byzantine period, from the fourth to sixth centuries A.D., there was a great deal of building activity on the south side of Jerusalem, south of the temple platform and including at least parts of the southeastern ridge. In Eudocia's time (450–460) the city walls were expanded to include the Pool of Siloam; at the pool she built a church. During the Byzantine period the city wall, of course, enclosed the southern part of the western hill and also crossed over the Tyropoeon Valley to connect with the wall of the City of David revised by Eudocia (as Shiloh suggests) in her extension on the southeastern ridge. Where the east-west wall across the Tyropoeon and the north-south City of David wall met at the southern end of the southeastern ridge, Bliss and Dickie discovered a gate which they calculated was used in three periods. One of these periods was the Byzantine, a date which Kenyon determined from her excavation at the same gate in 1961. The smooth dressed stones there were significant for her in determining that the gate was used in the Byzantine period. The tower just to the east of the main gate is certainly Byzantine, for it is built on a wall connected with an earlier Roman bath complex just to the south.[44]

Byzantine Churches on the Mount of Olives

Following the Last Supper, Jesus took the disciples down across the Kidron Valley to a place called Gethsemane, (Matt. 26:36; Mark 14:32; cf. Luke 22:39), where there was a garden (John 18:1). The word *Gethsemane* means oil press, indicating an instrument used for making olive oil. Such a term was naturally associated with the mount east of Jerusalem, the Mount of Olives, on which grew many olive trees. We do not know, of course, the exact spot where the Lord prayed. However, based on the statement of Matthew 26:36 which says that Jesus went to pray at "a place called Gethsemane," and Luke 22:39 which says that this prayer place was at the Mount of Olives, and John 18:1 which says, "he went forth across the Kidron Valley where there was a garden," we gather that the garden was on the lower western slopes of the mount, presumably in the vicinity where the present Garden of Gethsemane is located. There is a rock

---

44. Kenyon, *Digging Up Jerusalem*, p. 269, plate 6; Bliss and Dickie, *Excavations at Jerusalem*, pp. 88–93 and General Plan II; Shiloh, *Excavations at the City of David, I, 1978–82*, pp. 30–31.

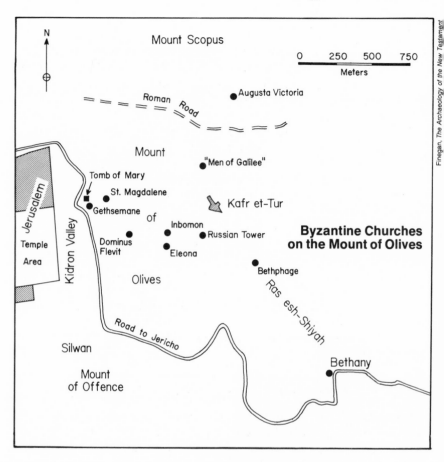

enclosed in the present Church of All Nations at the Garden of Gethsemane. This church is built over two earlier churches on the site. It could be that Jesus prayed at or near this mass of rock. The Bordeaux Pilgrim refers to a rock in this general vicinity. He says, as he begins to ascend the Mount of Olives, "On the left, where there are vineyards, is a rock where Judas Iscariot betrayed Christ." He also notes that not far away "about a stone's throw," are the tombs of Isaiah and of Hezekiah. The mass of rock which the Bordeaux Pilgrim speaks about could be what is called the Grotto of the Betrayal; it is located to the north of, and across the road from, the Church of All Nations.

Although Eusebius and the Bordeaux Pilgrim do not mention a church in the area, Aetheria (Egeria) indicates that in her time there was one there. She says, "They [the bishop and the people] descend

The Garden of Gethsemane. Notice Golden Gate in the background.

Ewing Galloway

The Church of All Nations in the Garden of Gethsemane.

from the Inbomon [The Ascension Church on the Mount of Olives] with hymns, and come to that place where the Lord prayed, as it is written in the Gospel [Luke 22:41], 'And he withdrew about a stone's throw and prayed, etc.' In this place there is a fine church." She goes on to indicate that after prayer the people moved on to Gethsemane. So from Aetheria's viewpoint there were two important Christian sites to be seen in her day: the place where Jesus prayed, commemorated with a fine church, and the place where Jesus was arrested, a place she calls Gethsemane. Following the idea that two places are to be distinguished (see the record of the Synoptics), one posits there was one place where Jesus entered with his disciples and another place where he withdrew to pray: "over there" (Matt. 26:36), "a little farther" (Mark 14:35), "about a stone's throw beyond them" (Luke 22:41). The Gospels indicate that Jesus then came back to the disciples, at which place he was betrayed. Jerome, in his revision of Eusebius's *Onomasticon* in 390, indicates that Gethsemane was at the foot of the Mount of Olives.

We can judge from this evidence that by Byzantine times the Christians thought of two important places the night the Lord was betrayed at Gethsemane: the place where Jesus prayed and where a Byzantine church was built, and the nearby place where he was betrayed and arrested. Traditionally the two places: the modern Church of All Nations built over earlier churches, and the Grotto of Gethsemane where Roman and Byzantine remains have been found, are very close. Corbo places them only about 290 feet apart.[45]

45. V. C. Corbo, *Ricerche Archeologiche al Monte Degli Ulivi* (Jerusalem: Franciscan Press, 1965), pp. 3–49, 85; B. Bagatti, *The Church from the Gentiles in Palestine* (Jerusalem: Franciscan Press, 1971), p. 229.

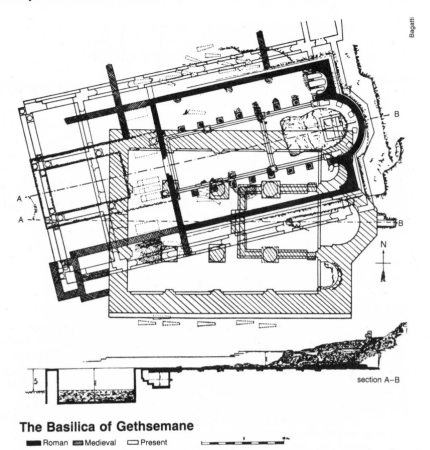

Bagatti

section A–B

The Basilica of Gethsemane

■■ Roman ▨▨ Medieval ▭ Present

The plan of the three churches at the Garden of Gethsemane, one imposed on the other. The solid black walls are from the basilica of the fourth century; the slanted line walls are from the twelfth-century church; the outline walls are those of the present-day Church of All Nations.

Whether these traditional spots are the exact ones where Jesus prayed and was betrayed is unclear. However, the locations for the events have to be found within the narrow confines of this lower region of the Mount of Olives, for Scripture says Jesus was at the Mount of Olives, and that he had "crossed the Kidron Valley," where "on the other side there was an olive grove, and he . . . went into it."

At the place traditionally called the place of the betrayal is the structure described as the Tomb of Mary. Theodosius says that at the Valley of Jehoshaphat (the Kidron Valley) there is the place where Jesus was betrayed and a Church of Mary, our Lord's mother. *The Anonymous of Piacenza* puts the place of betrayal in what he calls the

Valley of Gethsemane; then he comments that he found there "a basilica of St. Mary which, they say, was her house in which she was taken from the body." Arculf says that the Church of St. Mary had two stories, both round, and that in the lower story there was "the empty stone sepulcher of Mary in which for some time she rested." The *Jerusalem Breviary* also associates the basilica of St. Mary with her tomb. These writers thus give consistent testimony that the Church of St. Mary was in existence in the sixth and seventh centuries; the structure was probably erected in the fifth century. Finding the church in ruins, the Crusaders rebuilt it and constructed a large monastery next to it, which they called the Abbey of St. Mary of the Valley of Jehoshaphat. Although some trenching was done at the site in 1937, more extensive excavations (1972–73) have been carried out. Evidence obtained includes grave inscriptions. One is of Euphemia (late fourth or early fifth century) which has a cross inscribed at the beginning and end. The inscription had been reused as a paving stone. A second sixth-century grave inscription, also with a cross at the beginning and carrying the words "The Tomb of Kasios and Adios," was found west of the basilica of St. Mary. It too had been used as a paving stone. The excavation also found mosaic pavement of both the earlier church and of Crusader times. Although Arculf calls the church a round structure, actually it is cruciform. On the lower level to the right is the arcosolium chamber tomb of Mary. Today's church, called The Church of the Tomb of Mary or the Tomb of Mary, has an underground crypt called The Abbey of St. Mary. Remains of the Crusader abbey have been found to the west side of the tomb.[46]

The modern Church of All Nations (the Franciscan Church of the Agony) is in the present Garden of Gethsemane. This church was completed in 1924 and was built over two earlier churches. The earliest, built by Theodosius I in 385, was a basilica 65 feet long and 53 feet wide, with a nave, two side aisles, and triple apses. Several capitals, column bases, and parts of geometric mosaic floors were found in the ruins. This fourth-century church was oriented 13 degrees north of east to accommodate the large mass of rock which was at the front of the nave and altar. The mosaic pavement is predominantly geometric in design. Father P. G. Orfali excavated the ruins of this church in 1909–20.[47] This church was no doubt de-

---

46. B. Bagatti, *New Discoveries at the Tomb of Virgin Mary in Gethsemane* (Jerusalem: Franciscan Press, 1975) pp. 19–60; B. Bagatti, *The Church from the Gentiles*, p. 229; V. C. Corbo, *Ricerche Archeologiche*, pp. 76–80; Finegan, *Archaeology of the New Testament*, pp. 106, 107.

47. Mazar, *The Mountain of the Lord*, p. 247.

stroyed in 614 by the Persians. A second church was constructed at the side by the Crusaders in the twelfth century; they called it St. Savior. It was built several degrees to the right of the foundations of the fourth-century church and also included three apses. The modern church has been built on the foundations of the fourth-century church, and provision has been made for viewing some of the earlier floor mosaics.[48]

Southwest from the Garden of Gethsemane, about halfway up the Mount of Olives, is the Franciscan chapel called Dominus Flevit. The Latin term means "the Lord wept" (Luke 19:41). As the name indicates, this spot was set aside to commemorate the event of our Lord weeping over Jerusalem. Pilgrims in the early centuries often pointed to this place as the spot where the event took place. However, Scripture does not indicate the exact place on the western slope of the mount where Jesus made his lament. Ruins of a Byzantine church were found in 1954 under and next to the present Dominus Flevit. An ancient mosaic featuring a geometric design is still to be seen on the floor of the chapel.[49] A Byzantine capital was also found, and an inscription of dedication giving the name of the priest of the Anastasis in the Holy Sepulchre Church. Depending on literary sources, T. Milik dates this church to 675, just at the close of the Byzantine period.[50] It is possible, however, that this Byzantine church was one of the twenty-four churches Theodosius says were on the Mount of Olives in the sixth century. Another of these twenty-four churches may have been located almost 1,000 feet northwest of the Inbomon Church just to the west of the crest of the Mount of Olives next to the hospital that was built there in the early 1960s. The ruins of this unnamed church were uncovered in 1965 in bulldozing for the foundations of the hospital. Salvage excavation was done by the Near East School of Archaeology, Dr. Joseph P. Free of Wheaton College, Director. The excavators were Professor James Jennings of Wheaton College and Dr. Wilber Wallis of Covenant Seminary, St. Louis.

Southeast from the Dominus Flevit Chapel is the Eleona Church, located about 230 feet south and a little west of the summit of the Mount of Olives. This was built by Helena, mother of Constantine, and was called the Olive Grove Church or the Mount of Olives Church (the Greek word *eleona* means olive grove). Eusebius (*Life of Constantine* 3.43) remarks about this church:

48. Finegan, *Archaeology of the New Testament*, pp. 107–08; B. Bagatti, *The Church from the Gentiles in Palestine* (Jerusalem: Franciscan Press, 1971), pp. 203–06.

49. Finegan, *Archaeology of the New Testament*, pp. 100, 101.

50. *Encyclopedia of Archaeological Excavations in the Holy Land*, 2:617.

Ancient cave below
Eleona Church.

The mother of the emperor raised a stately structure on the Mount of
Olives also, in memory of his ascent to heaven who is the Savior of
mankind, erecting a sacred church and temple on the very summit of
the mount. And indeed authentic history informs us that in this very
cave the Savior imparted his secret revelations to his disciples.

Corresponding to Eusebius's statement, the Eleona Church was
built over a cave, the cave where Jesus is supposed to have taught
his disciples about the events of the Second Coming (Matt. 24). The
Bordeaux Pilgrim states that it was at the place "where before the
Passion the Lord taught the disciples." Aetheria says that "the cave
in which the Lord used to teach is there," and she used the name
Eleona for the church and locates it on the Mount of Olives. Another
cave there is called the Crypt of the Credo, since according to some
it was here that the apostles drew up the creed.

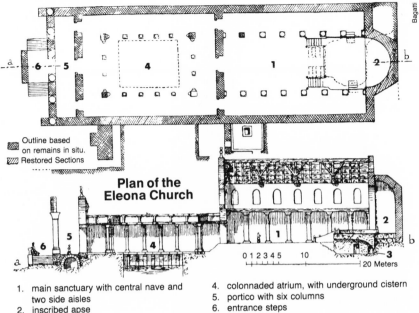

Bagatti

Outline based
on remains in situ.
Restored Sections

**Plan of the
Eleona Church**

0 1 2 3 4 5   10   20 Meters

1. main sanctuary with central nave and two side aisles
2. inscribed apse
3. cave under church
4. colonnaded atrium, with underground cistern
5. portico with six columns
6. entrance steps

In 1910 the Dominican Fathers began excavating the scanty remains of the Eleona Church. They projected that the church had a porch with six columns and three doors that led into a colonnaded courtyard under which there was a central large cistern. To the east of the courtyard were steps leading up to three additional doors which opened into the basilica itself. The central nave in the basilica was about 100 feet long, with two rows of columns and an aisle on either side. The central apse was at the east end. Small portions of mosaics were found in the north and south aisles and outside on the south side of the church. The church was similar in construction to the Church of the Nativity in Bethlehem.[51] The Eleona Church was destroyed by the Persians. In 1868 the present Church of the Pater Noster and the Church of the Creed were built on the site. The name Pater Noster (Our Father) is appropriate since the Lord's Prayer is inscribed in forty-six languages on wall panels there. The ancient cave and the east end of the Eleona Church with remains of its apse are under the Pater Noster Church.

About 230 feet north of the Eleona Church is the summit of the

51. B. Bagatti, *The Church from the Gentiles in Palestine*, pp. 184–88, figures 54–57.

Mount of Olives. Some believe it was here that Jesus ascended to heaven, but Scripture does not specify an exact location for this event. Luke 24:50–51 only says that he "led them out to the vicinity of Bethany . . . and was taken up into heaven." Nevertheless, early Christians believed that it was from the summit of the Mount of Olives that Jesus ascended, and it was here that the Inbomon Church, or the Church of the Ascension, was built. The Latin word *inbomon* is a translation of the Greek phrase meaning "upon the height." Aetheria mentions that on Palm Sunday the people went to the Church of Golgotha (the Holy Sepulchre), then to Eleona, and finally to the Inbomon, "that is, to the place from which the Lord ascended into heaven." The structure seems to have been there at least by the time of Jerome, who says that the pilgrim Paula passed through Tekoa and looked "upon the glistening cross of Mount Olivet from which the Savior made his ascension to the Father" (*Letter* 108.12). The inference is that this cross was affixed to the top of the

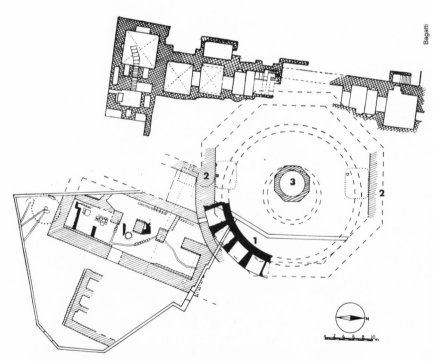

Plan of the Inbomon (Ascension) Church on Olivet

1. Wall G and black piers—A.D. fourth century—representing a circular church
2. Crusader walls (diagonal lines) representing the Crusader octagonal church
3. Crusader octagonal chapel now in the modern building walled in and capped with a dome

Levant

A recent structure over the Crusader Chapel at the ancient Inbomon Church.

Inbomon Church, and could be seen from Tekoa, 10 miles to the south. According to Peter the Iberian, the Inbomon Church was built by a devout lady named Pomenia.

The Inbomon Church was destroyed by the Persians. According to Arculf it was rebuilt into a large round church. In 1099 this church was destroyed by the caliph Abdel Hakim and rebuilt by the Crusaders in an octagonal form. Saladin, after his conquest in 1187, took over the church and restructured it into a mosque. Very little of the ancient remains of the Inbomon Church can be seen today. The area now is surrounded by an octagonal structure, 21 feet in diameter with a domed roof. This is used as a mosque. It was this small structure that the Crusaders used as a chapel.[52] However, then it was not walled up, and was open at the ceiling.

Southeast of the Inbomon Church is the site of Bethphage, identified by tradition as the place from which Jesus sent his disciples for the colt (Matt. 21:1; Mark 11:1; Luke 19:29). That this is the correct place for the biblical site may possibly be argued from the statement of Epiphanius Hagiopolita, a monk residing in Jerusalem (750–800). Basing his estimate on earlier tradition, he indicated that Bethphage was about 1,000 paces from the Inbomon Church. The site contains a Christian tomb, on which crosses are inscribed and in which were found fragments of Byzantine mosaic, but there is no evidence of a church. The modern Franciscan Chapel of Bethphage has been built on the site.[53] In the modern church one can see a portion of a fresco representing the two disciples with the donkey and the colt.

Southeast from Bethphage, down the eastern slope of the Mount of Olives, is the site of ancient Bethany and the modern village of al-'Azariyeh. The statements of the Bordeaux Pilgrim and Aetheria are important in determining the general location of Bethany. The Bordeaux Pilgrim says that Bethany was 1,500 paces from the Mount of Olives and Aetheria remarks that the place which she calls Bethany and Lazarium, was perhaps 1,500 paces or two (Roman) miles (less than two English miles) from Jerusalem, which geographically would place the site on the eastern slope of the Mount of Olives where the church and the modern town of al 'Azariyeh (the name has developed from Lazarium) are located.

The testimony of Eusebius is also important in identifying this site as the correct one for Bethany. He lists Bethany in this area as

52. Finegan, *Archaeology of the New Testament*, pp. 98–99; Bagatti, ibid., p. 66; V. C. Corbo, *Ricerche Archeologiche al Monte Degli Ulivi*, pp. 126–50.

53. Finegan, ibid., pp. 90–91; S. Saller and E. Testra, *The Archaelogical Setting of the Shrine of Bethphage* (Jerusalem: Franciscan Press, 1961), pp. 84–119.

the place where Jesus raised Lazarus and also says that "the place of Lazarus is still pointed out even until now." The phrase "is still pointed out" strongly suggests a long standing tradition. When Jerome revisited the Onomasticon, he changed the statement of Eusebius, adding "a church which has now been erected there points out his monument." Thus sometime after 330 and before 385, a church was built commemorating the raising of Lazarus from the dead.

Later Arculf (670) visited the site and describes what he calls "the little plain of Bethany surrounded by a large grove of olive trees where there is a great monastery and a great basilica built over the cave from which the Lord brought Lazarus, who had been dead four days, back to life".

The Franciscans who acquired the ancient site of Bethany in 1863 excavated there from 1949 to 1953, and found evidence that in general confirms the testimony of these early writers. At Bethany they have found remains of four ancient churches. The earliest, dating back to the fourth century, was 62 feet wide and up to 45 feet long, assuming the church extended an undetermined distance west into the area of the present day mosque. On this projection the excavators calculated that the first church was at least within 50 feet of the traditional tomb of Lazarus. The first church had lovely mosaic pavements featuring floral and geometric designs with small crosses (compare the similar mosaics at the Bethlehem Church of the Nativity), a nave, two side aisles, and an inscribed apse on the east. The second, a fifth-century church was built on the same basic plan as the first church. Its apse area extended 43 feet farther east than the fourth-century church. It is assumed that the second church extended west as far or farther into the area of the present day mosque. The indication on Saller's excavation plan of the Greek chapel adjoining the tomb of Lazarus, and the nearby mosque (another religious structure; quite frequently in Islamic periods churches were changed into mosques) may mean that the ancient churches extended west up to the Lazarus tomb. At any rate, a passageway connected the tomb on the west and the church on the east, however far apart they were. It was the second fifth-century church which Arculf no doubt saw. This church also had fine mosaic pavements with pleasing geometric designs, but without the presence of crosses whose use was prohibited by the Emperor Theodosius in 427. Also it did not have designs representing animal and human figures, a device so popular in the sixth century. The following factors may explain these omissions: a very strong earthquake occurred in 447 in the area and as a result the first church may have been severely damaged; around the middle of the fifth century, after

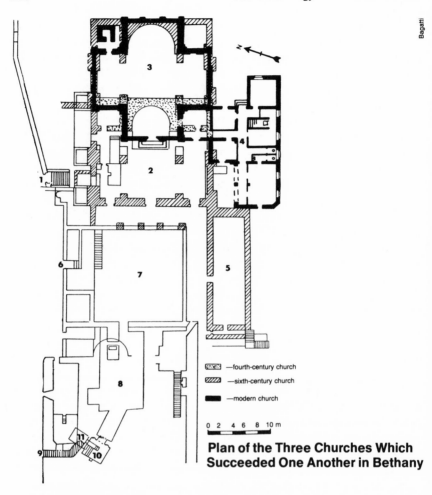

**Plan of the Three Churches Which
Succeeded One Another in Bethany**

1. present entrance from north
2. central nave of the fourth-century church and on a higher level that of the sixth-century church
3. apse of the sixth-century church
4. modern convent built over the medieval abbey
5. room with mosaic pavement of fourth century
6. present entry to mosque courtyard
7. mosque courtyard which previously was in part atrium and in part church of fourth century
8. below: room with cenotaph of Lazarus and entrance to tomb by corridor; above, apse of Crusader church erected over the tomb of Lazarus
9. present entrance (since sixteenth century) to tomb of Lazarus
10. Crusader period room erected in front of the tomb of Lazarus
11. tomb of Lazarus excavated in the rock and in covered stone work

the decree of Theodosius but prior to the time in the sixth century when animal and human figures were in common use, a second church was built over the first.

In the twelfth century the Crusaders modified the east end of the second church complex into the third church; a fourth church was built on the west end also in the twelfth century. Theodericus (1172) noted this when he wrote that there was a double church at Bethany: the one part the Church of St. Lazarus, and the other church honoring the burial place of Mary and Martha (by 1350 it also memorialized Simon the leper). This dual tradition may have been responsible for the two twelfth-century churches being built. The fourth church has continued to be known down to the present century; the crypt of the church is presently in the mosque (the upper part of the fourth church has long since disappeared). The third church on the east was known on into the seventeenth century and then again in the nineteenth century when the Bethany site was acquired by the Franciscans. A new Church of St. Lazarus also known as the Church of Mary and Martha, was built in 1954 on the east end of the complex. The present church, built in the form of a Greek Cross, preserves the apses of the first and second churches. Remains of the apse of the fourth-century church can be seen in the floor of the western arm. Parts of the apse of the second church are visible behind the altar in the eastern arm. Portions of mosaic pavement of the second church can be seen in the west side of the modern church, and farther to the west in the courtyard, the mosaic pavement of the first church is visible.

Particularly from a study of ancient clay lamps as well as other artifacts from the site, it is determined that the site was occupied from the sixth century B.C. to the fourteenth century; it flourished especially in the Byzantine period. In the vicinity of Bethany earlier Bronze Age tombs, Iron I and II pottery and other materials have been found.[54]

On the western slopes of the Mount of Olives, Clermont-Ganneau in 1870–74 investigated a tomb chamber called the Tomb of the Prophets. It contained extending fingerlike rooms with openings to a number of burial loculi. Other Byzantine burial areas have been found north of the Damascus Gate, in the Hinnom Valley, and at Mount Zion.

Indeed, the literary and archaeological evidence illustrates how intense were the building activities in Jerusalem in Byzantine times.

54. Ibid., pp. 92–94; Sylvester J. Saller, *Excavations at Bethany* (Jerusalem: Franciscan Press, 1949–1953), pp. 1–98; 131–37; 159, and figure 2.

The Early Islamic Periods
638–1099

In 639 the surging forces of Islam under their leader, Umar ibn el-Khattab, overwhelmed Jerusalem, and a new period in the city's history began. The new rulers were of the Islamic Umayyad dynasty. Although they were tolerant of Christians, this did not mean that the city would not change under their rule. There are no certain archaeological evidences yet of early Arab building activity along the western ridge of the city.[1] The only evidence of early Islamic activity Shiloh found at the City of David was in Area A 1 east of the Siloam Pool. Here Shiloh uncovered near ground level a number of walls and a stone pavement of the Islamic period. Islamic lamps and two Ayyubid coins found near the stone pavement indicate Islamic, and particularly Ayyubid, activity (late twelfth and early thirteenth centuries). Shiloh found that the structures related to the use of water installations there by Islamic peoples living farther up

---

1. Kenyon did not find any evidence of Islamic building activity at her Site L along the western wall in the Armenian Quarter until the Mamluk period following the Crusades (*Digging Up Jerusalem* [London: Ernest Benn, 1974], p. 280).

the Tyropoeon Valley.[2] However, there is considerable evidence of such activity in the temple area and to the south of the temple platform.

Today in the temple area—called in Arabic the Haram esh-Sherif (the Noble Sanctuary)—one sees two outstanding structures. The first, the Dome of the Rock, is located slightly to the west of center on the temple platform; the second, the al-Aqsa Mosque, is to be found at the south end of the platform a little west of center. These two structures are among the most important in all Islam. Abu-Hureira quotes Muhammad as saying: "Among all cities, Allah had singled out four for special esteem, and they are: Mecca—the city of all cities; Medina which is like a palm tree, Jerusalem which compares to an olive tree, and Damascus which is like the fig tree."[3] In citing Jerusalem, Muhammad is pointing to the temple area. This importance of Jerusalem for Islam is illustrated in the Muslim account which says Muhammad flew on his miraculous horse, Buraq, to this place by night, and from this place he ascended to heaven.

The reason for Islamic interest in the temple area is apparent when the historical background is examined. The Muhammedan caliphate was established in Mecca in 633, and following the death of Mohammad a struggle for power ensued among the Islamic leaders. Upon his rise to power, the caliph Umar ibn el-Khattab (634–644) conquered Jerusalem in 638; he showed intense interest in building a place of worship in the temple area. Christian witnesses speak of those early days of Islamic rule. Eutychius indicates that Umar cleared the sacred stone (the rock that is presently housed in the Dome of the Rock) which was cluttered with a great deal of debris. Umar also decided that the new place of worship should be so positioned that the stone would be located in the back of the structure. Theophanes (751–818) speaks of Umar's building the "temple" in Jerusalem but also reported that Umar encountered difficulty in his project. Umar was told that to succeed in his project he would have to remove the cross from the top of the Church of Ascension located on the Mount of Olives. So the cross was removed. The reference to a temple must be interpreted as referring to a place of prayer—that is, a mosque where prayer was made facing Mecca. Arculf confirms this when he calls Umar's temple a house of prayer, an equivalent to the Arabic word *masjid*, mosque, meaning literally a place of prostration. Arculf's words are expressive:

2. Yigal Shiloh, *Excavations at the City of David, I, 1978–1982* in *Qedem* (Jerusalem: Hebrew University, 1984), pp. 5, 31.
3. Benjamin Mazar, *The Mountain of the Lord* (Garden City, N.Y.: Doubleday, 1975), p. 261.

The al-Aqsa Mosque on the south end of the temple platform.

But in that renowned place where once the temple had been magnificently constructed, placed in the neighborhood of the wall from the east [i.e., the southern wall running from the southeast corner of the temple platform], the Saracens [i.e., people of Arabia] now frequent a quadrangular house of prayer, which they have poorly built, constructing it by raising planks and great beams on some remains of ruins; which house, it is said, can hold three thousand men at once.

The ruins on which the planks and beams were constructed may well refer to part of the Royal Portico, which suffered ruin at the time of the A.D. 70 destruction of Jerusalem. Assuming that this mosque was built on the southern end of the temple area, it would have had the sacred rock behind it (to the north) in the place Umar indicated it should be. We presume then that this structure was located in the same place as the al-Aqsa Mosque is today. Umar built this poorly constructed mosque with a wooden roof.[4]

In the eighth century this mosque was replaced by a better built structure, a work under the direction of the Umayyad caliph al-Walid (705–715), son of 'Abd al-Malik, who built the Dome of the Rock. Since the mosque was not as solidly built as the Dome of the Rock, it suffered earthquake damage from time to time and had to be rebuilt. Finegan lists three different rebuilding phases of the mosque following the al-Walid reconstruction. What could be called the third mosque was built by caliph al-Mansur (of the Abbasid Dynasty)

4. Kenyon, *Digging Up Jerusalem*, p. 275.

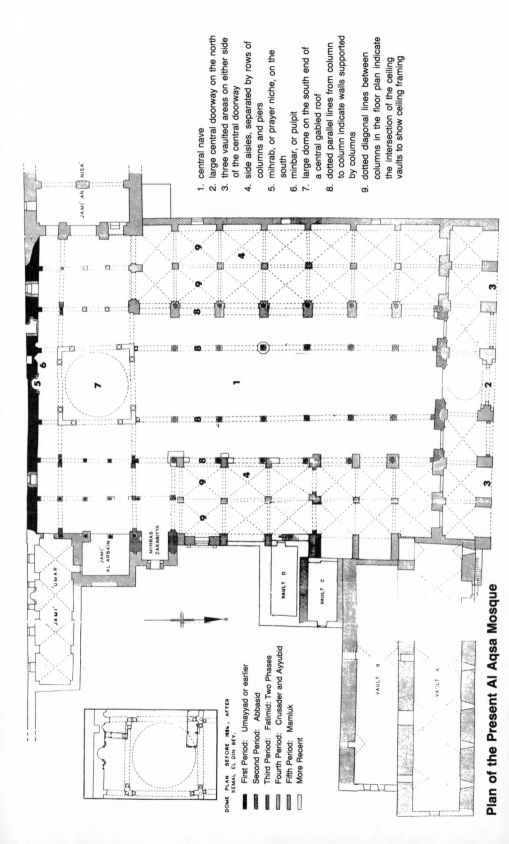

1. central nave
2. large central doorway on the north of the central doorway
3. three vaulted areas on either side of the central doorway
4. side aisles, separated by rows of columns and piers
5. mihrab, or prayer niche, on the south
6. minbar, or pulpit
7. large dome on the south end of a central gabled roof
8. dotted parallel lines from column to column indicate walls supported by columns
9. dotted diagonal lines between columns in the floor plan indicate the intersection of the ceiling vaults to show ceiling framing

JAMI AN NISÀ

JAMI' AN NISÀ

JAMI' AL ARBAÍN

MIHRAB ZAKARIYA

JAMI' 'UMAR

VAULT D

VAULT C

VAULT B

VA'ULT A

N

DOME PLAN BEFORE 1924, AFTER KEMAL EL DIN BEY.

First Period: Umayyad or earlier
Second Period: Abbasid
Third Period: Fatimid: Two Phases
Fourth Period: Crusader and Ayyubid
Fifth Period: Mamluk
More Recent

Plan of the Present Al Aqsa Mosque

about 771; the fourth by caliph al-Mahdi (Abbasid Dynasty) about 780; and the fifth by caliph al-Zahir (Fatimid Dynasty) in 1035.[5] R. W. Hamilton, in *The Structural History of the Aqsa Mosque*, indicates other times when changes, repairs, and additions to the mosque were made. Al-Mustansir reconstructed its facade in 1065. The Crusader Templar Knights used the mosque and added three central bays of the porch and other vaulted galleries (1099–1187). Among other things Saladin made repairs to the *mihrab*, the prayer niche (1187).[6] Further additions and restorations were made in the thirteenth and fourteenth centuries. This long history of building and repairs to the al-Aqsa Mosque covered seven hundred years, mainly under Islamic rule. The structure we see today is in the main the work of az-Zahir, and his mosque plan was probably much like that of his predecessor, al-Mahdi.[7]

Based on the description given by al-Muqaddasi[8] in 985 and on the archaeological remains of these earlier mosques, the plan of the mosque can be visualized as follows. The structure had a central nave and seven aisles on either side (it has only three aisles on each side today). There was a large central doorway on the north, with seven doors to the right and seven to the left. The inside aisles were separated by rows of columns and piers. The *mihrab*, or prayer niche, was characteristically located on the south end toward Mecca. There was a gabled roof over the central part of the structure, with a large dome rising behind it on the south end. The name of the mosque, Masjid al Aqsa, meaning "the Farthest Mosque," derives from the Qur'an account of Muhammad's journey to the seven heavens. He came from the sacred shrine, the Ka'bah at Mecca, to "the Farthest Mosque," the one in Jerusalem, the farthest place in that day for Arabs to worship.

The al-Aqsa Mosque today is located to the south of the Dome of the Rock at the south end of the temple platform. It is perpendicular to the south wall of the platform. Its dimensions are about 264 feet long and 180 feet wide, not including the side annexes. The north entrance includes a main arched entryway and a door. There are three vaulted areas to the north of the central entryway and three to the south.[9]

5. Jack Finegan, *The Archaeology of the New Testament: Life of Jesus and the Beginning of the Early Church* (Princeton: Princeton University Press, 1969), p. 124.

6. R. W. Hamilton, *The Structural History of the Aqsa Mosque* (London: Oxford University Press, 1949), p. 74.

7. Finegan, *Archaeology of the New Testament*, p. 124.

8. See Hamilton, *The Structural History of the Aqsa Mosque*, p. 72.

9. Finegan, *Archaeology of the New Testament*, p. 124.

Dome of the Rock.

The area of the *mihrab*, the prayer niche, is of particular interest. The *minbar*, or pulpit, consisting of a flight of stairs reaching a pulpit platform and located next to the *mihrab* was constructed in 1168 by an artist of Aleppo, Syria; it is carved in wood and inlaid with ivory and mother of pearl. The arched *mihrab* itself has marble columns on each side. It is part of a restoration at the south end of the mosque made by Saladin in 1187.[10]

The Dome of the Rock

The Dome of the Rock has erroneously been called the Mosque of Umar. It was not Umar but his successor, 'Abd al-Malik, Umayyad caliph of Damascus (685–705), who built a structure over the sacred rock. This structure was not intended as a mosque but a "place of witness"; it became known as the Dome (covering) of the (sacred) Rock—in Arabic, *Qubbet es-Sakhra,*—a sacred spot where the Herodi-

10. Ibid., p. 125.

an temple had earlier stood. Jacobson argues that the Arabs also constructed the Dome of the Chain structure, located just to the east of the Dome of the Rock, over the site of the ancient altar which stood in front of the temple.[11]

The plan of the Dome of the Rock is as follows: The circle with two interlocking squares inscribed within it is the governing principle of the plan as Creswell has pointed out.[12] Following this pattern the Dome of the Rock plan consisted of two such circles and sets of squares. The inner circle around the sacred rock set the circumference of the dome above it, and the points where the interlocking squares touched on the circumference of the circle determined the place where four massive piers were placed around the rock. Between the piers, three sets of marble columns interlocked with arches were constructed. The outer circle set the circumference for the eight corner points of the external walls of the Dome of the Rock. The sides of the two inner squares were projected to come out to eight points on the circumference of the outer circle, where they marked the midpoint in the construction of each of the eight segments of the external wall. Eight massive piers with two marble columns between each (sixteen in all) were constructed at the eight intermediate points inside the outer circle where the sides of the two squares intersected. Midpoint on every other one of the eight external walls entrances with small porches were built. Outside, below the dome and its exquisite frieze and sixteen windows placed around the drum, the roof gently sloped to the octagonal external walls. How exquisitely symmetrical! Possibly it was made, by the original design of 'Abd al-Malik, to resemble the plan of the Anastasis of the Church of the Holy Sepulchre (the inner diameters of the drums and the heights of the domes of both structures are almost identical).[13]

Around the inside wall of the Dome of the Rock an Arabic inscription gives the date for the basic structure; in our present calendar this date of 691 coincides with the reign of 'Abd al-Malik, who is credited with building the structure. The name of a later ruler, the Abbasid caliph al-Ma'mun (813–833), has been inserted into the inscription, probably because he later repaired the building. The extensive mosaic decorations in the interior of the building, mainly

11. David M. Jacobson, "Ideas Concerning the Plan of Herod's Temple," *Palestine Exploration Quarterly*, January–June (1980) pp. 33–40.

12. K. A. C. Creswell, *Early Muslim Architecture*, 2 vols (Oxford: Clarendon Press, 1932, 1940).

13. Jerry M. Landay, *Dome of the Rock* (New York: Newsweek 1972) pp. 67–71.

An interior view of Dome of the Rock,
featuring a close-up of one of the marble columns.

coming from the seventh century, and the inscription with its date
are the earliest existing examples of Muslim architectural embellishment; these examples are very well preserved. A major problem occurred in 1016, when the wooden dome fell in and had to be
reconstructed.

In 1189 Saladin added slabs of marble to the sides of the walls. In
1561 Suleiman the Magnificent, sultan of Turkey, whose name appears on the lower windows, added the exquisite blue, white, and

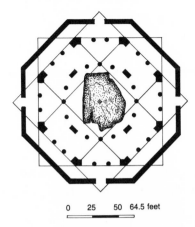

Plan of Dome of the Rock
The structure is composed of a series
of interlocking squares around the rock.
The inner pair of squares encompassing
the circle gives the circumference of the
dome above.

0   25   50 64.5 feet

green tile around the windows, as well as stained-glass windows. There are perforations at regular intervals in the windows and these are filled with colored glass. Passages from the Qur'an, written in a beautifully flowing style, extend around the structure like a Greek frieze.[14] The effect of all of this is aesthetically satisfying; it is a building of exquisite beauty. Doron Chen in a 1980 study relates the form and style of the Dome of the Rock to the tradition of classical art continued by a leading Byzantine school of architecture whose influence can be seen in the Justinian Church of the Nativity and the Church of the Holy Sepulchre.[15] In modern times a new aluminum dome with a copper covering was put up, and very recently the whole Dome of the Rock was refurbished by King Hussein of Jordan and rededicated in 1964.

A word should be said about the sacred rock now housed within the Dome of the Rock. The rock is about 58 feet long, 51 feet wide, and from 4 to 6½ feet high. Today there is an eye-level wooden fence around the rock to protect it. In past times channels and holes have been cut into the surface of the rock; one hole toward the south side penetrates through the stone into an underground cave. On the south side of the rock, stairs have been constructed for easy access down into the cave. The floors of the building are covered with lovely Persian rugs.

14. Finegan, *Archaeology of the New Testament*, p. 123; Jerry M. Landay, *Dome of the Rock* (New York: Newsweek, 1972), pp. 116–119.
15. Doron Chen, "The Design of the Dome of the Rock in Jerusalem," *Palestine Exploration Quarterly*, January–June, (1980) pp. 41–50.

Islamic Building South of the Temple Platform

Kenyon, at her Site C just south and east of the Church of the Holy Sepulchre, found a small amount of early Arab remains built over a layer of Byzantine material. Unfortunately, this material does not tell us much.[16]

On the other hand, the archaeological material from this period found directly south and southwest of the southern wall of the temple platform is revealing. Mazar argues that there is evidence here of an extensive Umayyad building, but Kenyon disputes the claim. Both have excavated in the area. In 1961–63 Kenyon in cooperation with Roland deVaux of the French École Biblique et Archéologique in Jerusalem, conducted excavations just inside the Dung Gate, near the southwest corner of the temple platform and in the southeast sector of the salient wall (the wall that runs south from the temple platform and then turns west). From her excavations she doubts that the three buildings claimed to be Umayyad structures are actually so. Rather, she thinks that what has been uncovered is actually the remains of two Byzantine buildings, one extending east-west and the other north-south. DeVaux concluded that these two structures were the remains of two hospices for foreign visitors and for the sick constructed by the emperor Justinian. Both DeVaux and Kenyon see in these structures a two-stage use: first as Byzantine hospices and then later in the Islamic period, first in the Umayyad Dynasty and then on into the Fatimid (969–1171). Argument for use in the Fatimid period comes from a glass weight with the name of Caliph al-Mustansir bi 'llah (1035–1094) which they found associated with a floor immediately above the earlier Islamic floor.[17]

Mazar, however, argues that the use of this building complex must be restricted primarily to the Umayyad period. It is reasonable to conclude that in this earlier Islamic era Arabs would build structures close to the site where the Dome of the Rock and the al-Aqsa Mosque were located. The results of Mazar's extensive excavation work to the west and south of the temple platform in the 1970s seem to support the contention that the Umayyads engaged in extensive building activity in this area.

South and southwest of the temple platform Mazar uncovered material which he says is in agreement with the plans of the Umayyad caliphs 'Abd al-Malik and his son al-Walid, who planned to make this area near the sacred shrines on the platform a religious

16. Kenyon, *Digging Up Jerusalem*, p. 275.
17. Ibid., pp. 276–77.

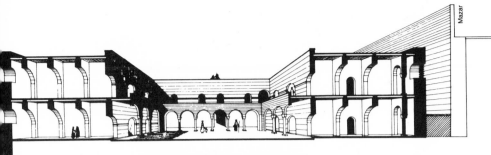

Umayyad Palace Building
Cross-section view facing west.

center. Mazar uncovered six buildings in the area. The most impressive was Building II, the largest structure, 280.5 by 313.5 feet, which had thick walls. Building II is located between the southern wall of the temple platform and the Turkish city wall. A paved street running east to the Double Huldah Gate separates this building from the temple platform. The structure seems to have been a Umayyad palace; it was a large square building with a central vaulted court, similar to the winter Umayyad palace near Jericho. The Jerusalem Umayyad palace did not have four corner towers like the palace in Jericho, but it had two stories. The upper one shows traces of a bridge linking its roof with the al-Aqsa Mosque for direct access through the southern wall of the temple platform which was on the south, or Mecca, side of al-Aqsa. Mazar remarks: "This fact leads our investigator [M. Ben-Dov] to believe that the palace was built by Caliph El-Walid I to allow him direct access to the mosque. Further evidence may be found in a Greek papyrus found at Aphro-

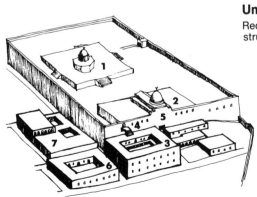

Umayyad Structures
Reconstruction of the Umayyad structures around the temple mount.
1. Dome of the Rock
2. al Aqsa Mosque
3. Umayyad Palace
4. bridge from the palace to the temple platform
5. double gate entrance to the temple platform below the al Aqsa Mosque
6. large building at the southwest corner of the temple platform
7. large building at the west wall of the temple platform

dito in Egypt which mentions artisans employed by the same caliph when he built a palace in Jerusalem."[18]

The Umayyad leaders restored the underground passage that led from the Double Huldah Gate north under what had been the Royal Colonnade, now the al-Aqsa Mosque. Mazar found that in building the palace the Umayyads reused large stone blocks and columns of earlier periods, particularly the Herodian period. The evidence for this is the palace's western wall, which looks similar to the Herodian platform wall. The Umayyads built directly over the earlier Byzantine buildings.

The Umayyad palace had a well-designed plan. Off the central vaulted courtyard were covered galleries on all four sides; the ceilings of the galleries rested both on the walls of parallel long halls and on a row of columns which surrounded the court. Of the structure's three important gates, the main one led to the east, a second to the west, and the third to the north toward the temple platform. The builders used fine geometric and floral designs.[19]

The Abbasid Dynasty succeeded the Umayyads in 750. Thereafter the important religious buildings on the temple platform were properly maintained, but quality of building to the south of the temple declined. The ruins found there, chiefly from the ninth century, show a poor quality of construction of the houses and other buildings; there was evidence of reuse of parts of Umayyad columns, capitals, and lintels. One reason for this decline may have been the fact that the headquarters of the Abbasid caliphate were now farther away, at Bagdad rather than Damascus; thus close attention could not be given to proper upkeep of the buildings. The devastating earthquake of 747–48 also added to the decline. As time went on, this area south of the temple platform became increasingly poor and sparsely populated. By the eleventh century the formerly prosperous Umayyad sector became the archaeological quarry for materials with which to repair the al-Aqsa Mosque and other buildings.

Mazar's excavations uncovered another building, located to the south of the palace, which may have been a hospice for wealthy visitors. West of the temple platform, to the southwest of Barclay's Gate, were found other colonnaded structures whose functions are not yet clear. A third large structure was located south of the temple platform and opposite the Triple Gate. Built at a lower level, it was surrounded by thick walls and contained a row of large columns. It may have been restored and used on into the Fatimid Dynasty (969–

18. Mazar, *The Mountain of the Lord*, p. 267.
19. Ibid., p. 268.

1171). This structure may be the Dar el-Akhmas mentioned in a document found in the ninth-century synagogue in Cairo, Egypt. That document mentions the southern gates of the temple platform and also a nearby structure called the Dar el-Akhmas; it calls the southern gates both by the Hebrew (Huldah Gate) and the Arabic (Ahwab el-Akhmas) names.[20]

On the eve of the Crusades, Nasir I-Khusrau in his *Diary of a Journey Through Syria and Palestine* indicates that many Muslims visited Jerusalem, especially those who were not able to visit Mecca. He also reports: "Christians and Jews came from all lands, the first to visit the Holy Sepulchre and the others the synagogues found there." According to his estimate, Jerusalem's population at this time was about 20,000.[21]

20. Ibid., pp. 270–71.
21. Ibid.

11

Crusader, Mamluk, and Turkish Jerusalem
1099–1918

Since much of what we see today in the Old City of Jerusalem can be attributed to Crusader, Mamluk, and Turkish activity, it is well to consider these three very different but interconnected periods together.

Crusader Jerusalem (1099–1187)

In July, 1099 Islamic Jerusalem fell to the European Crusaders. The effect on the city was dramatic. The invading attackers stormed the city and broke through the Islamic defense lines at Herod's Gate, located some 985 feet west of the northeast corner of the present north wall. Once the Crusaders were in control, their Latin Kingdom (as it was called) maintained its hold over the city for almost a hundred years.

The Crusader influence produced a number of changes, including change in the architecture of the city. An archaeological study of the remains of Crusader Jerusalem shows some of those physical and social changes.

277

Because of their intense interest in the holy sites, the Crusaders concentrated their attention on the temple area. But they did little work on the Herodian platform itself. One exception involved the Double Huldah Gate on the southern wall which the Crusaders walled up. Then they opened up a small gate, called the Single Gate, located toward the southeastern corner of the temple platform. They did this in order to gain access to the vaulted chambers under the

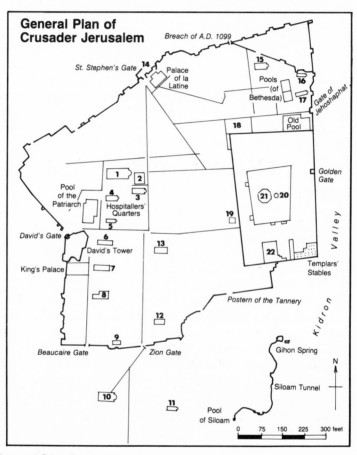

General Plan of Crusader Jerusalem

Churches and Other Religious Structures

1. Church of the Holy Sepulchre	9. House of Annas	17. Church of St. Anne
2. Bishop's House or Monastery	10. St.Mary of Mt. Zion	18. Church of the Repose
3. St. Mary la Latine	11. St. Peter in Gallicantu	19. Church of St. Giles
4. St. Mary la Grande	12. Church of St. Peter ad Vincula	20. Church of Jacob
5. Church of St. John the Baptist	13. Church of St. Martin	21. Temple of the Lord
6. Church of St. James	14. Church of St. Abraham	22. Templum Solomonis
7. St. Thomas Church	15. Church of St. Mary Magdalene	
8. St. James Cathedral	16. Church of St. Bartholomew	

The Church of the Holy Sepulchre
as pictured on a coin
dating ca. 1200–1225.

southeastern corner of the temple platform, now popularly known as Solomon's Stables. They used these underground galleries for stables for many years; the rings in the stone pillars used for tethering horses and camels, and the mangers found in the galleries, indicate this. These galleries, 40 feet below the surface of the temple platform, include 13 rows of vaults, 30 feet high, with 88 piers. The lower part of some of the piers shows Herodian stonework while the upper part displays Crusader rebuilding.[1] The Ophel area just to the south of the temple platform had been well inhabited in the Islamic period, but in the Crusader period it was depopulated and abandoned.

The Crusaders took over the Dome of the Rock and changed it into a church, the Church of the Knights Templar. They called it Templum Domini. Other changes included a fence around the structure and Christian crosses affixed to the dome and within the building.[2] They covered the sacred rock with marble slabs and placed an altar on it. The Crusaders also covered the interior walls with mosaics with Scripture verses and put Latin inscriptions on the external walls of the structure. In addition, they built an Augustinian monastery north of the Dome of the Rock and placed a number of altars in the court area of their temple.[3] At first the Crusaders used the al-Aqsa Mosque as the palace of Baldwin I, first Latin king of Jerusalem. Later it became the headquarters of the Knights of the Temple (Templars) and was called Solomon's Temple. They altered

1. Jack Finegan, *The Archaeology of the New Testament; The Life of Jesus and the Beginning of the Early Church* (Princeton: Princeton University Press, 1969), p. 126; Benjamin Mazar, *The Mountain of the Lord* (Garden City, N.Y.: Doubleday, 1975), pp. 274, 275.

2. Benjamin Mazar, *The Mountain of the Lord*, p. 275.

3. Meron Benvenisti, *The Crusaders in the Holy Land* (Jerusalem: Israel Universities Press, 1970), p. 70; Joshua A. Prawer, *The Latin Kingdom of Jerusalem* (London: L. Weidenfeld and Nicolson, 1972), p. 171.

the mosque by constructing the central bays of the porch and by building other vaulted annexes.[4] These additions survive in the area of the present Women's Mosque and the extension that goes into the Islamic Museum. The importance of the building to the Crusaders is seen in the fact that, with the Church of the Holy Sepulchre and the Citadel, it was represented on a coin of Baldwin I.[5]

The magnificent structure of al-Aqsa was ideal for the palatial residence of the first Latin king of Jerusalem. "The royal palace overlooked the ancient city of David, with the valley of Kidron below and the Mount of Olives beyond . . . . To the hardened warriors of France it must have seemed like a fable of the marvelous East come true."[6]

Although at the beginning of the Latin Kingdom, Baldwin I had his palace at the al-Aqsa Mosque, the Crusaders' center of authority and military power was the Citadel on the west wall of the city (the site of Herod's three towers). There is much in the Crusader defenses that is similar to the defenses constructed by Herod the Great many centuries earlier. In his excavations at the Citadel in 1934–40, C. N. Johns found remains of several Crusader buildings in levels above those representing the towers and fortifications of the Hasmonean and Herodian periods. The most famous Crusader tower at the Citadel is the one at the northeastern angle which is erroneously called the Tower of David, a misnomer probably based on the fact that Arculf in 670 called the adjoining gate the Gate of David.[7] This tradition was possibly carried over into the Islamic period when a *mihrab* (place of prayer), constructed on top of the large solid plinth of the Herodian tower, was considered the *mihrab* of David.[8]

More recently Magan Broshi found at the site remains of the southern end of the Crusader royal palace, the Curia Regis, constructed above Herod's palace;[9] Broshi found vaulted silos and wells in an area thought to be the basement of the palace and discovered on one of the walls a sculptured double cross (cross of Anjou).[10] It was to this site that the Crusader palace was moved from the al-

4. R. W. Hamilton, *The Structural History of the Aqsa Mosque* (London: Oxford University Press, 1949), p. 74.
5. Mazar, *The Mountain of the Lord*, p. 276.
6. Joshua Prawer, *The Crusader's Kingdom* (New York: Praeger, 1972), p. 110.
7. Finegan, *Archaeology of the New Testament*, p. 134; Mazar, *The Mountain of the Lord*, p. 277.
8. Benvenisti, *The Crusaders in the Holy Land*, p. 52.
9. Mazar, *The Mountain of the Lord*, p. 277.
10. Prawer, *The Crusaders' Kingdom*, p. 111, n. 2.

Aqsa Mosque, which by then was in a sparsely populated area of the city. This new palace, which lay in the area partly occupied today by the Armenian Patriarch's Garden,[11] was certainly connected with the Citadel, the center of military power. The new palace site was indeed important and impressive as far as location was concerned.

> To the north lay the Citadel, while on the west the palace overlooked the deep ditch which cut off the city from the surrounding plain, which extended to the cemetery of Mamillah. This was the traditional burial place of the city and under the Crusaders became the cemetery for the clergy of the Holy Sepulchre. On the east, facing the city within the walls, it overlooked the Greek monastery of St. Sabas and the Armenian monastery of St. James.[12]

It is difficult to postulate exactly what the Crusader palace here looked like.

To the north and west of their administrative center at the Citadel the Crusaders built a large square tower (115.5 by 115.5 feet) called the Tancred Tower at the juncture of the north and west walls of the Old City.[13]

With high religious motivation the Crusaders centered their attention on the churches of Jerusalem. Both Moslems and Jews were now forbidden to settle in the city.

Of course, the religious structure of foremost interest to the Crusaders was the Church of the Holy Sepulchre. In 1009 the structure had been destroyed by the caliph al-Hakim. Later it was rebuilt by the Byzantine emperor Constantine IX Monomachus (1042–54), who capped the church with a timber-domed rotunda. In 1099 the Crusaders found the wooden-roofed rotunda still there, and also the crypt of St. Helena on a lower level; the rock of Calvary was still visible to the south and east of the Rotunda. But the basilica was in ruins. The Crusaders built a basilica to the east of the rotunda and brought the rotunda and the rock all under one roof. From the main level of this church they built a stairway down into the crypt of St. Helena, which they made into a chapel. They changed the main entrance from the east side to the south side of the church and constructed a triumphal arch there. This was located across the court which was just in front of the rock of Calvary, and to the west

11. Benvenisti, *The Crusaders in the Holy Land*, p. 54.
12. Prawer, *The Crusaders' Kingdom*, p. 111.
13. Mazar, *The Mountain of the Lord*, p. 277.

of the entrance was a bell tower. Although there have been repairs and some modifications, this is the church that one sees today.[14]

The dimensions of the Crusader Church of the Holy Sepulchre were those generally found in Crusader churches. Prawer indicates that as a rule Crusader churches were about 115 feet long by 66 feet wide, measuring from the entrance to the apse. This could vary from an elongated quadrangle to almost a square. There were generally a nave and two side aisles; the aisles ended at the eastern end of the nave with three apses; the two side apses (north and south) were often smaller than the main central one. "The nave was divided from the aisles by a row of piers, usually massive and cruciform pillars with inserted round half-columns. The piers, which form a double arcade running from east to west on both sides of the nave, supported the arches of the nave and of the aisles on their capitals." The Crusader churches, however, did not have true cruciform transepts.[15] Following Coüasnon's plans, the Crusader Church from west to east included a rotunda and aedicule, a north-south transept, calvary, an apse, crypt of Helena, cloisters, and a monastery of rooms all around for a length of about 771 feet. The basilica area itself (including the apse, the area of Helena's crypt and the cloisters) would have been about 430 feet long and about 200 feet wide,[16] somewhat longer and wider than the general dimensions of crusader churches.

Other important Crusader churches in Jerusalem include the Basilica of St. Anne, located at the Pool of Bethesda. We have already seen that the earlier Bethesda Church there had probably been destroyed by the Persians in 614. The chapel which was built in its place was presumably also in ruins when the Crusaders came. The new Basilica of St. Anne built by the Crusaders was Romanesque in style, with a nave and two side aisles; it had three apses on its east end, a main central apse and a smaller one on either side. This structure was built in close proximity to the location of the fifth/ sixth-century Basilica of St. Mary; Saewulf in 1102 testifies to this:

> From the temple of the Lord you go towards the north to the Church of St. Anne, the mother of blessed Mary, where she lived with her

---

14. Finegan, *Archaeology of the New Testament*, pp. 171–72; Mazar, *The Mountain of the Lord*, p. 278; Prawer, *The Crusaders' Kingdom*, pp. 425–26; Charles Coüasnon, *The Church of the Holy Sepulchre in Jerusalem* (London: Oxford University Press, 1974), pp. 19, 20, 55–59; plate X; John Wilkinson, "The Church of the Holy Sepulchre," *Biblical Archaeology*, vol. 31.4 (July, August, 1978), p. 12.

15. Prawer, *The Crusaders' Kingdom*, pp. 419, 421.

16. Coüasnon, *The Church of the Holy Sepulchre in Jerusalem*, plate X.

husband, and where she brought forth her most beloved daughter
Mary, the savior of all the faithful. Near there is the Probatica [sheep]
Pool which is called in Hebrew Bethsayda, having five porches.

As for the Basilica of St. Mary, *The Anonymous of Piacenza* identifies
it as built on one of the porticoes of the Pool of Bethesda. Another
document (*Deeds of the Franconians Conquering Jerusalem*, 1108),
which gives an account of the Crusader conquest, states that the
Crusaders found the remains of the old pool with five porches "in
front of" the church. Thus we conclude that the Church of St. Anne
was built to the east of the Pool of Bethesda. The grotto under the
church is said to be the place where Mary was born. Today the
modern Church of St. Anne is built on the same site east of the pool.
At the pool the Crusaders also built a chapel over the ruins of the
earlier chapel and Byzantine church.[17]

Mention has already been made of the Church on Mount Zion
which later became the "great basilica" of which Arculf speaks. It
also was in ruins when the Crusaders came. They rebuilt it and
called it the Church of St. Mary, or the Church of Zion. The same
building complex contained the so-called Tomb of David and an
altar marking the spot where Mary was supposed to have died.
These were located in the lower story of the building, and the traditional Last Supper room was located in the upper story; this is at
the site of the Basilica of the Dormition.[18]

The ruins of the very interesting Crusader Church of St. Mary,
built by the Teutonic Knights (also called St. Mary of the Germans),
came to light through the excavations of N. Avigad in the Upper
City on the western hill. This building was located west of the southwestern corner of the temple platform. It had two wings, one the
church and the other a hospital or hospice for pilgrims. The structure has now been restored. Another hospital or hospice was built at
the site called the Muristan (a Persian word meaning hospital).
What is called the Muristan today is mainly an area lined with
shops located just to the south of the Church of the Holy Sepulchre.
Its dimensions are about 510 feet by 450 feet. It had been the site of
the Roman forum. In this area three churches had existed in earlier
times: the Church of St. Mary Latina in the northeastern corner of
the Muristan (today the site of the German Lutheran Church of the
Redeemer), the Church of St. Mary Magdalene just to the south of

17. Finegan, *Archaeology of the New Testament*, p. 145.
18. Finegan, *Archaeology of the New Testament*, p. 151; Mazar, *The Mountain of the Lord*, p. 278.

the Holy Sepulchre and the Church of St. John the Baptist in the southwest corner of the site. About the middle of the eleventh century Italian merchants restored the Church of St. Mary Latina which served as a monastery to care for the pilgrims until later in the eleventh century when it became too small. Another hospice in honor of St. John the Baptist was built. When the Crusaders came, they used this hospice of the Church of St. John the Baptist as the basis for their monastery and hostel-infirmary for pilgrims. They called it the Hospital of St. John. Its buildings were constructed in an L-shaped form and occupied the western and southern side of the Muristan square. Theodoric in the middle of the twelfth century describes the area:

> And here, on the south side of the church, stands the Church and Hospital of St. John the Baptist. As for this, no one can credibly tell another how beautiful its buildings are, how abundantly it is supplied with rooms and beds and other material for the use of the poor and sick people,—Indeed, we passed through this place, and were unable by any means to discover the number of sick people lying there; but we saw that the beds numbered more than one thousand.[19]

The Crusaders built hospitals, monasteries, and churches throughout the Jerusalem area. In the northern part of the Old City to the east of the Damascus Gate, in the area called the Muslim Quarter, they built the Jacobite Church of St. Mary Magdalene. It became a mosque and eventually was demolished; a school is now built on the site (al-Milawiya). The Church of St. Agnes was constructed near the Damascus Gate; today it is the Mosque of Milawiya. This quarter also included the Churches of St. Elias and St. Bartholomew.[20]

In the 1964–65 excavations by Crystal Bennett and Basil Hennessey at the Damascus Gate, ruins were found which seem to be the remains of the Church of St. Abraham. In an area outside the present gate, between the gate and the western tower, these excavations uncovered evidence of a rather simply built Christian chapel. Fragments of paintings were found, some still attached to the walls. This chapel, possibly the Church of St. Abraham, was located in Crusader times within the north wall of the city at a time when the Damascus Gate entrance jutted out to the north of the earlier Ro-

---

19. Benvenisti, *The Crusaders in the Holy Land*, pp. 58, 59. See also Finegan, *Archaeology of the New Testament*, p. 137.
    20. Ibid., pp. 71, 73.

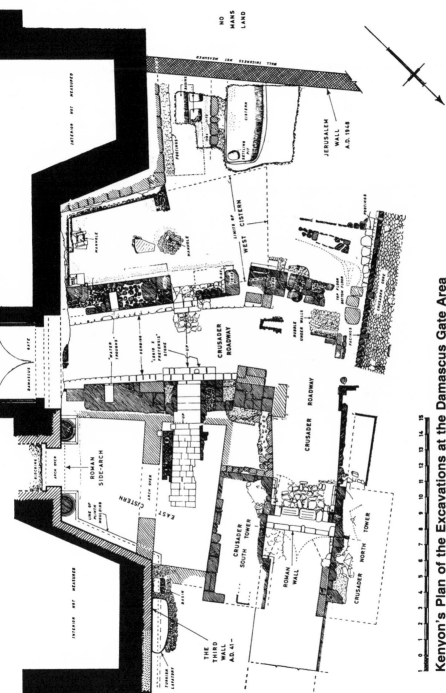

Kenyon's Plan of the Excavations at the Damascus Gate Area

Ruins of the Ramban synagogue.

man gate. The entrance complex then made a right angle turn so that the outer gate faced east.[21]

Kenyon feels that there is a distinct possibility that the Crusader city wall extended along the southern part of the western ridge. She also suggests the city wall then angled northeast to include a section of the city wall excavated by Bliss and Dickie, which section shows characteristic Crusader dressing. Kenyon thinks the Crusader city wall continued to angle northeast toward the southwest corner of the temple platform.[22]

Crusader churches were also constructed in the Armenian Quarter: the Armenian Church of St. James (their cathedral church); the Church of St. Thomas (now in ruins); the Greek Church and Hospice of St. Sabas (today a dwelling); the Church of James Intercisus (later the mosque of al-Yaqubiya); and the Church of St. Mark. The latter is now Syrian Orthodox and is situated on the boundary between the Armenian Quarter and the Jewish Quarter. In what is now called the Jewish Quarter the Crusaders built the Church of St. Martin (a carpenter's shop today), St. Paul's Church (location unknown), and the Church of St. Peter in Chains. The latter was situated between the Hurva Synagogue and the mosque on its south; this was possibly the site where the Ramban Synagogue was built.

21. Kathleen Kenyon, *Digging Up Jerusalem*, (London: Ernest Benn, 1974) pp. 278–79 and Figure 40.

22. Ibid., p. 23, Figure 6; p. 259, Figure 44; pp. 268, 279.

The Christian Quarter contained, among others, the Church of St. Chariton (later the Mosque of al-Khanqa), the Church of St. George, and the Church of St. Catherine.[23] In the Crusader period Jerusalem could rightly be called a city of churches.

The Crusaders were also active in building churches and monasteries on the Mount of Olives. They found in ruins the Church of St. Mary in the area of the Garden of Gethsemane, built about the fifth century. They rebuilt the church and beside it constructed a large monastery, the Abbey of St. Mary of the Valley of Jehoshaphat. In the 1937 excavations at the site, pavements and masonry found there gave evidence of the Crusader reconstruction. This monastery was wealthy and had a substantial endowment of land.[24] Nearby, on the site of the earlier Gethsemane Church, which commemorated Jesus' place of prayer in the garden, the Crusaders constructed a church partly to the south side of, and on an angle southeast from, the earlier fourth-century church.[25] The old Inbomon Church, the Church of the Ascension, on the summit of the Mount of Olives, was also rebuilt by the Crusaders and functioned as an Augustinian monastery; it was constructed in an octagonal rather than circular form, with an inner chapel left open to the sky.

The traditional location of Bethphage today, on the eastern slope of the Mount of Olives, is the one accepted by the Crusaders. The evidence for this is seen on a stone found in 1877 at the site which indicates Byzantine material. It displays inscriptions and depicts two disciples untying the donkey and its colt.[26] One can see this stone today in the Franciscan Chapel of Bethphage. At Bethany, farther down on the southeastern slope of the Mount of Olives, excavators have found evidence of Crusader rebuilding of the Church of St. Lazarus on the earlier Byzantine church. The Crusaders also built another church on the west end of the Bethany complex, a church which had a crypt connected to the tomb of Lazarus. Later the crypt became the el-Uzeir Mosque, which is still used today. The entrance to the tomb was reoriented to the north. South of the Bethany churches a large monastery or abbey about 205 by 164 feet shows evidence of Crusader stonemasons' marks, crosses, five-pointed stars, and letters of the alphabet.[27]

23. Benvenisti, *The Crusaders in the Holy Land*, pp. 71, 73.

24. Ibid., p. 73.

25. Finegan, *Archaeology of the New Testament*, p. 108; B. Bagatti, *The Church from the Gentiles in Palestine*, tr. E. Hoade (Jerusalem: Franciscan Press, 1971), pp. 205–06; M. Benvenisti, *The Crusaders in the Holy Land*, p. 73.

26. Ibid., p. 91.

27. Ibid., p. 95; S. Saller, *Excavations at Bethany* (Jerusalem: Franciscan Press 1957), pp. 6, 7, 67–71, 97–100.

Crusader Jerusalem and its environs was a Christian community of churches and monasteries. But all this was to come to an abrupt end in 1187, when the city was taken by Saladin. To be sure, for two short periods, 1229–39 and 1243–44, Jerusalem was again under the control of the Crusaders. Finally in 1247 Muhammedan Mamluks from Egypt conquered the area.

The Ayyubid and Mamluk Periods (1187–1516)

On October 2, 1187, Jerusalem fell to the Ayyubid ruler Saladin. Saladin took down the golden crosses on top of the Dome of the Rock and the al-Aqsa Mosque. He restored the *mihrab* (prayer niche) at the southern wall of al-Aqsa and made other repairs on the structure. One of the later Ayyubid sultans brought from Damascus for the mosque a lovely ebony minbar (pulpit) inlaid with ivory and mother-of-pearl.

After the brief periods when the Crusaders again held the city, Jerusalem finally fell again to the Egyptian Mamluk sultan. For 270 years the Mamluks ruled Jerusalem and the area through their governor in Damascus.

In their reconstruction at the temple platform and the nearby region the Mamluks introduced a number of architecture features that characterized Islamic building styles. These included: vaulted prayer niches, with the *mihrab* facing Mecca at the southern end, minarets, and installations to provide water for ritualistic purification.

Between the thirteenth and fifteenth centuries the Mamluk sultans built a number of beautiful multicolored buildings on the north and west sides of the temple platform. These buildings contained madrasas (colleges) which were surrounded by lovely cloisters. Mamluk architecture is well known for its alternating red and white building technique and its conch niches.

Mazar gives several examples of typical and extant Islamic art from the Mamluk period:

The Madrasa Arghuniyeh on Bab el-Hadid street (leading from the west to the Temple area). Facing it is the Muzhiriyeh, which has an entrance in a recessed trefoil arch with eight rows of stalactites.

The Madrasa Jauliyeh (named for Sanjar el-Jauliyeh, who supervised the work on Jerusalem and Hebron Islamic sanctuaries and who oversaw the work on the Dome of the Rock in 1319). This structure was located in the area of the Antonia fortress. The site is now occupied by the Omariya School, and is also the location of the first station of the Cross, from which the Franciscans make their weekly procession to the Church of the Holy Sepulchre.

The Madrasa Tankiziyeh was built by Emir Tankiz of Damascus over Wilson's Arch at the western wall in 1329. It is a two-story structure with a conch-shell niche over the doorway; it was constructed in the form of a cross and had accompanying courts and fountains. In later times it became a hostel for important officials, and was used in Turkish times as a high court.

Bab el-Qattanin, the Gate of Mohammed (1336), was also built by Tankiz; it was located just west of the Dome of the Rock at about the middle of the western wall. This exquisite gate leads west into the medieval Market of the Cotton Merchants, a street built of large ashlars taken from ancient walls and courts of this part of the temple area.[28]

At her Site L, along the western wall, Kenyon found excellent examples of fourteenth-century Mamluk buildings. The buildings showed evidence of vaulted halls with rooms extending off to the sides. The plan was that of an Arab Souk, or bazaar. This set of buildings may have been related to the hostel of the Hebron people, who, records of the Armenian Patriarchate indicate, are known to have lived in the area.[29]

After the capture of Jerusalem by Saladin, the Jewish population steadily grew; the core of Jewish residents congregated in the Upper City. This impetus toward Jerusalem was enhanced by Rabbi Moses ben Nahman (Nahmanides). He immigrated to Jerusalem in 1267 and inspired other Jews with his vivid writings concerning the desolate condition of the city. He built the first medieval synagogue in Jerusalem in 1267, reusing, as he says, an abandoned Crusader building.[30] That portion of the western wall of the temple platform known as the Wailing Wall, of importance since the Talmudic days, took on added importance for the Jews in this period.

During the centuries of Mamluk rule Christian and Jewish pilgrims continued to flock to Jerusalem, counting this an important part of religious worship. In the midst of this activity the plight of the city became increasingly desperate. Rabbi Obadiah of Bartenura, who came in 1488, said, "Jerusalem is almost wholly desolate and possesses no protective walls. No more than 4,000 of its inhabitants live in houses of their own and only seventy Jewish families, wretchedly poor, have remained."[31] Further evidence of the dilapidated condition of the city is seen in the archaeological findings at

28. Mazar, *The Mountain of the Lord*, p. 283.
29. Kenyon, *Digging Up Jerusalem*, p. 280.
30. Prawer, *The Crusaders' Kingdom*, pp. 246, 247; Mazar, *The Mountain of the Lord*, p. 284.
31. Mazar, *The Mountain of the Lord*, p. 286.

the Damascus Gate. Here the Mamluk entrance seems to have been built between remaining fragments of the Crusader walls and over the accumulated rubble there.[32]

The days of Mamluk rule came to an end near the beginning of the sixteenth century.

The Turkish Period (1517–1918)

The end of Mamluk hegemony over Jerusalem came in 1517 with conquest by Selim, the Ottoman Turkish sultan who rose in power over all the Middle East. In the centuries that followed, the Seljuk Turks generally were not able to put new life into the culture of the area. The one exception was Suleiman I, the Magnificent (1520–66), the son of Selim, who gave the Old City basically the look it has today.

One of the major tasks Suleiman set for himself was to rebuild the complete circuit of the city walls (1539–42); these followed the same course seen today. He built the walls on the foundations of those of earlier times. He also restored the Citadel as a military garrison, repaired the aqueducts bringing spring water into the city, and he rebuilt the gates. Peters cites Chelebi's enumeration of the rebuilt city gates in Ottoman times as follows (reading clockwise, from the southeastern corner): on the south side, Dung Gate and David's Gate or Sion Gate; on the west side the Jaffa Gate (known then as Abraham's Gate); on the north side, the Damascus Gate (also called Gate of the Iron War Mace) and the Sahira Gate (known by the Franks as Herod's Gate); on the east side, St. Stephen's Gate (known as the Gate of the Tribes) and the Golden Gate (called "an exposed double iron gate").[33] An inscription dating to the year 1538– 39 attributes the building of the Jaffa Gate to Suleiman.[34]

Mazar gives the lengths of the Turkish Old City walls as follows: southern wall (facing Mount Zion and Ophel), 3,700 feet; western wall, into which the present-day Citadel is built (facing West Jerusalem), 2,900 feet; northern wall (facing modern east Jerusalem), 4,270 feet; eastern wall (facing the Kidron Valley), 2,540 feet.[35]

32. Kenyon, Digging Up Jerusalem, p. 280.
33. F. E. Peters, Jerusalem (Princeton: Princeton University Press, 1985), pp. 480; 614, notes 6 and 8; See Chelebi, Evliya Tshelibi's Travel in Palestine, trans. St. H. Stephan (Jerusalem: Ariel Publishing House, 1980.)
34. Mazar, The Mountain of the Lord, p. 287; Kenyon, Digging Up Jerusalem, p. 280.
35. Mazar, The Mountain of the Lord, p. 287.

Portion of the east wall of the Walled City of Jerusalem. Note the upper parts in the wall added during the Turkish period. (Bedouin tents are in the foreground.)

Suleiman also used his building talents in embellishing the Dome of the Rock; he replaced the old mosaics on the outer surface of the building with faience tiles of blue, white, green, and yellow. The technique of coloring the tile was the well-guarded secret of Armenian craftsmen from Anatolia who were engaged in the work. In the nineteenth century the sultan Mahmud II (1808–39) regilded the surfaces on the inside of the Dome of the Rock and restored the tiles and marble on the outside.[36] After the destructive earthquake of 1545 the Church of the Holy Sepulchre was fully repaired.

Despite these building activities Jerusalem continued in its deteriorating condition. It did not attract expanding numbers of residents. According to estimates, in the early nineteenth century Jerusalem's Christian, Jewish, and Arab population totaled only 12,000; the city lacked many of the basic services needed for a progressing society. As the nineteenth century progressed, however, basic improvements were made in the road system and the water supply. In due course the flow of pilgrims increased, new churches and hos-

36. Mazar, *The Mountain of the Lord*, pp. 287–88; Finegan, *Archaeology of the New Testament*, p. 123.

pices were built, the Jewish community expanded, and many of the middle-class Arabs of Jerusalem began to move out of the Old City and build more substantial dwellings in the surrounding area.[37]

The modern twentieth-century Old City of Jerusalem looks much the same as it did centuries ago. Much excavation is in progress in and around the Old City, giving us the expectation that in the future we may have even better understanding of ancient Jerusalem.

37. Mazar, *The Mountain of the Lord*, pp. 288–91; Ruth Kark and Shimon Landman, "The Establishment of Muslim Neighborhoods," *Palestine Exploration Quarterly*, July–Dec., 1980, pp. 113–35.

Table of Equivalents

Length, Distance

1 meter	= 39.37 inches
1 meter	= 3.28 feet
1 kilometer	= .62137 miles
1 mile	= 1609.35 meters

Area

1 hectare	= 2.47104 acres
1 square meter	= 1.19598 square yards
1 square yard	= .836131 square meters
1 acre	= 4046.9 square meters
1 square mile	= 2.59 square kilometers

Weight

1 kilogram	= 2.20462 pounds
1 gram	= .0353 ounces
1 metric ton	= 1000 kilograms

Volume

1 liter	= 1.05668 quarts
1 quart	= .94636 liters
1 gallon	= 3.78543 liters
1 pint	= .95 liters

Glossary of Technical Terms

abacus Uppermost member of the capital of a column.

acropolis Official or royal part of an ancient city, often an elevated portion of the city.

acroterion (pl. *acroteria*) Ornament or figure at the corner or apex and lower angles of a pediment.

aedicula Decorated niche in a wall or a small chapel.

agora Marketplace or public square of an ancient Hellenistic city.

alabaster Hard translucent variety of gypsum or calcite, often white and translucent and sometimes banded.

amphitheater Building with seats all around the arena or central area; for gladiatorial shows and other public performances.

amphora Large two-handled, open-mouthed vase, with an oval body tapering toward the base; commemorative for victors of the games or used for oil, wine, etc. Sometimes quite large.

amphoriskos Miniature amphora.

anta (pl. *antae*) Slightly projecting pier or pilaster which terminates the side wall of a cella or temple building; columns standing between two antae are spoken of as "in antis."

antefix Decorative upright ornament at the eaves of a tiled roof; placed sometimes also along the top of the ridge of the roof.

apse Vaulted semicircular or polygonal recess of a building, particularly of the end of a church at the other end from the main entrance. Sometimes a church had three apses.

architrave (or *epistyle*) Lowest member of a classical entablature: a lintel member or beam carried from the top of one capital of a building to another; in ionic entablature the architrave is in three parts (also called *fascia*), with each succeeding horizontal member projecting farther out than the one below.

arcosolia A tomb structure having an arched recess containing a bench or bed below the arch. See *loculus*.

area Sector of units of excavation and consists of a group of closely related, usually contiguous, squares. Areas are numbered with capital letters, e.g., Area A, Area B, etc., and squares numbered with Arabic numbers, Area A, Square 1. In some systems of excavation what is called an Area in the above description is called a Field, and instead of the smaller unit of squares described above, that unit is called an area, e.g., Field 1, Area 1.

area supervisor Under the excavation director and the chief archaeologist/ field director, an area supervisor responsible for the overall operation of an area. This person determines the strategy to be followed in the area as a whole, and then counsels the square supervisors on methods to be employed to implement that strategy. An area supervisor will typically supervise an area containing four to seven active squares.

ashlar masonry Regular masonry of stone squared on all faces, with horizontal courses and vertical joints.

atrium Main or central room of an ancient Roman house, open to the sky and usually with a pool for the collection of rainwater; a courtyard surrounded by porticoes in the front part of an early Christian church.

balk Balk is a strip of unexcavated earth (and any other material), usually one meter wide, which separates squares within an area. A balk is made up of the outer 0.50 meter strip of each edge of each square. Subsidiary balks can be made of particular units within a square.

balustrade Railing or ornamented parapet with supporting regularly spaced short columns or pillars.

basilica Used as the court of justice and administrative center in Roman times. It was generally a long rectangular building with two rows of pillars or columns dividing it into a central nave and two aisles. The design of the basilica influenced that of the royal portico on the temple mount, and that of synagogue and church architecture, giving the characteristic nave and aisle form.

bead and reel Convex molding with the form of elongated beads alternating with disks placed on edge, or with spherical beads or both.

bema Platform; for public speaking.

capital Uppermost member of a column or pillar, supporting the entablature; one of the most distinctive members of the architectural order.

cavea Semi-circular auditorium of an ancient theater, so called because it was originally excavated in a hillside.

cella Interior, enclosed main room of an ancient temple, called *naos* in Greek.

ceramicist Ceramic expert, usually a member of the archaeological staff, who conducts the first analysis of the pottery as it comes from the field.

chancel The part of the church in front of the nave, consisting of the pulpit and altar area.

colonnade Series of regularly spaced columns, usually capped by capitals supporting an entablature.

corbel Courses of stones, set in a wall, each projecting slightly beyond the course below; when continued, the top courses can be joined by a capstone (corbel arch).

Corinthian Grecian decorative order having a bell-shaped capital with rows of acanthus leaves, a style adapted to Jewish and church architecture.

Corinthian order Capital decorated with acanthus leaves and volutes, said to have been invented in Corinth.

cornice (also called the *geison*) Crowning member of the entablature: a projection designed to throw rain water from the face of a building; the diagonal cornices of a pediment are spoken of as "raking."

corona Cornice's projecting member, with a vertical face.

crater (or *krater*). Bowl with wide mouth, and a body with two handles projecting vertically from the juncture of the neck and body; used for mixing wine and water.

crepidoma (or *krepidoma*) Stepped foundation platform of a Greek temple.

cyclopean masonry Rough, massive masonry employed in the Bronze Age for the walls of cities and citadels.

cylix (or *kylix*) Drinking cup in the shape of a shallow bowl, with two horizontal handles projecting from the opposite sides, often terminating with a stem and foot.

dado Lower portion of a wall when treated as a continuous wainscot.

debir (*devir*) Holy of Holies, in the Jewish tabernacle and temple.

dendrochronology Dating technique based on the study of growth rings in trees.

dentils Closely spaced, small rectangular blocks in a cornice's bed-mold, which represented originally the ends of roof-beams.

Doric order Simple or plain capitals, with abacus and an echinus sloping in toward the column below, developed in Dorian countries; frieze consists of metopes and triglyphs (*q.v.*).

drum One of the cylindrical blocks of which the shaft of a column is composed.

echinus Convex molding just below and supporting the abacus of a capital, as in a Doric capital.

egg and dart (or *egg and tongue*) Ornament to enrich an ovolo or an echinus, consisting of an alternating series of oval and pointed forms.

elevation Drawing of a structure or other feature from a given side.

engaged column Semi-detached column.

entablature Superstructure carried by the columns, consisting of architrave, frieze (often omitted in the Asiatic Ionic order), and cornice.

entasis Slight convex curve of a column, to correct an optical illusion or for a pleasing effect.

episkenion Upper story of the scene building.

exedra Semi-circular stone seat or recess.

exodus Exit, departure of players from place of action; passage to go out by; final song sung when the chorus is marching out.

faience Colorful glazed earthenware or pottery.

feature Major coherent element of an ancient site, such as a room, a courtyard, a pit, or an industrial installation. A feature may be confined to one square, may extend to several squares, or may encompass an entire area.

field book Basic recording book provided for every square excavated. It is composed of locus sheets (see below) and graph paper, the use of which provide for a thorough, integrated record of all the facts discerned about any given locus.

field laboratory Houses the first stages of the analytical process of artifactual data. Here two steps are performed: cataloging and preliminary analysis.

fillet Flat band or molding.

flotation A method of wet sieving. A soil sample(s) from the excavation is placed in a container and immersed in water. Pure soil passes through the sieve. The lighter materials (the light fraction) float above the screen and are skimmed off; the heavier materials (the heavy fraction) caught by the screen insert are then collected.

flutes Vertical channels in the shafts of columns, separated from each other by an arris (or sharp ridge) in the Doric order and by a fillet in the Ionic and Corinthian orders.

forum Marketplace and place of official business and assembly in an ancient Roman city.

foundation trench Consists of a section of ground excavated in antiquity for laying in a foundation of a wall or other installation and the refill of earth, sherds, and other material to fill in the remaining space next to the wall. The latest pottery in the foundation trench should represent the founding date of the structure.

frieze Middle member of the entablature between the architrave and the cornice, usually decorated with sculpture in low relief, or any sculptured horizontal band.

gable See *pediment.*

goufa (gufa, goufah, or gufah) A basket made of old tire casings for carrying earth in an excavation.

guttae Small peg-like cylinders under Doric regulae and mutules.

hechal (*hekhal*) Sanctuary of the Jewish temple.

hellenistic Jews or other orientals who used the Greek language and manner, but were not Greeks. Hellenism could be regarded as a symbiosis of Greek and oriental culture in the near east.

hemicycle Semicircular recess.

hydria Water jar having a short neck and large angular body, with three handles, two horizontal just below the shoulder, and one vertical from the lip to the shoulder.

hyposkenion Room below the platform of the stage.

intercolumniation Space between the columns of a colonnade.

Ionic order Capital decorated with volutes (or spiral scrolls) and usually supporting an entablature with a continuous frieze; the style of Phoenician or Egyptian origin was known in Palestine as far back as the ninth or eighth centuries B.C.

iron age Period following the bronze ages in which iron came into use. It heralded a major agricultural and economic revolution, an upward surge in the standard of living, and a marked difference in social organization. It corresponds to the Israelite period (1200–586 B.C.) in biblical times.

kalpis Hydria jar with rounded forms.

kantharos Wine cup with a deep bowl, and foot and two high-curving handles; used in celebrations for Dionysus.

khirbet Arabic word for the ruin of an ancient settlement.

kokim See *loculus.*

krepis or **krepidoma** (or *crepis* or *crepidoma*) Stepped platform forming the floor and sub-architectural features of an ancient classical building, such as a temple.

kylix See *cylix.*

lekythos Slender vase with narrow neck, flared mouth, narrow base with foot, and a high curving handle rising from below the neck and then descending to the shoulder; used for oil and perfume.

level Altitude above sea level based on computations in relation to the nearest surveyor's bench mark available.

lintel Horizontal member spanning an opening, such as a door or window.

loculus (or *kokim*) Horizontal recess or niche in a burial cave or a rock-cut tomb; plural = *loculi*. Often a tomb will contain both loculus (kokim) and arcosolia burial places.

locus Fundamental unit in the recording system. It can be defined as any discernible soil layer or "thing" (wall, pit, hearth) within or related to a given soil layer. Identified by arabic number, coded.

logeion (Gr. *speaking place*) Podium or platform of the Hellenistic stage.

metope Rectangular panel (often sculptured) between the triglyphs in the Doric frieze.

monolith Single block of stone.

Munsell Color Chart Objective color designation derived from the standard Munsell Soil Color Charts by which soil and other colors can be described. These charts are published by the Munsell Soil Company (1954).

mutule Projecting slab on the soffit (underside) of a Doric cornice.

narthex Vestibule or passage between the main entrance and the nave of a building, as of a church.

nave Main longitudinal section of the church from the main entrance or narthex to the chancel.

numismatist Expert in ancient coinage who examines, cleans, identifies, and reports on coins recovered from a site.

nymphaeum Place dedicated to the nymphs with a fountain or running water.

obsidian Dark volcanic glass, translucent in thin splinters, which are sharp-edged and therefore useful in the manufacture of knives, etc.

odeion (Gr.), **odeum** (Lat.) Roofed building for musical performances.

oinochoe Wine jug with a vertically extended and rounded body, short foot, and a round or trefoil mouth, and with a high curved handle from the lip to the shoulder.

opisthodomus Small room in the rear of a temple, used for a treasury.

orchestra Circular dancing place of a Greek theater, where the chorus performed.

order Architectural system composed of the columns and entablature (Doric, Ionic, Corinthian).

ossuary Depository box for the bones of the dead.

ostracon Ancient inscribed potsherd.

ovolo Convex molding form, in section one-quarter of a circle or ellipse.

parapet Low balustrade; a protective wall.

parascenion (Gr.), **parascenium** (Lat.) One of two symmetrical wings of the *skene* which projected forward toward the orchestra of a Greek theater.

parodos (pl. *paradoi*) Lateral entrances to the orchestra of the theater; songs of the chorus sung while entering.

pedestal Base supporting a column or statue.

pediment Triangular frame, above the entablature at either end of the temple, formed by raking and horizontal cornices; within this area often stood sculpture in the round.

period General historical division of cultural domination on an ancient site. Identified by name, e.g., Iron Age, Hellenistic, Roman, etc. These period divisions may correspond to the strata and phases of this and any other particular site, but such correspondence is not automatic.

peripteral Term given to a temple, whose cella is surrounded by a peristyle (or row of columns).

peristyle Colonnade surrounding a building; or an inner court lined with a colonnade.

phase Stage in the history of construction within a given stratum. Major phases are identified by a capital letter, with lower case Greek letters used for minor subdivisions, e.g., Phase A of Stratum XV. The term *phase* is also used to designate constructional or occupational levels during excavation and subsequent study, up to the point where stratum numbers can be assigned. Thus EB (Early Bronze), phase 1; EB, phase 2, etc., may be employed until the EB stratification and its relationship to the earlier and later strata are determined.

pier Free-standing rectangular support or short wall having the function of a column or pilaster but mostly of heavier mass.

pilaster Shallow rectangular column, free-standing or engaged or semi-detached in a wall.

pillar Vertical stone structure used as support or ornament.

plan Any drawing of a structure or other feature viewed from the top.

plinth Bottom of a column base or podium.

plinth course Projecting course of stone at the base of a wall.

podium Low wall or continuous pedestal for columns or wall; a raised platform.

porch Entrance, vestibule.

poros Tufa, a kind of marble, but lighter.

porphyry Dark red or purple rock of feldspar crystals.

portico Structure with a roof supported by columns, or piers; usually a porch of a building.

pottery pail tag Tag, prepared in the square, which accompanies and identifies a pottery pail through the pottery registration process. Associated artifacts and ecofacts also carry the same tag and locus number as the pottery pail. The original tag remains with the same sherds during the storage and study phases. A record of the pottery container tag is retained on the locus sheet.

pottery reading Reading of the pottery at the site headquarters is the first stage in pottery analysis. At this point a tentative date is given to the sherds, important pieces of which are saved for further study and drawing.

pottery registry Depository of all ceramic information. It serves as a catalogue, as a record of the preliminary analytical results, and as a guide for future processing of the material.

preliminary report Prepared by the senior archaeologist and the director of the expedition and members of the core staff, a summary report of the results of a single season of excavation. It gives a general presentation of field results, suitably illustrated, but with a minimum of interpretation.

pronaos Porch or vestibule at the front of a temple.

propylaeum (pl. *propylaea*) Monumental entrance gate to a temple area (*temenos*) or other enclosure. A simple building of this type is known as a *propylon*.

proscenium Colonnade or decorative arch between *skene* and orchestra of a theater.

prostyle Temple with portico of columns in front.

prothyron Porch in front of the main door.

psykter Jar with an ovoid body tapering at the neck and set on a high foot, used for keeping wine cool.

pyxsis Vessel (normally pottery) usually of cylindrical shape, wide mouth and having two handles attached vertically along the top edge of the shoulder (one on either side). The Greek prototype is highly decorated. Used for oil.

regula Narrow strip under the Doric taenia, beneath which are carved the guttae (small peg-like cylinders).

rhyton Ancient Greek drinking horn, of pottery or bronze, with the base in the form of human or animal head.

sealed locus Area in which there is no extraneous material from later periods and thus represents a deposit from a single occupational phase.

section Scale drawing (usually 1:25) of a perpendicular balk face (both main and subsidiary balks) which shows each occupational phase and soil layer that are to be seen in the balk. Each section is cut contiguously at right angles to the other three sections of the square thus giving a complete record of the vertical relationship of the planes to one another.

sima (or *cyma*) Uppermost member in the classical architectural order; the gutter on the gables and flanks of a building.

skene (Gr.), **scaena** (Lat.) Temporary building, booth for the players; later the permanent backstage building of the Greek theater.

skyphos Deep wine cup with two horizontal handles near the rim, and a flat base or a foot.

socle Projecting member at the foot of a wall; for example, in the Bronze Age, the courses of field stones laid on the ground to raise the sun-dried bricks of a house wall as far as possible above potentially damaging rainwater. Also a base for a column or pedestal; a plinth.

square Immediate subdivision unit of an area, regardless of its size and shape. Although squares can vary considerably in size, they are usually five or six meters on a side. Squares are designated by arabic numbers; thus Square 1, etc.

square supervisor Person responsible for the planning and execution of the day-to-day operations in one particular square and the recording of all evidence gathered there.

stele Tombstone, or any stone slab used for sculptured reliefs or inscriptions.

stereobate Base on which a building is erected; the substructure.

stirrup jar Small round pottery vessel with a false center spout, with two handles extending from this spout, one on either side, to the shoulder. The true spout opening is on the edge of the shoulder. The Greek prototype is highly decorated.

stoa (Gr.), **porticus** (Lat.) Building whose roof is supported by one or more rows of columns parallel to the rear wall and used as a promenade, meeting place, or shop.

stratigraphy Study of the arrangement of rock and/or soil layers together with the study of their origin, the order of their deposition, and their functional and chronological relationships to one another.

stratum Subdivision of the period, based on stratigraphic evidence of a major cultural break, connected with a series of loci or layers, and supported by ceramic, architectural, and object data. Often a stratum is marked at its beginning and end by radical changes, such as destruction layers. Identified by upper case roman numerals, e.g., Stratum XV: Late Roman II–III (ca. A.D. 193–324).

structure Consists of a group of features, such as a house, public building, road, etc., which form a major architectural unit in one of the occupational phases.

stylobate Pavement on which columns stand, such as the upper step of a temple.

subsidiary balk Secondary balk produced to connect stratigraphically an isolated feature or lateral element within the interior of the square to one of the main balks.

taenia Projecting fillet (or band) of the Doric entablature separating the frieze from the architrave.

tell Ancient mound in the Middle East, composed of the remains of human habitation built up by successive levels of human occupation and destruction.

temenos Sacred enclosure in which one or more Greek temples stood.

torus Large convex, circular molding, commonly forming the lowest member of the base of a column or that directly above the plinth; sometimes a double torus.

triangulation Surveying technique designed to locate unknown points in relation to two or more known points. The distance to an unknown point is measured from two known points. This describes two arcs around the known points. Their point of intersection within the area is the location of the unknown point.

triglyph Projecting member, with vertical channels and chamfers, that separates alternately the metopes of the Doric frieze course.

trochilos or **scotia** Deep concave molding between two fillets (or strips) as in an Attic column base.

tuscan order Simplified Roman Doric order with unfluted columns and lack of other decorations except moldings.

tympanum Triangular interior wall of the pediment, enclosed by the raking and horizontal cornices.

unguentarium (pl. *unguentaria*) Small vessel of pottery, glass, or stone to hold ointments or perfumes, often with elongated necks.

velum Canvas roof, used as a sunshade over the auditorium in the Roman theater.

vestibule Anteroom or passage hall next to the outer door of a house.

volute Spiral scroll of an Ionic capital.

vomitoria Entrances from the covered passages leading to the different sections of the auditorium, with wide openings which "vomit" or "spit out" the numerous visitors.

Bibliography

Books

Albright, W. F. *The Archaeology of Palestine*. Baltimore: Penguin, 1960.

Amiran, Ruth. *Ancient Pottery of the Holy Land*. Jerusalem: Massada Press, 1969.

Arndt, W. F.; Gingrich, F. W.; Danker, F. W. *A Greek-English Lexicon of the New Testament*. Chicago: University of Chicago Press, 1979.

Avi-Yonah, Michael. *The Madaba Mosaic Map*. Jerusalem: Israel Exploration Society, 1964.

————, ed. *Encyclopedia of Archaeological Excavations in the Holy Land*. 4 vols. Englewood Cliffs, N.J.: Prentice-Hall, 1976.

Bagatti, B. *The Church from the Gentiles in Palestine*. Translated by E. Hoade. Jerusalem: Franciscan Press, 1971.

————. *L'Eglise de la gentilité en Palestine*. Jerusalem: Franciscan Press, 1968.

————. *New Discoveries at the Tomb of Virgin Mary in Gethsemane*. Jerusalem: Franciscan Press, 1975.

Bahat, Dan. *Carta's Historical Atlas of Jerusalem, An Illustrated Survey*. Jerusalem: Carta, 1983.

305

Baly, Denis. *Geographical Companion to the Bible.* London: Lutterworth, 1963.

———. *The Geography of the Bible.* New York: Harper and Row, 1974.

Barrois, G. A. "Valley of Rephaim." In *The Interpreter's Dictionary of the Bible,* edited by George A. Buttrick, 4:35–36. New York: Abingdon, 1962.

Benvenisti, Meron. *The Crusaders in the Holy Land.* Jerusalem: Israel Universities Press, 1970.

Bliss, F. J. and Dickie, A. C. *Excavations at Jerusalem, 1894–1897.* London: The Committee of the Palestine Exploration Fund, 1898.

Brown, Francis, Driver, S. R., and Briggs, Charles A., eds. *A Hebrew and English Lexicon of the Old Testament.* Boston: Houghton Mifflin, 1907.

Chelebi. *Evliya Tshelibi's Travel in Palestine.* Translated by St. H. Stephan. Jerusalem: Ariel Publishing House, 1980.

Corbo, V. C. *Ricerche Archeologiche al Monte Degli Ulivi.* Jerusalem: Franciscan Press, 1965.

Coüasnon, Charles. *The Church of the Holy Sepulchre in Jerusalem.* London: Oxford University Press, 1974.

Creswell, K. A. C. *Early Muslim Architecture.* 2 vols. Oxford: Clarendon Press, 1932.

Douglas, J. D., ed. *Illustrated Bible Dictionary.* Vol. 1. Sydney: Hodder and Stoughton, 1980.

Finegan, Jack. *The Archaeology of the New Testament: The Life of Jesus and the Beginning of the Early Church.* Princeton: Princeton University Press, 1969.

———. *Light from the Ancient Past.* Princeton: Princeton University Press, 1959.

Gallery Book of the Palestinian Archaeological Museum for the Stone and Bronze Ages, p. 63, no. 866.

Guy, P. L. O., and Engberg, Robert M. *Megiddo Tombs.* Chicago: University of Chicago Press, 1938.

Hamilton, R. W. *The Structural History of the Aqsa Mosque.* London: Oxford University Press, 1949.

Harris, R. L. *God's Eternal Creation.* Chicago: Moody, 1971.

Hayes, John W. "Hellenistic to Byzantine Fine Ware and Derivatives in the Jerusalem Corpus." In *Excavations in Jerusalem, 1961–1967,* in A. D. Tushingham. Toronto: Royal Ontario Museum, 1985.

Hollis, F. J. *The Archaeology of Herod's Temple.* London 1934.

Jeremias, Joachim. *The Rediscovery of Bethesda.* Louisville: Southern Baptist Seminary, 1949.

Kenyon, Kathleen. *Archaeology in the Holy Land.* London: Ernest Benn, 1960.

———. *Digging Up Jerusalem*. London: Ernest Benn, 1974.

———. *Jerusalem: Excavating 3000 Years of History*. New York: McGraw-Hill, 1967.

———. *Royal Cities of the Old Testament*. New York: Schocken Books, 1971.

Lamon, Robert S., and Shipton, Geoffrey M. *Megiddo I: Seasons of 1925–34, Strata I–V*. Chicago: University of Chicago Press, 1939.

Landay, Jerry M. *Dome of the Rock*. New York: Newsweek, 1972.

Loud, Gordon. *Megiddo II: Seasons of 1935–39*. Chicago: University of Chicago Press, 1948.

Mare, W. Harold, "I Corinthians." In *The Expositor's Bible Commentary*, edited by Frank E. Gaebelein, 10:175–297. Grand Rapids: Zondervan, 1976.

May, G. H., and Engberg, R. M. *Material Remains of the Megiddo Cult*. Chicago: University of Chicago Press, 1938.

Mazar, Benjamin. *Jerusalem Revealed*. Jerusalem: Israel Exploration Society, 1975.

———. *The Mountain of the Lord*. Garden City, NY: Doubleday, 1975.

Meshorer, Ya'akov. *Jewish Coins of the Sacred Temple Period*. Tel-Aviv: Am Hassefer and Massada, 1967.

Miller, J. Maxwell, and Pinkerton, Jack M. *Archaeological Survey of Central and Southern Moab*. Atlanta: Emory University, 1979. Unpublished.

Moore, E. A. *The Ancient Churches of Old Jerusalem: The Evidence of the Pilgrims*. Beirut: 1961.

Moorey, R., and Parr, P., eds. *Archaeology in the Levant*. Warminster, England: Aris and Phillips, 1978.

Parrot, Andre. *Golgotha and the Church of the Holy Sepulchre*. London: SCM Press, 1957.

———. *The Temple of Jerusalem*. London: SCM Press, 1957.

Payne, J. B. "Chronology of the Old Testament." In *The Zondervan Pictorial Encyclopedia of the Bible*, edited by Merrill C. Tenney, 1:829–45. Grand Rapids: Zondervan, 1975.

Prawer, Joshua A. *The Latin Kingdom of Jerusalem*. London: W. Weidenfeld and Nicolson, 1972.

Peters, F. E. *Jerusalem*. Princeton: Princeton University Press, 1985.

Pritchard, James B., ed. *Ancient Near Eastern Texts Relating to the Old Testament*. Rev. ed. Princeton: Princeton University Press, 1955.

Saller, Sylvester J. *Excavations at Bethany*. Jerusalem: Franciscan Press, 1957.

———. *The Jebusite Burial Place in the Excavations at Dominus Flevit*. Part 2. Jerusalem: Franciscan Press, 1964.

―――. *Second Revised Catalogue of the Ancient Synagogues of the Holy Land*. Jerusalem: Franciscan Press, 1972.

Saller, Sylvester, and Testa, E. *The Archaeological Setting of the Shrine at Bethphage*. Jerusalem: Franciscan Press, 1961.

Schaff, Philip. *History of the Christian Church*. Vol. 3. Grand Rapids: Eerdmans, 1956.

Schick, S. *Die Stiftshutte, der Tempel in Jerusalem und der Tempelplatz der Jetztzeit*. Berlin: 1896.

Shiloh, Yigal. *Excavations at the City of David, I, 1978–1982 in Qedem*. No. 19. Jerusalem: Hebrew University, Ahva Press, 1984.

Shipton, Geoffrey M. *Notes on the Meggido Pottery of Strata*. Vols. 6–20. Chicago: University of Chicago Press, 1939.

Simon, J. *Jerusalem in the Old Testament*. Leiden: E. J. Brill, 1952.

Smith, George Adam. *Jerusalem*. 2 vols. London: Hodder and Stoughton, 1908.

Tufnell, Olga; Inge, Charles H.; Harding, Lankester. *Lachish II (Tell ed-Duweir), The Fosse Temple*. London: Oxford University Press, 1940.

Tufnell, Olga, et al. *Lachish IV (Tell ed-Duweir), The Bronze Age*. London: Oxford University Press, 1958.

Tushingham, A. D. *Excavations in Jerusalem, 1961–1967*. Toronto: Royal Ontario Museum, 1985.

Vincent, L. H., and Abel, F. M. *Jerusalem Nouvelle*. Vol. 2. Paris: Libraire Lecoffre, J. Gabalda et Cie, 1954–56.

Weill, R. *La Cite de David*. Paris: Institut Francais L'Archeologie de Beyrouth, Bibliothèque Archéologique et Historique, 1947.

Wright, G. E. *Shechem, The Biography of a Biblical City*. New York: McGraw-Hill, 1965.

Yadin, Yigael, et al. *Hazor II, An Account of the Second Season of Excavations, 1956*. Jerusalem: Magnes Press, Hebrew University, 1960.

Note: Citations from Josephus are from the volumes of the Loeb Classical Library. A number of other ancient literary sources come from the *Corpus Christianorum, Series Latina, CLXXV, Itineraria et Alia Geographica* (Turnholti: Typographi Brepols Editores Pontificii, 1965), and from the Anti-Nicene, Nicene and Post-Nicene Church Fathers.

Periodicals

The following list is a composite of periodicals that were cited in this book. The list may also be used as a guide for further reading on the subject of mid-eastern archaeology.

Articles

Aarons, Leroy, and Goldie Feinsilver. "Jerusalem Couple Excavates Under Newly Built Home in Search of Their Roots." *Biblical Archaeology Review* 8.2 (1982): 44–49.

Amiran, R. "The First and Second Walls of Jerusalem Reconsidered in the Light of the New Wall." *Israel Exploration Journal* 21 (1971): 166–67.

Avigad, N. "The Epitaph of the Royal Steward from Siloam Village." *Israel Exploration Journal* 3 (1953): 152.

———. "Excavations in the Jewish Quarter of the Old City of Jerusalem, 1970." *Israel Exploration Journal* 20 (1970): 134–35.

———. "Excavations in the Jewish Quarter of the Old City of Jerusalem, 1971." *Israel Exploration Journal* 22 (1972): 193–95.

———. "How the Wealthy Lived in Herodian Jerusalem." *Biblical Archaeologist* 2.4 (Dec. 1976): 23–35.

Avi-Yonah, M. "The Newly Found Wall of Jerusalem and Its Topographical Significance." *Israel Exploration Journal* 21 (1971): 168–69.

———. "The Third and Second Walls of Jerusalem." *Israel Exploration Journal* 18 (1968): 123–25.

Bahat, Dan. "The Wall of Manasseh in Jerusalem." *Israel Exploration Journal* 31 (1981): 235–36.

Bahat, Dan, and Magan Broshi. "Jerusalem, Old City, the Armenian Gardens." *Israel Exploration Journal* 22 (1972): 171–72.

Baramki, D. C. "An Ancient Cistern in the Grounds of Government House, Jerusalem." *The Quarterly of the Department of Antiquities in Palestine* 4 (1935): 165–67.

Barnett, R. D. "The Nimrud Ivories and the Art of the Phoenicians." *Iraq* 2 (1935): 179–210.

Bayewitz, David A. "The 'Fountain of Siloam' and 'Solomon's Pool' in First Century C. E. Jerusalem." *Israel Exploration Journal* 29 (1979): 92–100.

Ben-Dov, M. "Found After 1400 Years—The Magnificent Nea." *Biblical Archaeology Review* 3.4 (Dec. 1977): 32–37.

Benoit, P. "L' Antonia d' Herode le Grand et le Forum Oriental d' Aelia Capitolina." *Harvard Theological Review* 64 (1971): 135–67.

Broneer, Oscar. "Corinth." *Biblical Archaeologist* 14.4 (Dec. 1951): 80–83.

Broshi, Magan. "Evidence of Earliest Christian Pilgrimage to the Holy Land Comes to Light in Holy Sepulchre Church." *Biblical Archaeology Review* 3.4 (Dec. 1977): 42–44.

Chen, Doran. "The Design of the Dome of the Rock in Jerusalem." *Palestine Exploration Quarterly* (Jan.-June 1980): 41–50.

Dor, Ben. "Palestinian Alabaster Vases." *Quarterly of the Department of Antiquities in Palestine* 11 (1945): 93–112.

Fleming, James. "The Uncovered Gate Beneath Jerusalem's Golden Gate." *Biblical Archaeology Review* 9.1 (Jan.-Feb. 1983): 24–37.

Galling, Kurt. "Die Necropole von Jerusalem." *Palestinajahrbuch* 36 (1936): 90–95.

Geva, Hillel. "The Western Boundary of Jerusalem at the End of the Monarchy." *Israel Exploration Journal* 29 (1979): 84–91.

Giacumakis, G. "The Gate Below the Golden Gate." *Bulletin of the Near East Archaeological Society* ns. 4 (1974): 23–26.

Graesser, Carl F. "Standing Stones in Ancient Palestine." *Biblical Archaeologist* 35.2 (June 1972): 34–63.

Hennessey, J. B. "Preliminary Report on Excavations at the Damascus Gate, 1964–66," *Levant* 2 (1970): 22–27.

"Hesbon 1974." *Andrews University Seminary Studies* 14.1 (Spring 1976): 103–06.

Jacobson, David M. "Ideas Concerning the Plan of Herod's Temple." *Palestine Exploration Quarterly* (Jan.-June 1980): 33–40.

Kark, Ruth, and Shimon Landman. "The Establishment of Muslim Neighborhoods." *Palestine Exploration Quarterly* (July-Dec. 1980): 113–35.

Kaufman, Asher S. "The Eastern Wall of the Second Temple at Jerusalem Revealed." *Biblical Archaeologist* 44.2 (June 1981): 108–15.

Kenyon, K. "Excavations in Jerusalem, 1965." *Palestine Exploration Quarterly* (July-Dec. 1966): 85–87.

Lancaster, G., L. Harding, and B. S. Isserlin. "Four Tomb Groups from Jordon." *Palestine Exploration Fund Annual* 6 (1953): 14–26.

Maisler, B. "Cypriote Pottery at a Tomb-Cave in the Vicinity of Jerusalem." *American Journal of Semitic Languages and Literatures* 49 (1932–33): 248–53.

Mare, W. Harold. "Archaeological and Literary Evidence Regarding Building Remains and Worship in the Early Church." *Bulletin of the Near East Archaeological Society* ns. 1 (1971): 13–16.

Mazar, Benjamin. "Herodian Jerusalem in the Light of the Excavations South and South-west of the Temple Mount." *Israel Exploration Journal* 28 (1978): 230–34.

"1984 Abila of the Decapolis Excavation." *Bulletin of the Near East Archaeological Society* 24 (Winter, 1985): 32–33.

Pettinato, Giovanni. "The Royal Archives of Tell Mardikh-Ebla." *Biblical Archaeologist* 39.2 (June 1976): 46.

Rabinovich, Abraham. "The Temple Puzzle." *The Jerusalem Post Magazine* (March 28, 1980): 12.

Rahmani, L. Y. "Ancient Jerusalem's Funerary Customs and Tombs, Part Two." *Biblical Archaeologist* 44.4 (Fall, 1981): 229–35.

Sasson, Victor. "The Siloam Tunnel Inscription." *Palestine Exploration Quarterly* (July-Dec. 1982): 111–17.

Schein, Bruce E. "The Second Wall of Jerusalem." *Biblical Archaeologist* 44.1 (March 1981): 21–26.

Shaheen, Naseeb. "The Siloam End of Hezekiah's Tunnel." *Palestine Exploration Quarterly* (July-Dec. 1977): 108–09.

————. "The Sinuous Shape of Hezekiah's Tunnel." *Palestine Exploration Quarterly* (July-Dec. 1979): 105–08.

Shanks, Hershel. "Report from Jerusalem." *Biblical Archaeology Review* 3.4 (May-June 1977): 23.

Shiloh, Yigal. "The City of David Archaeological Project, the Third Season, 1980." *Biblical Archaeologist* 44.3 (Sept. 1981): 162–65.

Stein, Murray. "How Herod Moved Gigantic Blocks to Construct the Temple Mount." *Biblical Archaeology Review* 7.3 (May-June 1981): 42–43.

Stigers, Harold G. "The Interphased Chronology of Jotham, Ahaz, Hezekiah, and Hoshea." *Journal of Evangelical Theological Society* 9 (1966): 81–90.

Ussishkin, David. "Original Length of the Siloam Tunnel in Jerusalem." *Levant* 8 (1976): 82–95.

Wilkinson, John. "The Church of the Holy Sepulchre." *Archaeology* 31.4 (July-Aug. 1978): 13.

Index